American Dreams in
MISSISSIPPI

AMERICAN DREAMS

CONSUMERS, POVERTY, & CULTURE, 1830–1998

IN MISSISSIPPI

Ted Ownby

The University of North Carolina Press

Chapel Hill and London

© 1999 The University of North Carolina Press
All rights reserved
Set in Minion and Block by Keystone Typesetting, Inc.
Manufactured in the United States of America
The paper in this book meets the guidelines for permanence
and durability of the Committee on Production Guidelines
for Book Longevity of the Council on Library Resources.
Library of Congress Cataloging-in-Publication Data
Ownby, Ted.
American Dreams in Mississippi: consumers, poverty,
and culture, 1830–1998 / Ted Ownby.
   p.   cm.
Includes bibliographical references and index.
ISBN 0-8078-2479-8 (cloth: alk. paper).—
ISBN 0-8078-4806-9 (pbk.: alk. paper)
1. Consumption (Economics)—Mississippi—History.
2. Rural poor— Mississippi—History. 3. Afro-American
consumers—Mississippi—History. 4. Consumers—
Mississippi—History. 5. Mississippi—Economic consumers.
I. Title.
HC107.M73C66   1999
339.4'7'09762—dc21   98-30825
                      CIP
03   02   01   00   99   5   4   3   2   1

TO SUSAN

CONTENTS

ILLUSTRATIONS

TABLES

ACKNOWLEDGMENTS

Through the years I have learned from my colleagues and students in the History Department and the Southern Studies Program at the University of Mississippi. Southern Studies colleagues Bob Brinkmeyer, Lisa Howorth, Tom Rankin, Ann Abadie, and Bill Ferris have all offered help, as have History Department colleagues Robert Haws, Winthrop Jordan, Nancy Bercaw, Sheila Skemp, Charles Eagles, Chiarella Esposito, David King, and Michael Landon. As my colleague in both History and Southern Studies, Charles Wilson has shared sources, ideas, encouragement, and sympathy about why it takes so long to finish a book. Susan Glisson was available for conversations about editing, and Karen Glynn in the Southern Media Archive helped identify the most useful photographs. Some extraordinary graduate students in both programs have assisted with the research. I thank Paul Anderson, Jim Baggett, Joe Bonica, Cristina Bortolami, Scott Holzer, Greg Hospodor, David Libby, Bruce Mactavish, Traye McCool, Leigh McWhite, Sam Morgan, David Nelson, Mark Newman, Peter Slade, Scott Small, Sarah Torian, Bert Way, and Bland Whitley. Mactavish, Holzer, Wiley Prewitt, Corey Lesseig, and Farrell Evans supplied me with sources from their own research.

At the University of Mississippi, grants from the Graduate School, the Office of Research, the College of Liberal Arts, and the Ventress Order have helped fund my research.

The University Press of Mississippi graciously allowed me to publish material I adapted from "The Snopes Trilogy and the Emergence of Consumer Culture," published in *Faulkner and Ideology*, ed. Donald M. Kartiganer and Ann J. Abadie (Jackson: University Press of Mississippi, 1995).

Other scholars who have offered help include John Higham, Edward Ayers, Kenneth Bindas, Victoria de Grazia, Daniel Horowitz, Jack Temple Kirby, Joanne Robinson, Connie Schultz, Tricia Rose, and Cheryl Thurber. My thanks to good and patient friends at the University of North Carolina Press, Lewis Bateman, Pamela Upton, and Alison Tartt.

Above all, I thank my family. Like many fifteen-year-olds in our culture, Meghan Salmon sees no moral ambiguities in shopping. My parents, Bill and Mary Ownby, have seen my own interests in consumer goods change over the years. Susan Ditto makes life interesting and exciting every day, and I dedicate this book to her.

American Dreams in
MISSISSIPPI

INTRODUCTION

This project began with William Faulkner's Montgomery Ward Snopes. Faulkner grounded so much of his work in the slow agricultural rhythms of Mississippi life that a hustler and pornographer named Montgomery Ward immediately stands out as a comic contrast to most of his work. Montgomery Ward, the mail-order house in Chicago, signifies novelty, urban culture, and a distant impersonality. Few people associate Mississippi history with any of those things.

When historians study Mississippi, and usually when they study the American South, they tend to study things that are old, often to see how and how long those old things continued. Rightly or wrongly, Mississippi seems to represent the past, partly because so many Americans think of poverty, farm life, and racism as old things and abundance, urban and suburban life, and multiculturalism as American hopes for the future. This book studies behavior that, like Montgomery Ward Snopes, does not seem to have southern roots, and it studies how that behavior changed.

Questions of goods and spending money ultimately concern the American Dream or, more properly, several American dreams. Consumer culture has developed as a series of social and personal ideals—or dreams—that emerged at different points in American history. This work asks how four of the most powerful dreams have fared in Mississippi.

The Dream of Abundance. The dream that America can be a place without poverty and hunger has been a recurring theme in American history. From early dreams of America as a material paradise to comparative writing from Tocqueville to Werner Sombart, to famous words by Franklin Roosevelt to the scholarly work of David Potter and countless others, the notion of Americans as a People of Plenty has worked as a source of identity and usually optimism.[1] The many writers and reformers who wonder how poverty they associate with third-world economies can exist in the United States are among the clearest proponents of an American identity rooted in abundance.

The Dream of a Democracy of Goods. Emerging in the nineteenth century was the dream that goods could allow people to cut across traditional lines of status by allowing everyone who could afford it to have similar goods, or at least to share the experience of shopping. The dream of a democracy of goods began most clearly in cities and towns among a growing antebellum middle class, but it fully emerged later in the nineteenth century among an urban working class whose members shopped in department stores and aspired to changing identities available through consumer goods. For both the antebellum middle class and the working class in the late nineteenth century, part of the dream of shopping has involved the movement of women into exciting new areas of shopping. Many Americans have feared the dream of a democracy of goods for the possibility that it will flatten out differences among people of diverse backgrounds, while others take pleasure in seeing aspects of ethnic or working-class life from blue jeans to rock music turn into fashions popular far beyond the groups that originated them.[2]

The Dream of Freedom of Choice. Americans have come, at different times and places, to place great emphasis on shopping. Many take pleasure in the process of selecting goods as part of the meaning of freedom. Whether they are fascinated with the stores themselves or shop in catalogs that encourage people to imagine how goods will help them become new people, the process of selecting goods allows shoppers a pleasure in redefining themselves. The rise of an advertising industry dates this dream in the early twentieth century.[3]

The Dream of Novelty. For individual consumers, the dream involves a romantic, necessarily unquenchable thirst for the new experiences promised not simply by consumer goods but by the novelty of progressing from one product to the next. As Colin Campbell has argued, attaching personal fulfillment to the next product one can buy, and then the next, places consumers in the position of the nineteenth-century romantic, dreaming of "something evermore about to be." At its logical extreme, this dream demands constant change and creates hope that today will always be better than yesterday and that tomorrow will be even better. It is the economic system and cultural ideal of what Martha Wolfenstein calls "fun morality," which turns the child's fascination with new experiences into a social ideal for all ages.[4]

Together, the four dreams assume a future full of progress. The dream of abundance assumes a future of ever-increasing wealth and comfort. The dream of democracy suggests progress toward greater inclusiveness in that abundance. The dream of choice suggests an increasing range of goods. The dream of novelty is an individual dream of ever-changing desires, fascinations, and satisfactions.

The history of Mississippi would seem to have little in common with the four American dreams. Poverty of different kinds has characterized the economy of the state. For most of its history, the state has had a tiny middle class, and farms have prevailed in importance over towns and cities. Its dominating social ideal, enforced by slavery and then by a series of laws designed to control black Mississippians, until recently discouraged notions of equality and punished those who expressed them. And much of the cultural life of the state has concentrated more on the past than the future. The way the dream of novelty always looks forward to the next possible pleasure would not seem to find a comfortable home among people whose cultural leaders repeatedly call on the ghosts of the past to define moral behavior and group ideals.

This incongruity is precisely why we should study the importance consumer issues have had in the history of Mississippi. Instead of asking the common question of what is distinctive about southern or Mississippi history, we should examine what goods meant to different Mississippians as individuals, within their communities, and as forms of communication and miscommunication. The story of consumer behavior ultimately involves questions of conversations—conversations between blacks and whites, poor and rich people, men and women and children, rural people and urbanites, and conversations in the minds of uncertain individuals.[5] It is essential to see which American dreams were meaningful—to whom, how, and why—in a state which for so long has seemed to lie outside most American dreams.

Three issues dominate this work. What place did consumer goods have in different experiences of rural life? How did Mississippians use goods and shopping to think about the meanings of freedom? How did Mississippians use goods and shopping to think about concepts of race and relations? In answering those questions, this work ranges from the 1830s to the 1990s.

The first three chapters analyze the place of goods in agricultural settings. Members of farming households feared debt so intensely that they worried that buying goods threatened the independence of their households. Farming men did most of the shopping at general stores, which remained sleepy establishments for most of the 1800s. Slaves took advantage of their rare opportunities for buying goods to reshape their own identities, and wealthy men and women enjoyed shopping in cities. But men tended to see interests in goods and shopping as vices of the weak and not something that should truly trouble them as responsible heads of households. After emancipation, African Americans, who as slaves had known almost all of Mississippi's problems *except* debt, came to fear debt and worried that the general stores and plantation stores were sites for their own oppression and white men's recreation.

The fourth chapter details the entry of new stores and new ways of shopping into Mississippi. Department stores, cash stores, five-and-dime stores, and automobile dealers promised new goods, new experiences, and new methods of shopping. Much of this chapter seems less specific to Mississippi than any other section of the book. The issue of how Mississippians responded makes up the rest of the book.

The final four chapters and the epilogue investigate cultural questions of how different groups interpreted the changing roles goods and shopping might play in a changing Mississippi. In the early decades of the twentieth century, the changes that rocked social life called on Mississippians to investigate old identities and consider new ones. Declining opportunities for owning farms and declining demand for farm labor, increases in cash-paying jobs and migration from the region forced Mississippians to call into question the ideals of farmers, would-be farmers, and planters, and any ideals they had about the virtues of rural life.

Identities rooted in making money and spending it offered possible new alternatives. But what were the costs? Dorothy Dickins, the leading home economist for the state of Mississippi, gradually changed from an old perspective that women should stay at home and contribute to household independence to a consumer perspective that valued new goods and even the possible benefits of going into debt. Mississippi's many blues musicians dramatized a life of mobility and city life that saw goods as part of the freedom of people to put on new identities and to reject the demands of agricultural poverty. The state's four greatest writers showed different perspectives on goods and perspectives, but each of them—William Faulkner, Richard Wright, William Alexander Percy, and Eudora Welty—believed consumer goods had the potential to subvert for good or bad the class and racial conventions that had long dominated rural Mississippi. For them, whatever old topics they addressed in their work, consumer goods stood as what was new and either intriguing or threatening.

Finally, the civil rights boycotts of the 1960s involved, among other things, conversations about the place of goods in Mississippi race relations. Were protestors asking for a full place inside the stores they were boycotting? Or were they rejecting the goods and experiences of shopping in favor of higher, more lasting values?

A recurring question in this book asks how issues of goods and shopping relate to issues of race relations. It might seem easy to suggest that the logic of buying and selling should work against any distinctions other than the ability to pay for goods. But questions of economic relations and ideas about race have intermingled in Mississippi in intricate and sometimes surprising ways. Throughout American history, men and women who identified themselves as white people have projected their fears about their own worse sides on other groups, especially those identified as blacks. As Winthrop Jordan has shown, those projections involved understandings of both the self in notions of sexual self-control and the society in notions of Christian civilization.[6] By also understanding cultural components of economic behavior, we can see how ideas of race played a role in the justifications of poverty among African Americans. Different groups of white Mississippians have repeatedly claimed that black Mississippians were the true consumers—impulsive, fun-loving, indulgent, and wasteful. In their desire to see themselves as responsible parts of independent rural households, many white men and women identified consumption as a weakness that threatened both their own image of themselves and served to identify the vices they saw as part of being black.

For African Americans in Mississippi, the contradictions involved in shopping and buying goods caused considerable tension. On one hand, the role slaveowners and postbellum employers forced on most African Americans was one in which buying goods on the scale of modern consumers was not an option. Beginning most clearly under slavery but continuing long after emancipation, landowners and employers expected African Americans to look the part of the poor. Without the force of the legal system, those in power maintained the general goals of sumptuary laws from a much earlier age. On the other hand, one way for African Americans to rebel against those expectations was to be consumers. Freedom could mean defying both material poverty and the expectations of racists by shopping for goods and displaying and enjoying them. Substantially complicating that strategy was the belief common among whites that African Americans were at heart the most indulgent of people who could not have money without spending it immediately. Combining images of the consumer and the primitive was easy enough for white southerners who believed blacks needed protection from themselves. But for African Americans, it posed a significant dilemma. To spend and enjoy scarce resources was to confirm what many whites expected; to live on the economic margins with few goods and little novelty was to do what most whites wanted them to do. In the twentieth century, many black Mississippians discovered they could reject old Mississippi identities as subservient workers by embracing and reshaping American identities as consumers.

Many scholars have condemned consumer culture as an end to either fairness or independence in the economy, and they have often viewed people's interest in goods as a substitute for something more meaningful. Although many Mississippians have made the same point, the perspective that the democratization of shopping and the growing importance of goods represent the end of something distinctively positive in Mississippi is not easy to accept. When were the good ol' days when work was more satisfying, when values were more lasting, and when personal relationships were more meaningful? The history of economic oppression in the state makes almost any such nostalgia hard to accept.

Those of us who write about the history of shopping and consumer goods feel the power of at least four critiques of American materialism. An ascetic critique has long asserted that the pursuit of wealth and the enjoyment of goods have the potential to corrupt both the individual and society through the pursuit of self-indulgence and frivolity rather than things that really matter. A radical critique faults consumer culture for valuing only the labor that produces marketable goods and for hindering the development of working-class consciousness. A regionalist critique worries that consumer culture leads away from local tradition and uniqueness and toward a bland homogenization of all cultures. And an elitist critique views the profit-driven bottom line of consumer culture as the most insidious opponent of good taste and inspired great art.

I have some sympathy for the first three of those critiques, and I have a deep and inherited understanding of the ascetic's rejection of luxury goods, doubts about name-brand goods, and fears of credit card debt. Nonetheless, I believe that my job as a scholar is to appreciate sides of life I may find troubling and, sometimes, to understand sides of myself I may distrust or dislike. Thus, this book does not begin or end with assumptions that consumer goods, shopping, and advertising are always harmful forces in Mississippi life. I have some sympathy for the idea that goods and shopping offer the potential for liberation from painful realities and confining identities. This work tries to treat with care and sympathy both those who chose to spend money for pleasure and liberation and those who chose not to do so. The villains of the piece are those who denied other people the freedom to make that choice and those who identify goods and shopping as vices of the weak-willed and self-indulgent.

CHAPTER ONE

Men Buying Cloth

THE LIMITS OF SHOPPING

AMONG NINETEENTH-CENTURY

FARMERS

If you entered a Mississippi general store in the nineteenth century, your experience would have a great deal to do with your own identity. If you were a wealthy man or woman, you would judge the selection limited and its quality questionable by the standards you had learned from urban travel and trade with city merchants. If you were a slave, you would take pleasure in a rare opportunity to make choices and enjoy unusual sensations, but you would also be suspicious of any freedoms you seemed to have. If you were a woman in a free farming family, you would notice that most and probably all of the people in and around the store were men, and many of the men seemed to be there more to enjoy themselves than to buy things. If you were one of those men, you would feel more at home than any other visitors, but you would worry that buying things at the store might be putting you too deeply in debt. And if you owned the store, you would consider yourself an emissary of cosmopolitan culture, and you would be a bit frustrated that too few of the locals wanted to hear your message about the virtues of new goods.

In antebellum Mississippi, and in much of the later nineteenth century as well, the great majority of free people did their shopping at such general stores. Throughout the antebellum period, most people in the state could not choose from a great variety of stores. Only in larger towns, especially those on bodies of water, could potential shoppers choose from a variety of specialized stores. Along with general stores, residents of wealthy and well-settled Adams County could shop at saddlers, five jewelers, and several clothing stores and hardware stores. In Hancock County on the Gulf of Mexico, residents could do business not only at general stores but with a tailor, two dealers in shoes and boots, and a saddler. On the Tombigbee River, Columbus offered a number of clothing stores, a rare millinery shop, two jewelers, two confectioners, two florists, a music store, a bookstore, four carriage makers, two gunsmiths, and three saddle shops along with a number of dry goods stores and groceries.[1]

Few other counties in Mississippi had many stores other than general stores, groceries, and occasional plantation supply stores and commission merchants. According to a guide to businesses published in 1854, twelve groceries and three dry goods stores served the 1,500 people and 100,000 cattle in Greene County in the Piney Woods area. In the more settled northeastern Tippah County, Ripley had nine general stores, Salem had three, and three tiny communities had single general stores. The central Mississippi county of Winston had seventeen general stores and nothing else. In Bolivar County in the Delta, according to the guide, "there are no merchants, as the planter generally supplies himself by the year in New Orleans," but supply boats occasionally traveled up the Yazoo River with goods.[2]

By the 1880s, the variety of stores had grown, but more in number than kind. More stores concentrated exclusively on selling clothing, more sold candy and drugs, and there were even a few toy stores. The most important change by the 1880s was the rapid growth in the number of millinery shops. Usually the only stores in their towns run by women, eighty-seven millinery shops in Mississippi in 1883 sold hats to women. Despite the growing variety, however, general stores reigned as the dominant institution, appearing in virtually every community large and small. For example, two general stores were the only businesses in Daleville, population 50, in Lauderdale County. The Delta town of Riverton had five general stores and no other businesses. Twenty general stores, two saloons, and a farming supply store served Crawford and its 250 people in Lowndes County. Only larger towns showed signs of variety. The 754 residents of Shubuta could buy goods at twenty general stores and also at two drug stores, two stores of farming supplies, two confectioners, and two jewelers.[3]

Owners of general stores considered it their responsibility to bring comfort, choice, and contact with change to people in rural, isolated areas. In traveling to order their goods in northeastern or European cities, or even simply going to New Orleans or St. Louis, they believed they were emissaries for their customers, bringing back what was new and exciting. Newspaper advertisements almost always emphasized that goods came from distant urban centers. Merchants noted that they had "eastern goods" or "northern goods." Many mentioned that goods had their origin in specific cities—New York or Philadelphia,

London or Paris. In Yazoo City in 1851, Nunnally and Company advertised the sale of "our new and extensive stock of merchandise, direct from the Eastern cities, which was selected with great *care* by our Mr. Nunnally."[4]

Seeing themselves as part of and agents for cosmopolitan culture, owners often wrote home from buying trips to tell family members about particularly stylish goods they were buying for the family. Thus they tied their own identities to the goods themselves and to their part in knowing what was the latest thing. For example, merchant John Houston Bills traveled to England and France in 1851 to buy goods for his store in western Tennessee. In Paris he bought dry goods and jewelry and also paused to buy a dress for his wife.[5] In 1877 T. V. Gill wrote her store-owner husband about some calico he had bought her on a trip: "It is making up very pretty as your selections allmost invariably do."[6] In 1870 a woman in Arkansas likewise asked a relative who was on an urban buying trip to choose a bonnet or hat for her sister. "I don't mean to flatter you at all, but really you have *splendid* taste, at least *all* of us think so."[7] That merchant, William Paisley, later wrote his wife about examining "fine furniture" on a buying trip to St. Louis. He "could but almost covet the nice things in that line for ourselves, but hope we will be able to have such things after a while."[8] Thus, when store owners went to supply their stores, their identities were wrapped up in furnishing both their own families and their customers with the latest goods from cosmopolitan cities. Consumers themselves, they made the clothing and homes of their families serve as advertisements for the new goods they hoped to sell.

General store owners almost desperately wanted women to become shoppers. Elite fashions for women changed most frequently and dramatically, so in offering the latest goods, store owners hoped to bring to women in Mississippi both a connection to cosmopolitan culture and the expectation of constant change. For example, a store owner setting up a business in the late 1820s on the western Tennessee frontier said his main goal was to "please the customers particularly the Ladies."[9] Newspaper advertisements repeatedly stressed that women were valued customers. A store owner in Kosciusko advertised in 1851 that he had just received a large shipment from New York. "The Ladies are particularly invited to call and examine my fine stock of Dress Goods, Bonnets, etc."[10] In Yazoo City, Morris Reiman had just received a shipment from New York and invited "the ladies in particular . . . to call and examine" the stock of French, English, and German goods.[11]

General store owners were especially frustrated that their rural, farming customers rarely paid in cash. Agricultural people typically did business by making purchases on credit and paying at the end of the crop year, and store owners believed this stifled their desire and ability to buy new goods. Believing cash payments held the key to a rapid turnover of goods and adherence to the changes in styles, one store owner after another tried to minimize their customers' use of store credit. In Greenwood three men opening a store in 1845 hoped "to execute all the various branches of their profession in a style, (how well soever it may be elsewhere done) *inferior to none*. Their terms invariably cash, they desire their performances to correspond with the *taste of the times*; and to be in close affinity with that *progression*, which so prominently characterises their business in the nineteenth century from the little '*vine and fig-leaf*' operations of their great '*antedeluvean prototype*.' "[12] Isaac Marks opened a new general store in Yazoo City in 1851 with an advertisement that "he is determined to sell for Cash, at as low rates as the same articles can be had for anywhere."[13] The owner of a new dry goods store in Hernando claimed in 1869 that he would sell "exceedingly low for CASH, and cash only. We take this method of making known our terms that all may know them, and not ask to buy on account, thus saving us the disagreeable duty of refusing them."[14] Such merchants thought their customers needed education in how to buy. Without it, they believed, farmers would let their natural caution hold them back both from paying honest debts and buying new goods.

Many stores offered discounts to customers who paid with cash. One store in the village of Tchula, for example, promised in 1839 "to reduce our prices from 50 to 25 per cent. for good money."[15] A store in Coffeeville in 1844 cut prices between a quarter and a third for cash customers.[16] Two Kosciusko stores in 1850 promised to sell for "the most favorable terms for Cash, or to responsible persons, on the usual credit" and to sell for cash only to "punctual customers."[17]

The Roggenburger Brothers used verse to describe their store in antebellum Coffeeville. The advertisement brought together several ways the stores offered cosmopolitan culture to the farm folk.

> Jim along to brothers Roggans',
>   They can suit you to a pin;
> New boots, hats, and shoes and stockings,
>   Cheap as dirt—almost—for "Tin."
> Prime dry goods, of every sort,
>   From the North, they've just got in;
> Earthen, hard ware, ne're before bought,
>   In our town, so low—for "Tin."[18]

The brothers offered a variety of goods that were inexpensive, but they stressed their northern origin and their recent arrival. Selling for "tin" suggested they were trying hard to sell for cash rather than credit.

General store owners, to summarize, hoped to bring Mississippians into a consumer economy by urging their customers to pay cash, by encouraging women to become shoppers, by linking rural areas to cosmopolitan centers, and by offering not merely goods but access to changes in fashion. But were they successful? What actually happened at these stores? Who went to the stores, why, and what did their trips mean to them?

Life at the general stores was above all male. Throughout the nineteenth century the tremendous majority of visitors and customers were men. They saw the stores first as places to buy supplies as inexpensively as possible, second, as places for male recreation and only third, if at all, as places to enjoy freedom of choice and connection to cosmopolitan fashion.

Since most store ledgers simply listed their accounts by name, it is not surprising that the large majority of accounts in a male-dominated society were in the names of men. Only a tiny percentage of accounts were in the names of women in the antebellum period. By the 1890s, women had more than 10 percent of the accounts, but men were still the dominant figures in the stores. It might seem likely that women visited stores more often than those figures indicate and made purchases under the names of their husbands, but a few ledgers that recorded precisely who visited the stores make clear that the stores were male institutions. Ledger entries that identified female customers—usually nameless—as the wives or daughters of the men who held accounts only signified further that the men in charge considered women to be outsiders.

Men made the space in and around the stores sites for recreation. As Coldwater resident Boyce House recalled of the early 1900s, "For the men, Pritchard's was the center of town life." House recalled men sitting inside and on the porch talking about politics and telling "droll stories."[19] In his detailed study of postbellum general stores, Thomas Clark emphasizes how often white men talked about politics, told jokes, or shared gossip, often while playing checkers or whittling and spitting tobacco. Men still offered to stand stallions for stud outside stores, and younger men and boys saw the area outside the stores as gathering places for wrestling, running races, and eventually playing baseball.[20] At many but certainly not all stores, the alcohol that storekeepers served in the rear offered strong taste and powerful after-effects that made trips to the store special occasions. In fact, it seems clear that white men bought and drank a great deal of the alcohol consumed in the area on such trips.

With the combination of male-dominated business, male sport, male drinking, and male crowds, many women chose to stay away. Women who lived in towns knew when men would be coming from the farms and avoided the area around the stores. White women raised in small towns in southern and western Tennessee recalled that, as girls, they were denied access to male crowds. Born in 1893, novelist Evelyn Scott recalled that women and all children in Clarks-

TABLE 1. *Accounts at General Stores, by Gender*

	Men	Women	Men & Women	Unclear	Percentage Men
German Berry's Store (Steen's Creek, Miss.) 1831	152	2	0	7	98.7
Mount Prospect Trading Post (Bassfield, Miss.), 1838	203	11	0	0	94.9
Burwell Corban General Store (Corbandale, Tenn.), 1852–56	496	41	0	8	92.4
F. H. Campbell Store (Lodi, Miss.), 1890–91	158	21	0	0	88.3
F. B. Furr Store (Oxford, Miss.), 1893–94	203	12	0	0	94.4
W. S. Hankinson Store (Yokena, Miss.), 1894	253	57	2	8	81.7
Love's Station Store (DeSoto Co., Miss.), 1900	691	90	3	8	88.5
Henderson's Store (Preston, Miss.), 1905	238	43	1	12	84.7
John Albert King and Sons Store (Egypt, Miss.), 1909–10	126	19	0	4	86.9

Sources: German and Joseph T. B. Berry Ledgers, Mount Prospect Trading Post Account Book, John Albert King and Sons Store Records, MDAH; Love's Station, Mississippi, Ledger Book, UMem; Henderson's Store Records, W. S. Hankinson Daybooks and Ledgers, UK; F. B. Furr Store Ledger, UMS; F. H. Campbell Store Ledger, Prewitt Family Collection, Winona, Miss.; Burwell J. Corban Papers, SHC.

Note: The category "Men & Women" includes joint accounts held in both names.

dale, Tennessee "were, almost invariably, forbidden the street" when crowds of men gathered in town. Even in the tiny town of Bucksnort, Lila May Pamplin recalled that a woman would not go into towns crowded with men. "She would have been scandalized if she did." In Germantown in the 1870s, according to Plautus Lipsey, "drunkenness was so common that it was never considered safe for a lady to go down on the streets on Saturday."[21]

TABLE 2. *Customers at General Stores, by Gender*

	Men	Women	Unclear	Percentage Men
John P. Davidson General Store (Talladega, Ala., 1835)	554	75	64	88.1
Clay and Sinclair's General Store (Ripley, Tenn., 1859)	547	47	15	92.1
Vaiden General Store (Vaiden, Miss., 1871)	294	32	4	90.2
M. Jones Mercantile Store (Mt. Vernon, Ark., 1875)	691	45	10	93.9

Sources: John P. Davidson & Company Daybook, William McCorkle Papers, SHC; Vaiden General Store Ledger, UK; M. Jones Mercantile Store Journal, UMem; Clay and Sinclair's General Store Account Book, TSLA.

The women who lived in towns avoided stores when the farming men took over. Even more significantly, most women in the countryside rarely came to town to do their own shopping. Julia Arledge Thigpen, raised in rural southern Mississippi in the 1870s, recalled that her home was twenty-three miles to the closest railroad stop where her father went to shop. "Making this 23-mile round trip was so strenuous, taking two long hard days in rough riding wagons, that women seldom went. In our family, our father made the trips to town about two or three times a year. We would give him a list of things we wanted. He did the buying for the whole family. If he bought things we did not like, it was too far to go to exchange them so we just made the best we could of it."[22] A Delta resident recalled that thirty years later, "opportunities for shopping were extremely limited for the rural housewife of the early 1900s and trips to town were indeed infrequent."[23] As late as the 1920s, a study found that in the largest, poorest rural white households, women "hardly ever left home."[24] Even the women who did some of their own shopping visited the stores far less frequently than most men. Of the twelve women who shopped at the F. B. Furr store in Oxford in 1893, only one went into the store more than three times in one month, and most of the twelve visited less than once a month.[25]

It would be easy to stress the abundance and variety of the foods men found at the general stores. Thomas Clark, for example, emphasized the wide range of general store goods in the title of his 1944 history, *Pills, Plows, and Petticoats*.[26] The owner of a Noxubee County dry goods store listed his entire inventory in 1846. A. H. Jones listed relatively little clothing—stockings for men, women and

Leigh's Chapel Store, Tipton County, Tennessee, in the early 1900s. Many stores were important as gathering places for men as well as places for buying new goods. (Looking Back at Tennessee Collection, Tennessee State Library and Archive)

children, boots and shoes, suspenders, gloves, hats, bonnets and caps, over-coats, men's dress pants and vests, men's drawers, cravats, and shirt collars. He offered a few personal accessories—handkerchiefs, fans, parasols, and um-brellas—and a supply of household goods such as tablecloths, carpeting, blankets, dishes and glasses, towels, trunks, a chest, and some chairs. The inventory did not mention much farming equipment, perhaps including it under the generic term "hardware," but the store had traps, a good selection of rope, chains, a shotgun, and bags of shot. The store also had a few books and some medicine. More complete was Jones's supply of sewing equipment—pins, buttons, thimbles, ribbons, thread, and fringe. Above all, the store offered cloth—bolts and bolts of cloth. The inventory listed forty-nine different kinds of cloth, emphasizing the store had "a great deal" of jeans, ginghams, and flannel.[27] An 1842 advertisement for William C. Beck's store in Holly Springs gives a clear picture of the variety of goods. Beck sold groceries, plantation goods, and dry goods. Among the groceries were sugar and coffee, flour and meal, spices, fish and pork, wine, candles, soap, tobacco, nuts and candy. Plantation goods included powder, shot and lead, nails, chains, hoes, stoneware, and buckets.

TABLE 3. *Purchases Made by Sixty-seven Customers at the F. H. Campbell Store, Lodi, Mississippi, 1889–1891*

	Number	Percentage of Total
Men's clothing	57	3.9
Women's clothing	68	4.6
Children's clothing	21	1.4
Clothing, no clear gender	82	5.6
Shoes	233	15.9
Cloth	426	29.1
Sewing implements	306	20.9
Kitchen equipment	84	5.7
Books, pencils, etc.	64	4.4
Personal decorations	77	5.3
Household decorations	46	3.1
Total	1,464	100

Source: F. H. Campbell Store Ledger, Prewitt Family Collection, Winona, Miss. My thanks to the Prewitt family for allowing me to use the ledger, and to Scott Holzer for his work compiling the charts.

Among dry goods, Beck offered bonnets, cups, saucers and plates, sewing goods like pins and needles, and, above all, a great variety of cloth.[28]

Listing inventories may give an impression that stores held more excitement and offered more fascination than they actually did. In fact, the great majority of customers bought a small range of goods. The purchases customers made in 1890 and 1891 at Campbell's General Store in Lodi illustrate what they bought most frequently. The store offered the typical variety of dry goods, from pocket knives to dishes to men's suits to cloth. By a considerable margin, the goods customers bought most often were small purchases of cloth, costing less than a dollar. The next most common were sewing notions—pins, needles, ribbons, and thread. Precisely half of the purchases were either cloth or sewing notions.

This concentration on goods used in sewing reveals the close connection nineteenth-century Mississippians made between consumption and production. Men bought cloth, took it home, and women in their households made clothing from it. Especially for men, few of whom were involved in sewing, this was simply buying supplies as they would buy tools or seed; it was not shopping for goods that brought pleasure, excitement, or intrigue. Choosing among an array of bolts of cloth and small boxes of buttons, farm men wanted above all to buy cheaply and to check off the items on their list.

Dry goods store in Bolivar, Tennessee, 1913. Except for the bicycles, most of the goods were behind counters where only the clerk could reach them. (Looking Back at Tennessee Collection, Tennessee State Library and Archive)

Women who made rare trips to stores bought cloth and sewing goods far more than any other goods. Their purchases, like those men made, were small, and they almost never made exceptionally large purchases. Three-quarters of the women who visited the Jones Mercantile Store in Mount Vernon, Arkansas, in 1875 bought cloth, ribbons, buttons, or thread. Four bought plates, pickle dishes, forks, and knives, and seven bought shoes. But the large majority made purchases they could use in making their contribution to the independence of the household.[29]

The men and occasional women who visited the general store found themselves in a long, narrow building that resembled a hallway. Goods were piled to the ceiling on shelves on both sides. Most were behind counters, and many others were in barrels. Men entered the stores, and either handed the shopkeeper a list or simply told him what goods he wanted, and the shopkeeper retrieved the items. Customers did not often walk among the goods, wondering about possible choices, imagining how they might change their lives with new goods.

One of the clearest signs that general store customers seldom adopted the point of view of the modern consumer always searching for new pleasures was the tiny number of high-priced purchases they might have considered luxuries.

TABLE 4. *Most Expensive Individual Purchases at Stores, 1831–1894*

Store and Date	Items Purchased
German Berry's Store (Lowndes Co., Miss., 1831)	Cloth, salt, shoes, fur hats
Mount Prospect Trading Post (Bassfield, Miss., 1838)	Blankets, salt, cloth, one fur hat
Corban General Store (Corbandale, Tenn., 1853)	Shoes, boots, cloth
Clay and Sinclair's General Store (Ripley, Tenn., 1859)	Pants/vest, bonnets, coats, cloth
Vaiden General Store (Vaiden, Miss., 1871)	Suits, coat, cloth, saddle
M. Jones Store (Mount Vernon, Ark., 1875)	Cashmere coat, cloth, boots, meat
Campbell Store (Lodi, Miss., 1889–90)	Shoes, suits
F. B. Furr Store (Oxford, Miss., 1893–94)	Paint, suit, coats, dinner set

Sources: German and Joseph T. B. Berry Ledgers, Mount Prospect Trading Post Account Book, MDAH; Burwell J. Corban Papers, SHC; Clay and Sinclair's General Store Account Book, TSLA; Vaiden General Store Ledger, UK; M. Jones Mercantile Store Journal, UMem; F. H. Campbell Store Ledger, Prewitt Family Collection, Winona, Miss.; F. B. Furr Store Ledger, UMS.
Note: The table lists the most expensive items any individuals purchased on single trips to the stores. The items are listed in descending order, with the most expensive purchases first.

The most expensive luxury purchases men made at stores were men's suits and coats. The man who paid $7.50 for a fur hat at a Bassfield, Mississippi, store in 1838 was unique.[30] Far more typically, customers who made large single purchases were buying not special goods but bulk quantities of subsistence goods like cloth, shoes, and salt.

The habit of purchasing expensive goods only on extremely rare occasions suggests that general store customers did not tend to view shopping as exciting or particularly special. No doubt men welcomed opportunities to see male friends and to leave behind farm work, farm supervision, and the behavior expected in a family setting. Food, tobacco, and alcohol offered immediate enjoyment. And coming home with a wagon full of goods offered the experience of being the provider of taste and pleasure for women and children—the experience of being a patriarch even for owners of the smallest farms. However, the diaries and letters of all but the wealthiest white men in nineteenth-century Mississippi include few references to shopping. Seldom did they make any mention of buying goods at general stores, and on those rare occasions they used language that was straightforward and anything but romantic. Every day in 1886, for example, Arthur Rice recorded activities on his farm, usually mentioning nothing but the weather and the crops. The only time he mentioned any personal activities away from the farm was on April 15. "Suit clothes got today."[31] In an equally simple diary entry, a Tennessee farmer and preacher made clear that cost was his most important concern in buying goods for his wife. "Bought a pair of Shoes for wife. paid one dollar & 40 cents."[32] Mississippi farmer and brickmason Walter Overton put his purchases in the same mundane light when he recorded, "Bought a pair of shoes and gave for them $.95."[33] This was language without introspection, moralism, or intrigue; it was the language of checking items off a list, not language with room for desire or fascination.

Newspaper advertisements did little to suggest the stores were centers of mystery or excitement. Even when their advertisements stressed that goods were new and came from distant cities, store owners recognized and addressed the most important concerns of their customers for inexpensive, useful goods. Most advertisements simply named items, sometimes but not often with their prices. Goods appeared on long lists, fittingly enough in stores where farming men came with lists to fill. For example, E. M. Greaves described the stock in his store in Greenwood in a straightforward way. "We have in store and will keep constantly on hand, a good assortment of Staple and Fancy dry Goods, Groceries & c., which we offer for sale on the very best terms." For twenty-three lines, the advertisement then listed goods in unadorned language that used no adjectives beyond "fine," "coarse," and a few colors.[34] One of the most consistent claims was simply that goods were inexpensive. The Blue Store boasted in 1850 that it was "the Cheapest Store at which to buy bargains in Kosciusko."[35]

Stores did not even become places of shopping excitement at Christmas. Throughout the antebellum period and into the postbellum years, Mississippi storekeepers saw no reason to run special Christmas advertisements. Most newspapers passed through December without mentioning the holiday except to warn men against drunkenness. In fact, the end-of-year lists of property available because of unpaid taxes probably said more about farmers' place in the cash economy than any mentions of Christmas spending. One store owner in Hernando in 1869 offered the opposite of Christmas cheer. W. A. Raines viewed the holiday as a year-ending reminder of things more important than fireworks and candy. "Christmas!—Christmas is near at hand, and all those indebted to me for past indulgence, are respectfully requested to come forward and settle their accounts." Raines promised no new credit to those who left unsettled bills.[36]

The exceptions were adults who bought Christmas presents for children. Mitchell's Fancy Goods in Holly Springs advertised in 1851 that "Christmas is coming: Be merry for Christmas only comes once a year." The store offered toys, candy, and fireworks, apparently expecting all of the gifts to be for children.[37] A year later, a general store in Kosciusko offered "For Christmas, Cranberries, Almonds, Apples, Raisins, Pecans, Oranges, Newark cider and a variety of other nick nacks."[38] Christmas was thus a time of indulgence, but it consisted largely in men indulging themselves in drunkenness and indulging children with small gifts for their immediate enjoyment.

If Christmas offered no special pleasures for the men who shopped at the general stores, if newspaper advertisements did little more than list goods, if shoppers rarely bought expensive luxury items, and if men probably took more pleasure from seeing male friends than buying cloth for women to sew, what were shoppers thinking about as they came to the stores? As men filled their orders, they thought about debt. Were they putting their households at risk? Would this year's crop cover the cloth and shoes and tobacco they were buying? If they splurged and bought a suit, would they have to pay interest this year? If they had to leave goods for someone off their list, who would go without shoes, or cloth for a dress, or a collar for a shirt?

Debt was the central reality for general store customers.[39] Advertisements that claimed to sell for credit only to "responsible persons" challenged farming people to consider if they rated such consideration. As in many agricultural economies, most customers chose their goods, the storekeeper recorded each purchase and the unpaid cost in a ledger, and the customer hoped to pay at the end of the crop season. At one store in Noxubee County, only about a seventh of the customers from 1837 to 1839 paid any cash except between December and February. In fact, half of the customers paid no cash at all, either leaving their bills for the following year or paying with cotton or corn.[40] At one general store in central Tennessee in 1832, virtually no customer paid any cash until December. The poorest members of the free antebellum population were often wage laborers who did not have cash and could not get store credit.[41] By the end of the century, the growing number of wage earners was beginning to free up more cash to spend, but debt remained a crucial concern. At Love's Station General Store in DeSoto County, Mississippi, shoppers in 1901 purchased about six times as many goods on credit as they bought with cash.[42] At a store in Warren County in 1898, only a tenth of the customers made any cash payments.[43] At Campbell's Store in Lodi, only eight of sixty-three customers in 1890 paid any cash outside the cash-rich months of November, December, and January.[44]

Going into debt meant giving up the personal independence so valued in the antebellum South. It meant working for someone else, losing control over one's family, facing the possibility of financial ruin, and knowing that no prosperity was ever secure. In a slave society, it meant being in a position that resembled the powerlessness of slaves. For Virginians in the late colonial period, as T. H. Breen has argued, debt was the primary sin, just as selfishness and conflict were the primary sins for Puritans in colonial New England.[45] Mississippians tended to see the same moral gravity in debt, even as so many went deeply into it. One writer used the ultimate metaphor: that death was the "one debt due from all living that sooner or later must and will be paid."[46]

As Breen suggests, debt-free independence was central to the notions white men had about freedom and manhood. The language of debt as a threat to manhood was perhaps even more crucial to political and economic thinking in the Mississippi area. Those who were deeply in debt feared that by not being in control, they could not really act as the equals of other men. On the western Tennessee frontier in 1832, William Duncan used especially powerful language in worrying he had "been raped by old claims all of which I have endeavored to pay when presented. I have no other wish under heaven than to discharge every debt I ever owed or now may owe."[47] Duncan felt not merely unmanned but attacked and defeated and thus less a man than those who had power over him. Significantly, in being unmanned or raped, such men feared they were not properly protecting their families.

In an impassioned letter to a store owner in postwar Arkansas, one debtor displayed how the inability to pay debts threatened his honor and masculine control along with his finances. Sim Williams wrote store owner William Paisley, "You have a right to think me a d— scoundrel or anything else & I could not blame you if you were to take the coat off my back & strip me entirely and sell my clothes." The notion of a man "stripped" by his debts was one more sign of the links between manhood and independence. In a culture based on personal honor, "damned scoundrel" was duelling language, but by applying it to himself, Williams showed he did not consider himself a man who deserved respect. He continued by quoting a letter from Paisley. "You say that you hope that I will 'not ask or expect further indulgence.' I can't ask you to wait longer, but I am telling you the truth when I tell you that I have only 15 cents to save my life." Admitting to destitution, Williams suggested he did not deserve to be indulged—a condition white men had tended to reserve for women, children, and, prior to emancipation, slaves. The pitying tone of the letter came from Williams's acknowledgment that he was neither a man of independence nor a man of honor who could expect equal treatment from other men.[48]

Debt presented an interesting dilemma for whites in Mississippi. In parts of the country less devoted to production for markets, the fear of debt often meant people concentrated on growing food crops before thinking of profits. While farmers and planters in Mississippi saw self-sufficiency as a noble ideal, in general they had settled the state in hopes of pursuing the wealth available through cotton and slaves. As Bradley G. Bond writes, "The market was always present in the Deep South; it was the midwife at Mississippi's birthing."[49] Many Mississippians could not pursue wealth without going into debt, and they were too attracted to the chances the state offered to eschew debt for land and slaves. Thus if debt threatened their independence and their manhood but also offered their only chance for wealth, they focused their fears and condemnations of debt on those debts that helped buy consumer goods.

It is no coincidence that many Mississippians used the same term to describe both the time needed to pay debts and the expenses they considered frivolous. Both were *indulgences*, and in the language of nineteenth-century political and religious thinking, indulgence was both economically dangerous and sinful. In diaries, sermons, political speeches, and letters to children, Mississippians repeatedly warned themselves and others about the temptations of spending too much on the mere pleasure of goods. Exasperated by his debts in 1850, for example, Needham Whitfield condemned himself: "I just feel like I have done enough to indulge myself the balance of my life or at least determined to keep out of debt and be more moderate."[50]

Other language Mississippians used to criticize spending habits had moral sides as well. A young woman who threatened to spend her new family into poverty seemed "extravagant."[51] A young man had to defend himself against his father's impression that he was "still travelling in the old rut—extravagance."[52] A young man confessed he had long been "improvident" in spending, but pledged to reform when he got married.[53] The possibilities to make money quickly in the early years offered temptations to spend quickly as well. Duncan McKenzie wrote that an acquaintance was "on the extravagant list. any man may make money but it is the fewest that can keep it."[54]

It was primarily their ties to credit that gave general stores, their owners, and their employees a shady reputation among farm people. Store owners often seemed and felt themselves to be outsiders in the communities where they lived, and planters and farmers, especially in the antebellum period, tended to see selling goods as a frivolous and perhaps untrustworthy profession. D. McKenzie wrote sadly of an acquaintance who had "commenced that light and gaudy occupation of selling Silks laces [illegible] and callicoes from a pedling waggon. . . ."[55] Storekeeping seemed to threaten the independence so many white men craved. On the Mississippi frontier in 1830, a young man named Thomas Clark worked in a store owned by "my masters as I may call them." Clark complained that he did all of the work for his idle employer and enjoyed himself only when he "escaped the store" and went into the countryside.[56]

The biggest problem was that storekeepers dealt in credit, and free Mississippians hated debt even as they went deeply into it. Descriptions of financial life in the stores were almost always full of suspicion. Living outside Greenville, A. J. Paxton made clear the distinction between the goal of independence and resistance to the dangers of credit. When a merchant pressed him for his debts, Paxton claimed to have replied, "You can have what I've got but my children and I are not going to work for you."[57] Day after day, storekeepers faced distrust and the tension inherent in a situation in which customers might see them either as friendly benefactors or greedy predators. Storekeeper Clark wrote in 1832 that "our Counting Room is now full of Loud noisey young men that distrust me."[58] A store owner in north Mississippi wrote his partner that although money was tight, he was able to make some collections in January 1854. "I am dunning tight & madding some."[59]

Some store employees saw their work as a sign of conniving, corruption, and immorality. In January of 1861, store owner Thomas Webber lay in a Byhalia bed suffering from illnesses he contracted while he tried frantically to collect some debts. He was "pressed almost out of my mind for money" and had to rely on some shaky friendships to forestall a collapse. As this twenty-six-year-old contemplated his problems and those of the South, he despaired, "Life has few charms for a man Situated as I am determined to quit the dry goods business[.] It will kill any man of my temperament in the whole world."[60] Ten years earlier, another storekeeper despaired that the Aberdeen region was "a cursed, infernal, devilish & hellish country to collect money in."[61] In the Delta, farm owner Clive Metcalfe helped out at a store for a few days in 1889 and complained, "This is a hard world when a man has to deal with and associate with creatures whom it is impossible to elevate the mind above a cuss word. God forbid that I will have to do it allways."[62]

The status of so many store owners and peddlers as ethnic outsiders in Mississippi made them particular targets for disdain among farm people already ready to distrust creditors. A farmer in antebellum Amite County was irritated by the number of traveling salesmen who felt free to stay at his home. After having overnight visits from Jewish, French, Dutch, and Irish peddlers in less than two months in 1841, L. M. Boatner decided to start charging them for room and board because "such characters are becoming so common that we do not feel bound to support them for nothing. Pedling is resorted to by foreigners and we are not sure that some of them are not spies."[63] A Mississippi native joined his hatred of dependence with conventional beliefs about Jews to complain from Texas, "Now that I am working for Jews I have no time that I can call my own not even Sunday as a day of rest and recreation."[64] After a Delta flood in 1890, Henry Ball took some pleasure in seeing "bunches of Jew clerks, coats off, and doing perhaps the first honest work of their lives."[65]

The story of Jewish life in nineteenth-century Mississippi revolves around stores and storekeeping. Jewish immigrants from German-speaking areas of Europe came to the state in the antebellum period, followed by Russian and Polish Jews later in the century. Many had backgrounds as storekeepers and tailors, most had faced legal restrictions against owning land, and relatively few had backgrounds in plantation agriculture. Thus, many began as traveling peddlers before the more successful settled in towns to open stores. In some towns, there were only a few Jewish residents, most of whom owned and worked in stores. By the 1840s, John Mayer, Aaron Beekman, and David Moses ran three of the largest stores in Natchez. By the end of the Civil War, Vicksburg was home to ninety Jewish families and about thirty-five Jewish-owned stores.[66]

Jewish merchants living in Mississippi towns tried to find their niche in a society dominated by farmers and planters, most of whom took their Protestantism seriously. They made no secret of their Jewish identity, and only a few changed their names to make their status as outsiders less conspicuous. Isaac Flower, for example, changed his name from Isaac Blum, a German and Yiddish term for flower, and started the Flower Clothing Company in Lexington. More followed the lead of Ettenger and Tandler, who described their dry goods store in Holly Springs as "the Jew's Store."[67] It was hard for storekeepers to shake the old stereotype of Jewish merchants as selfish creditors whose religion and background made them untrustworthy, but some went to great lengths to challenge it. For example, C. H. Blum had a general store in Nitta Yuma and used two approaches in his advertising to reassure customers they could trust and do business with him. First, customers who bought goods worth over $2.50 received free hymnals "suitable for Baptist or Methodist," and those who made purchases over $5.00 received Bibles. Second, "Our Mr. Blum has purchased a picture, a true piece of art, and well worth your inspection. The picture represents the Last Supper, or the Lord taking the last Sacrament with the Apostles." Each customer could vote for his or her own church, and on Christmas Day, Blum gave the painting to the church with the most votes. This gesture said with no great subtlety that a Jewish merchant posed no threat to the money or religion of Christian farmers. Far from trying to find ways to cheat them, C. H. Blum was showing he was willing to give things away.[68]

Despite such efforts to reassure customers, the position of selling goods was thus a tenuous one. On the one hand, merchants brought customers in contact with goods they wanted. On the other hand, merchants in an agricultural

Joseph Perlinsky, owner of Perlinsky's Store for Men in Canton, Mississippi. One of many Jewish immigrants to run successful stores, Perlinsky started as a tailor's apprentice in Poland, migrated to Mississippi, and opened his store in 1872. (Mississippi Department of Archives and History)

society often seemed to be outsiders—people with different backgrounds operating with a different and sometimes threatening set of rules.

General stores, to summarize, rarely played the roles their owners hoped. They partially and often only barely fulfilled their goal of bringing cosmopolitan fashion to rural areas. Men continued to shop in ways that showed they were more interested in inexpensive utility than in changing fashions. With little interest in those changes, they did not become the dreaming consumers who hope to use their next purchases to redefine themselves. Store owners who wanted to convert their customers to cash payments were dreaming themselves. Cash came slowly to most farming Mississippians, and they parted with it painfully. Most general store owners who hoped to encourage women to shop met frustration as well. Throughout the nineteenth century, women did little of their own shopping in general stores, although that was beginning to change by the end of the century. Instead of meeting the store owners' lofty goals of bringing cosmopolitan culture to the farm people, the stores remained institutions that above all served the needs of men who valued independent farm life more highly than any pleasures goods might bring. Goods were dangerous, they were indulgences, they were frivolous. If they brought temporary pleasure to the men and—far less often—the women who bought them, they also threatened the independence so many white Mississippians saw as their definition of the good life. Over the course of the nineteenth century, stores and their shoppers changed, but only gradually. Store owners demanded more cash payments and offered a wider variety of goods. In the postbellum period, as Chapter Three will show, former slaves went into the stores, but they rarely felt at ease in white-owned stores. As long as Mississippi farm life revolved around rural rhythms, male control, and the fear of debt, stores remained sleepy sites where the dreams of consumer culture were slow to develop.

Farming women had little control over how money was spent, but they had a great deal to say about the goods their families used, wore, and ate. Living in a society where almost everyone understood his or her place in the world through the prism of a household, they understood and shared men's efforts to keep households independent.[69] They had their own relationship to goods—a relationship that, like men's, feared that too much indulgence in the life of cosmopolitan fashion could endanger things they valued more than a new dress.

Farm women did little shopping in nineteenth-century Mississippi. When they went into general stores, they bought cloth and sewing tools more than any other products. Hardly ever did they buy expensive goods for themselves, and farming men did not buy expensive clothing for the women in their families. Ready-made clothing for women was not often available and, to the men who bought things for women to sew, not desirable. Shoppers in a Jackson, Tennessee, general store in 1859 made more than four times as many purchases of clothing for more than five dollars for men as they made for women. Thirty years later in Lodi, Mississippi, five men made clothing purchases of more than five dollars for men, but no one bought articles of women's clothing for nearly that amount.[70]

Tensions were almost inevitable in a situation where men bought the cloth that women used in their sewing. Women who rarely shopped could make specific requests, but most men decided how the family spent its money. The potential for conflict showed in the diary of Nannie Jackson, a poor farm woman in the Delta area of Arkansas. In ten months in 1890 and 1891, Jackson went to the store six times, more often than most rural women in the nineteenth century. More frequently, she asked her husband or other men to shop for her. Some purchases led to memorable arguments with her husband William. The night after she bought some cloth and thread on credit, "it looked like Mr Jackson got mad because I bought what I did today but I can't help it if he did."[71] Two weeks later, the argument continued. Her husband "accused me of mean things because I was going to send to Redford by Mr. Morgan to get some white goods to make Sue & I a white dress apiece oh but I would he had treated me with silent contempt for 6 months than to talk to me as he did this evening."[72] We can only speculate whether they were arguing about the expense of the goods Nannie Jackson wanted or about her attempt to make decisions William assumed were his to make.

Most nonslave women, like most men, identified household independence as the key to their family's happiness and future. Women used the same tortured language as men to describe their fears of debt. A middle-class woman in Water Valley combined her worries about debt with her reticence about expressing those worries. Dora McFarland wrote friends, "I am almost crazy about the future when I see no means coming in to insure independence of living for months to come. Mr. McFarland often says he wishes I was like any other woman under the sun, all of whom (he thinks) trust such troubles wholly to their husbands, and themselves take life easy and are happy."[73] In Washington County, Martha Blanton worried that her husband might be putting the family into debt, but she feared she could do little about it. "I know one thing; if he is not able to judge for himself about such matters, I have no right to advise, but I am opposed to debt certain."[74] After the Civil War and the death of her husband led to large debts, Octavia Otey despaired in 1871, "I owe so many debts that I am crazy about them. we have to go through with some privations it is true and deny ourselves all pleasure outside of our house but it hurts me to keep people from their just dues. . . . here they are, my debts, my own acts and they crush me to the earth."[75]

Wishing to stand above the lure of luxury and self-indulgence that could create or increase such debts, women in free households tried to sew as many clothes as possible. Sewing helped contribute to the household economy, and it helped to thwart the development of tastes toward expensive fabrics and clothing.[76] Countless entries in diaries show the moral and economic importance women placed in sewing as part of their contribution to the independence of the household. A teenager we know only as Miss Hardeman spelled out the significance she placed on sewing in New Year's resolutions she made for 1859. Hardeman planned to allot three days each week for nothing but sewing.

> 1st Monday. Repair clothing of every kind and put them in place—annex a penalty to the omission of this duty.
> 2nd Tuesday. If a garment is commenced, work diligently with a view to completion within the week.
> 3rd Wednesday. If we should be dress-making, use every exertion to complete it in as short a time as possible. Be patient, diligent and industrious.[77]

Clear moral compulsion governed such rules; Hardeman's second rule seems close to the biblical notion to do with all her might whatever her hand found to do.

Vivid examples of the moral obligation not to allow anything frivolous to interfere with the duty of sewing lay in sermons and in the letters parents wrote to their daughters. One father wrote his daughter in 1862 to "keep good order at all times. . . . permit no laughing and talking on sewing evenings."[78] Methodist minister Charles B. Galloway stressed the opportunities to use sewing to relieve suffering. Among the virtues he saw in the New Testament character Dorcas was the fact that "many skinny little limbs were made warm and comfortable by her industrious hands."[79] When such men discussed the sewing or spending of women, their language ranged from the heroic to the subversive, but it always tended toward extremes. Women could either be the virtuous Dorcas, using needle and thread to spread comfort and uphold freedom, or the temptress Eve, endangering freedom with tastes for extravagant new pleasures. Woman's weakness ran toward indulgence, her strength toward heroic self-denial.

In considerations of household independence, the opposite of sewing was wasting money on cloth and clothing. Evangelical preachers loved to condemn women's tastes for luxurious and frivolous clothing, often in ways that joined the weaknesses of the upper classes with what they saw as the special weaknesses of women. Both, they believed, tended toward self-indulgence and pretension. Methodist leader William Winans condemned the ability of clothing to stimulate pride among the wealthy. "Some claim a distinction for the dress they wear—perhaps for the color of a ribbon or the richness of a lace, the chasing of a bracelet or the brilliancy of its jewels."[80] A Baptist in northern Louisiana suggested a book of religious literature to his daughter because "it shows the folly & wickedness of some persons passions for dress in its true light."[81] A preacher in Holly Springs attacked the upper-class ideal for women and tied it to tastes for clothing. "Be not ambitious to be considered a belle. It is the fate of most belles to be foolishly vain, think of nothing and care for nothing beyond personal display."[82] An Arkansas man, writing proudly in his diary about the happiness of his family, attributed it in large part to the sacrifices of his wife, whose "own pleasure has no existence apart from what may be the pleasure of the others. . . . When our revenues are low and no means and opportunities of recruiting them, she curtails the expenses of her wardrobe and household accordingly, [illegible] without a murmur."[83]

"The Country Girls," a poem the *Lexington Union* printed in 1838, developed the same point at considerable length. The unnamed poet began his picture of the ideal female with the importance of sewing as a way to avoid the expense and frivolity of fashion.

> I love the country spinster,
>   Who turns the buzzing wheel,
> Who plies, with busy hands the card,
>   With merry hum, the reel.
> I love the country seamstress,
>   Who makes the household gear,
> And who, with industry and art,
>   Prepares the homespun wear.

The poet continued that such women "wear their own wrought homespun / And gew-gaw show reject" and have "No studied vicious taste" and no corsets to "cut the waist." The poet ended with an ode to women who are

> Faithful to all relations,
>   As mothers, daughters, wives—
> As sisters kind, as lovers true,
>   And virtuous their lives.[84]

Such poetry seems likely to have been the work of a man whose household benefited from high levels of production. When women wrote about sewing and spending, they used less grandiose language. It was indeed a duty, women said, but along with duties came burdens, and they often chided themselves for doing less than they should. It was a day-to-day duty, but it was rarely a heroic act with biblical meaning. The moral side of women's commitment to sewing shows most clearly in their diaries, where they described sewing as their "work" or their "duty." Mahala Roach, a wealthy woman living outside Vicksburg, recorded an extraordinary amount of sewing. In 1868, she sewed on at least 155 days, more than half of the days that were not Sundays. Referring to sewing as "my work," Roach scolded herself for not doing as much work as she could.

Discussing sewing on December 31, she promised, "will *try* to be more indus-trious next year." She complained about her own work habits: "I have been too lazy to live, almost too lazy to read, have done no sewing, nothing useful but nurse the babies." Fifteen years later, she still worried that she had not sewed "both because my eyes hurt, and that I am lazy." She considered her inactivity a "shameful waste of time."[85] Evangelical women often connected the need to economize to the moral dangers of luxury. Nancy Willard, a devout Baptist in northwest Louisiana, lashed out at the pretensions and high style of the local elites. In a long series of letters, she scoffed at church members who hosted dancing parties. "When I was A child they were not allowed to ware A ruffle on their garments much less go to a dancing party." Even more objectionable than ruffles was the hoop skirt. Willard snorted to a friend, "Take care for they are large you can hear them strike the seats and scrape the door casing as they flaunt in and out."[86]

For many women, especially younger women, deciding if they could care about fashion without becoming indulgent and pretentious was an important part of developing their own personalities. Temptation lay in luxury, and lux-uries threatened the goal of household independence. One extended example shows a young woman who struggled to find her own place in the material world. Maria Dyer was born in 1833 into a fairly wealthy cotton-growing, slaveowning family outside Macon, Mississippi. The diary she started keeping in her late teens shows how hard she found it to choose between two perspec-tives. On the one hand, she saw sewing as part of a duty that had moral significance. She felt guilty when she did not do her sewing, once complaining, "I made a few lazy efforts to sew but haven't done anything." On another day, she "sewed very well. Have been trying to do my duty to-day."[87]

On the other hand, Maria Dyer loved to shop. Sometimes she went into Macon, and once or twice she made the trip to Mobile. In almost an anthem for consumer culture, she summed up the romantic ability of consumer spending to relieve momentary unhappiness with the phrase, "Had the blues. I bought me a dress." Taking obvious pleasure in buying, owning, and displaying her goods, when a shipment of new clothing arrived from Mobile, she spread them out in her room and noted, "We have quite a display of finery and fine-ness." At times a real-life Scarlett O'Hara, she once spent the morning "dressing and undressing. finally we made our choices & went to the fair."[88]

Dyer was torn between her desire for luxury and the pleasure of shopping, on the one hand, and her commitments, on the other, to the notions of sewing as a duty and display as a sinful extravagance. She took seriously sermons about the virtues of humility, and once recorded with apparent agreement that her preacher "gave it to the girls about their laziness and extravagance." The tensions came to the surface at a church service in 1852 when she openly renounced some of her finest clothing. "I had been troubled about my shawl (crape and embroidered). I always felt that it was finer than I wanted to wear & I could not tell whether it was the Sperit which told me not to wear it; or whether twas a notion of my own. perhaps a temptation. I made the sacrifice in class. I did not feel the happiness I anticipated but I thought it might be because I was so reluctant to give it up."[89]

In the nineteen-year-old Dyer, the side that demanded religious humility and household independence won out over the side that yearned for novelty and fashion. The winning side believed it was not merely prudent but moral to avoid luxury in the name of simplicity and production. During the Civil War white women turned sewing, simplicity, and home production into a homespun crusade. It became a badge of religious simplicity and Confederate dedication to display clothes of one's own making. As a Louisiana woman wrote a friend, "I have been wearing homespun dresses this winter to save my calico. . . . in the last eighteen months I have not worn anything better than a calico." Mary Overton noted in December 1861 that she was doing the first spinning of her life. Mary Willard wrote in 1862, "You aught to hear the Women talk about spinning we are out of looms."[90]

Sewing their own clothing had meanings beyond preserving the independence of the household. Women shared sewing and patterns and sewed for each other. For many women, sewing was a material expression of sisterhood that combined production with creativity and friendship. According to historian Caroll Smith-Rosenberg, middle-class Victorian women resisted some of the effects of male domination through frequent visiting and letter-writing that created a sisterhood that offered them roles other than wife and mother.[91] In rural Mississippi, sewing served the same purposes. Women often sewed together. Ten-year-old Belle Strickland recorded in her diary in 1865, "I sewed on my doll dress this evening and sewed some tonight and Miss Lizzie and Miss Cora read some and Mrs. Watson sewed."[92] Eighteen-year-old Jane Jones also wrote of the ways sewing connected different generations. "Mother & myself made a dress for Aunt Abby. I then went out and wove a good deal."[93]

Mississippi women frequently sewed clothes to send to friends and relatives. The mail must have been full of garments being shipped as gifts from woman to woman. In 1876 a young woman wrote her aunt that another relative "is well, and is knitting Tina some little woolen stockings, she has made Marrie and myself, a Jacquet trimmed them with black velvet."[94] Sisters Martha Blanton and Jane Smith sent each other one garment after another and were part of a larger circle of female family members who did the same. Blanton asked her sister to "tell Mama I received two beautiful little Hoods or Bonnets last week for which I thank her sincerely," and Smith wrote later to wonder, "Why don't Sister Anna send us some sewing to do for her children. Tell her to do so; send it by one of the packets, and I will be sure to get it. If you are pressed with work, Sister and I will gladly assist you this winter."[95]

Sewing offered important opportunities for women in free households. They could take comfort in helping preserve debt-free independence for the family, satisfying notions of female duty, resisting temptation and self-indulgence, and enjoying a material expression of sisterhood. But many women, especially wealthy women, rejected some of these values and shaped themselves instead as consumers. These were the women who agreed with Maria Dyer when she had the blues and bought a dress.

A clear example was Lucy Irion. She was born in Bolivar, Tennessee, in 1843 and spent most of her life in Mississippi. Irion grew up having to sew but found it difficult to view an economic necessity as a moral obligation. After her family left their home due to economic problems in the early 1850s, she "used to think it very hard that I must sit in Aunt's room day after day & knit the negroes' socks when the sun shone so brightly & the birds sung so sweetly. I blamed Sis many times when she refused to let me play."[96] The notion that making clothes was part of female duty stayed with her. When the family's finances improved enough to send her to Corona College in Corinth, Mississippi, she frequently recorded moral and economic importance she saw in sewing. One day she combined it with Bible reading. "I read my chapters regularly and fixed my worsted dresses."[97] Later she "arose early & performed my usual duties & sewed steadily till dinner."[98]

Believing that sewing was a duty and recognizing the problems of debt, Irion shared with Maria Dyer a fear of the moral and economic dangers of expensive clothing. She ran up a high clothing account in 1859 but promised to reform. "I am not going to by anything scarcely next Session, but I *did try* to be saving this last session." She emphasized the religious side of the issue, praying, "God help me to be a good girl."[99]

After she married and her family's finances improved, she came to believe that the best clothes were those that conformed to the latest northeastern and European fashions. Beginning to describe her interest in clothing as "woman-like,"[100] Lucy Irion Neilson filled her letters and diary with discussions of changing fashions and possible purchases. Shortly after the Civil War, she greeted her first visitors in years with a pesky series of questions. "Above all, what *sort of clothes* were in their ample trunks? Ah, weak human-nature & especially *woman*-nature, but, remember, dear Journal, I had been in Secession for four long years, & all my silks and muslins had positively refused to be turned upside-down & wrong-side out any more. . . . Delightful visions of fresh ribbons, rich laces, & soft fleecy organdies flitted thro' my brain & then a pang followed to think how 'tacky' I would appear on my first call!" Her husband gave her "a handful of green-backs," and she went to Columbus in the state of mind storekeepers no doubt wished was more common. "How delighted I was when I went shopping. . . . How I gloried in the thought! I purchased some sweet, lush-looking dresses, & a 'perfect love of a hat'! My self respect was raised several degrees when I went out, *dressed up, fresh & new.*"[101]

This was the desire of the consumer society. Wrapping up self-respect with freshness and novelty and new clothing, she was espousing a clear statement of the romantic concept of taking pleasure in the change that new goods could bring. Five years later, Neilson was complaining that she felt shabby for wearing the same "few dresses so constantly," and she asked her sister to keep her informed about the latest styles. "I find myself getting anxious to know how the gay world proposes tricking up their heads this season."[102]

CHAPTER TWO

Wealthy Men, Wealthy Women, and Slaves as Antebellum Consumers

Lucy Irion Neilson was the kind of southerner William Henry Holcombe of Natchez meant when he claimed in 1850, "The Northerner loves to make money, the Southerner loves to spend it."[1] Like many statements of southern identity, this maxim referred only to the region's ruling class. The wealthy could buy luxury goods sold in cities, either by traveling to New Orleans or Mobile or Memphis or by dealing with cotton factors who bought goods for them. In the antebellum period, they were the only free people who could buy goods without worrying about losing their independence, and even many of them were not so sure. This chapter deals with the two groups for whom debt was not the main concern in thinking about goods in antebellum Mississippi—the extremely wealthy and the slaves.

Robert Gordon, owner of Lochinvar, a large plantation in north Mississippi, fit Holcombe's definition of a southerner. In the summer of 1851, he and Mary Gordon took a trip to Boston in June and to London, Paris, and Glasgow in July and August. On the first leg of the trip, as Robert Gordon wrote in his diary, they "spent this day in Boston shoping & gave measurements to have some clothes made for Jas. and myself. Mary bot. Bonnet & Dress." A few days later they were "engaged looking at carriages—A great variety Can't decide what we like best." In Glasgow and Paris, the Gordons went shopping after he "drew fifty pounds of my Bankers." Finally, back in London, he drew 200 more pounds and "spent the day in shopping getting clothes."[2]

The tour by the Gordons reveals how wealthy Mississippians bought and thought about their goods very differently from most people in the state. Men and women often shopped together, and women could be at least as important in the shopping experience as men. Planter family consumers spent large and even huge sums of money. They considered merchants their friends and apparently had little of the resentment toward the sellers of goods that tended to characterize relations between farmers and general store merchant-creditors. They shopped around in different stores, bought luxury goods, and sometimes bought goods just for the fun of it.

A comparison of the goods owned by different groups of white households helps illustrate just what constituted luxury goods in antebellum Mississippi. A study of probate inventories of 112 people in Lawrence and Yalobusha Counties shows what wealthy people owned in the 1830s, 1840s, and 1850s. Located in the south-central and central parts of the state, Lawrence and Yalobusha Counties were cotton plantation areas, but neither had the extraordinary wealth of some Mississippi regions. For the convenience of comparison, the 112 inventories were divided into three groups by wealth.[3]

One of the most striking differences among the three groups involved vehicles—wagons, buggies, and carriages. Fourteen percent of the poorest group and 43 percent of the middle group owned vehicles, but 74 percent of the wealthiest had vehicles. While some members of the poor and middling group owned wagons, only the wealthy had expensive carriages, about a quarter of them owning vehicles costing more than a hundred dollars.

More private goods also divided along clear lines of wealth. Only one of the thirty-eight poorest members of the sample owned a carpet, while 20 percent of the wealthiest had carpeting. Forty-five percent of the poorest had chairs, about two-thirds of the middle group, and four-fifths of the wealthiest had chairs. Forty percent of the poorest group owned beds, while more than 90 percent of the other two groups had at least one bed. Most striking is that the wealthiest group averaged about 5 beds per household, while the middle group averaged about 2.5 beds. Among the poorest group, that minority who had beds had just 1.5 per household.

Specific examples of the goods belonging to three men from Yalobusha County can illustrate the precise differences in the possessions antebellum Mississippians owned. Small farmer Richard Godfrey died in 1852 with a little less than $200 worth of property. Rare for people of his low income, he owned two beds. But his other household goods were typically sparse. Five inexpensive chairs surrounded an old table. His only other furniture consisted of a desk valued at seventy-five cents and two inexpensive boxes that probably served as both containers and tables. He had two ovens, a pot, a teakettle, a pair of fireplace implements, a razor, and a shaving brush. Aside from a cheap pair of spectacles, all of his other goods consisted of livestock, corn, and farm tools. Virtually all of his belongings seemed dedicated to either production or inexpensive subsistence.

Thomas Carby, an example from the middle group, died in 1851 with an estate of $1,736.25. A farmer and surveyor, Carby owned a variety of goods that contrasted dramatically to those of Richard Godfrey. He owned one of the few pianos in his county and could afford a carriage valued at $350. He owned a little carpeting, two clocks, a "fine lamp," a large mirror, some vases and candlesticks, and several blinds and curtains. In a dining area, Carby had six mahogany chairs, a dining table, and, unlike Godfrey, could set the table with a few glasses and plates, knives and forks, as well as an older set of tinware. Carby had a wardrobe, a bureau, two bedroom chairs, two feather beds, and a trundle bed for a child. Finally, his household included a sofa and a variety of tables. The rest of his goods lay in farm products and farming and surveying equipment.

Michael Melton died with a substantial estate worth about $5,500, four-fifths of which consisted of five slaves. The wealthier man had more luxury goods than his farming neighbor, Carby. For example, Melton could entertain in a room with one of the few dining room carpets in Yalobusha County. Whereas Carby had seven forks and knives and apparently no spoons, Melton could afford to serve guests with a dozen ivory-handled knives and forks and full sets of silver tablespoons, teaspoons, dessert spoons, a pair of sugar tongs, and two butter knives. And where Carby had tableware valued at about five dollars, Melton had glasses that were alone worth twenty dollars. Unlike the other two men, Melton had a parlor—a receiving room nineteenth-century Americans typically loaded with ornate furniture. Melton's parlor had carpeting, a mahogany center table, a pair of spittoons, and on the walls framed pictures of Washington and Lafayette and maps of the United States and the Holy Land.[4] Many of his goods were simply more expensive than Carby's. His marble-topped dressing bureau was worth thirty dollars, twenty-two dollars more than the wooden bureau in Carby's house. And with four beds and twenty-four chairs, he had more goods. Unlike the inventories of most Mississippians, including Carby and Godfrey, the inventory of Melton's goods described some of them with points of origin; the teaspoons were German, the bedsteads were French.

The goods people like Michael Melton owned help delineate the meanings of luxury in antebellum Mississippi. To whom did plantation families expect their goods to communicate, and what did they want them to say? A too-simple scholar's dichotomy could divide wealthy people into groups who used their spending power to express leadership and involved their larger communities in the fruits of their wealth, and groups who used goods primarily to enjoy themselves privately and to communicate that enjoyment with other elites. In the colonial South, that distinction tends to divide Virginia and South Carolina. In Virginia, planters built mansions on hills and expected the rest of white society literally to look up to them and to approach them for debts, favors, dances, horse races, and barbecues, while promising to descend to perform public-spirited political service in return. In South Carolina, many elites lived in Charleston as absentee landlords in houses cut off from the street and any public view and enjoyed their luxury goods with little public connection to the rest of white society.[5]

In the Mississippi inventories, two points stand out as distinctive features of luxury goods. First is the importance of display. Wealthy Mississippians chose to display luxuries to express permanence and elitism. Many enjoyed using luxury items in offering hospitality. Second, luxury goods offered private pleasures unavailable to the rest of the population. As the shopping trip by Robert and Mary Gordon showed, goods connected the wealthy to Euro-American cosmopolitan culture. Unlike the farm men who took occasional trips to general stores to buy cloth and worry about debt, the Gordons had the sheer pleasure of shopping as individuals or couples. Probably less important, goods also allowed wealthy people more privacy inside their homes.

Wealthy Mississippians hoped to express leadership with their homes, carriages, and home furnishings. Many scholars have stressed the effort by the wealthy, as Eugene Genovese suggests, to put on a well-financed show to earn the respect of the rest of the population. "Every dollar spent by the planters for elegant clothes, a college education for their children, or a lavish barbecue contributed to the political and social domination of their class." Genovese notes, significantly, that much of the notion that the wealthy had goods that suggested "quality" came not from the rest of the white population but from the slaves.[6]

The mansions of the wealthy communicated messages to other white Mississippians. The expense and the permanence of the structures said the rich were there to stay, while the small wooden houses of smaller farmers suggested impermanence. This was crucial in a time when one or two bad crops inspired thoughts of migrating to Texas. The materials of the mansions, the fact that they had architects, and the elaborate design that made some of them such remarkable social statements, all had to do not merely with enjoying wealth but displaying it. In Natchez, the earliest home for extreme wealth in Mississippi, elites built homes on tree-lined hills, in part to create a dramatic show for those approaching the mansions and in part to remind those working down below that there were those who had the power literally to live above them.[7]

Deep in English gentry tradition, luxury vehicles served as symbols of elitism, marking their riders as people who deserved respect as they approached their earth-bound inferiors.[8] Often ornate with wood carving, carriages allowed their travelers the potentially contradictory possibilities of having privacy while being on display. Many vehicles immediately announced the identity of their owners, but did so without forcing the inhabitants of the homes on wheels to get out and socialize with other travelers. Mississippians loved to talk about carriages as objects of either desire or derision. In 1857 Martha Blanton described taking her daughters and family guests to a series of upper-class parties and dances. "I wish I had a carriage to carry them about in, but the next extravagance of mine will be for their [her daughters'] benefit as well as my own."[9] According to a man in western Alabama, a relative made an unmistakable statement with her vehicle. "She drives a fine carriage & horses & is disposed to keep up as good style as any one in the Country."[10] Susan Sillers Darden, an extremely wealthy member of a planter family in the Natchez area, commented frequently on carriages as she traced the comings and goings of upper-class society in the 1850s. "Jack came with his carriage; it is pretty." In another diary entry, she wrote, "Mr. Montgomery got his new carriage home Monday; it cost $375.00 in New Orleans." A friend "has a new carriage & horses; the carriage cost $1050.00; the horses, $800.00." Owners of the carriages put great significance in the appearance of their vehicles. Darden noted that when her husband returned from Natchez one night, he brought a new carriage, "trimmed with lilac and orange morocco cushions; gave $575.00."[11] One could buy carriages in Memphis with "tops trimmed with red velvet."[12]

Did such attention to appearances suggest that their owners expected their carriages to command respect or simply that they could afford luxuries? An ardent critic of the wealthy in northwest Louisiana showed her contempt of any such attempts when she sneered at such expensive and showy displays of elitism. "The grandeur of Bosier Parrish the Bust heads is rolling past here in their 1000 dollar carriages."[13] However, a scene in Aberdeen, Mississippi, suggests that elites at least thought their carriages suggested something about leadership. When political figures John Quitman and Henry S. Foote came to town in 1851, thirteen men and thirteen women led them through the streets in what an observer termed "a very imposing spectacle." The women wore black riding habits, the men carried small flags. "Then last of all came the carriages, about fifty in number."[14] Thus, the homes and the carriages made clear statements about who was in charge and who was not, involving all in at least the experience of viewing exteriors of elites.

The carpeting, numerous chairs, and expensive china in Michael Melton's house were helpful in entertaining guests and seem to have been part of a lively social life. None of the goods in the houses of Carby or Godfrey suggested they could play the role of host. But Melton had the goods that allowed him to make guests feel comfortable and special. Twenty-four chairs could seat a large crowd around a dinner table set with silver. The crowd could drink from the expensive glasses. The dining room rug marked the area as a place where something important might take place. A statement by Adams County planter Charles Whitmore that he wanted a carpet that was "substantial showy" indicates that such luxuries made a statement and did not simply keep the floors warm.[15]

Despite their obvious interest in displaying their wealth, did rich Mississippians like Melton invite the rest of the population to drink wine and eat their food, to dance in their mansions, to watch their race horses, to feel a sense of awe in the presence of their obvious betters? Little evidence suggests they were especially concerned with trying to involve the rest of the free population in the fruits of their wealth. A great deal of their hospitality seemed directed at fellow elites rather than the rest of the population, and the frequent grumbling in colonial Virginia about the necessity of "swilling the planters with bumbo" does not seem to have been a significant concern in Mississippi.[16]

Instead, what seems to have mattered more than cultural leadership were private pleasures and a system of communication about cosmopolitanism that was available only to elites. The French and German goods in Michael Melton's home said to him and anyone who saw them that his household was connected to an international culture—a culture that shifted with new fashions and would shift again. It was this system of communication that so clearly differentiated the wealthy in Mississippi from people like Thomas Carby who were comfortable enough but had no clearly identifiable luxury goods. Melton probably bought or ordered new goods fairly often, knew the origins of his goods, and could expect and hope for newer and better goods every year.

Even the language wealthy Mississippians used to describe their purchases and the process of buying them differed from the straightforward, unmodified descriptions of buying supplies that tended to turn up in the diaries of farmers and smaller planters. Robert Gordon did not simply buy a carriage. Enjoying the romantic side of consumer culture, he looked at a "great variety" of carriages and pondered which he should "like best." Likewise, when Dugal McCall, owner of plantations in both Mississippi and Louisiana, took a steamboat to New Orleans in 1850 to do some shopping, he "went out to buy things. bough[t] of Sampson & Kean and others such things as I wanted."[17] By emphasizing that he bought goods at several places and that he was buying not merely what his household needed but what "I wanted," he distinguished himself from the common farmer who rode in his wagon to buy supplies at the general store.

Even more different from the purchases of most farmers were the amounts such planters were willing to spend on such trips. Gordon drew on bankers throughout the Northeast and Europe. McCall spent $325 on his trip to New Orleans. He showed the difference between city shopping and shopping at small-town general stores two months later when he paid about eight dollars for two coats, a hat, and some shoes at a store in Rodney, Mississippi.[18] When north Mississippi planter Francis Leak took a trip to Memphis in 1841, he paid a cotton factor $144.53 in cash for a large order of clothing, shoes, cloth, and wine.[19] Dick Eggleston owned a plantation in Wilkinson County in the 1830, but he hardly ever bought anything but drinks in stores in his home county. Instead, he made large purchases in New Orleans. After one trip, he recorded, "I was very busy in New Orleans, paid James Agilvie & C[o]. $139 for groceries of last year, J. W. Oakley & Co. $30.50 for dry goods & Rogers [illegible] & Co $4.12 1/2 for hardware in 1829. . . . paid Bonnie & Baker $41.50 for clothes, $6 for a coat $5.50 for a bonnet & $9 for a cloak for Betsy."[20]

Shopping in cities like New Orleans connected wealthy Mississippians to a large world of possible imports. Choices of goods were extraordinary in a city where ships came, as early as the 1840s, from Liverpool, London, Glasgow, Grenock, Cowes, Falmouth, Belfast, and Cork in the British Isles, Bordeaux, Marseilles, Nantz, Rouen, Le Havre, and Cette in France, Gottenburg, Amsterdam, Rotterdam, Bremen, Antwerp, Hamburg, Stockholm, St. Petersburg, Gibraltar, Genoa, Trieste, and Spanish cities, as well as the West Indies and U.S. cities such as New York, Boston, Providence, Philadelphia, and Baltimore.[21]

The goods wealthy men and women identified as special and exciting almost always came from cities and not from local general stores. Their luxuries came from Memphis, New Orleans, New York, or farther. The fact that most of their expensive goods came from places most Mississippians never visited helped mark those goods as signs of elitism. *Their* goods changed year to year, while the goods of the rest of society, white and black, did not. For example, Jane Randolph wrote from her southern Mississippi plantation in 1839 to ask her sister "to purchase a few articles for me in Orleans, that is if you come that way. there is nothing in Woodville worth buying."[22] Stores in Woodville certainly had things to offer, but Randolph considered new and stylish goods the only ones "worth buying." New Orleans stores held the same appeal for Anna Coffee in northwestern Alabama. In 1846, she described a woman whose husband "has fitted out a complete wardrobe of finery, and sent to her from New Orleans." She later mentioned a judge who "came home by way of Mobile and Orleans. Brought his wife some handsome presents."[23] Just after the Civil War, a woman in central Mississippi tied fashionable and hence desirable goods to their urban origin. "Cousin Susie dresses elegantly; she has the prettiest cloak I ever saw, that Uncle got her in New York."[24]

More often than they bought goods while traveling, wealthy Mississippians ordered luxuries from cotton factors. In the antebellum South, most planters contracted with factors to sell their cotton, and many relied on those factors to serve as creditors and to make purchases for them. Factors had offices in New Orleans and Memphis and Mobile that connected planters to the international markets of cotton buyers and sellers of goods. As Harold Woodman writes in the best work on the subject, the factor served as "the cotton planter's commercial alter ego, his personal representative in the marketplace."[25] That relationship made factors, among other things, shoppers for the planters. Factors claimed that the dealers from whom they bought goods, in an advertisement Woodman describes as typical, were "well supplied with all descriptions of foreign and domestic merchandise direct from Europe, and from the markets and manufactories of the North, and are prepared to supply their customers on the most liberal terms."[26]

Advertisements for urban wholesale stores went into detail about how their goods linked buyers to European centers of fashion. Far from the small-town general store advertisements that simply described goods as having come from eastern cities, Memphis store advertisements in the late 1840s trumpeted that customers could buy saddles from England and Spain, clocks from England and France, hats, caps, boots, and shoes from England and France, satin scarves and handkerchiefs from India, French leggings, English "Tally Ho" razors, Italian medicated soap, French embroidered muslins and party dresses, Swiss lace, Canton crepe shawls, Parisian violin strings, and Prince Albert buggies. One store advertised watches of "the same quality and style as those worn by the nobility of Europe."[27]

Cotton planters routinely wrote business letters that included requests for goods, and many allowed factors considerable freedom to secure the furniture or carriage or clothing that conformed to current styles. The goods the planters bought through their factors, the amounts they spent, and the detailed language both planters and factors used in discussing possible purchases all showed a fascination with the latest cosmopolitan styles. For example, when a New Orleans factor wrote south Mississippi planter Lewis Clarke about a possible purchase of a buggy, he assumed Clarke would want only the best. The factor could buy a superior buggy "for from $350 to $400. Can get one not so good for $235 to $300, but cannot recommend the latter. . . . [G]ive me a little discretion, and I will select one for you and I think I can please you."[28] Adams County planter Charles Whitmore, who sold watches and gold rings for his Scottish cotton factor, wrote to Liverpool to order a long series of goods. He asked for a "claret cold surtout coat, velvet collar, with white or light sleeve lining," an olive coat of the same kind, "one pair brown pantaloons good casimere," and "one pair fancy oxford grey pantaloons good casimere." He also wanted "well selected fancy silk vests" and "two pair *best quality* fancy Striped Cottonade." Finally, Whitmore asked for a "really handsome, large pattern, bold colored" Kidderminster carpet with a "modern finish."[29]

Because of their trips to cities and even their frequent dealings with cotton factors, planters were, if not urbanites, people with strong urban ties. In a city such as Memphis that developed primarily as a site for wholesale dealers to buy cotton from planters and sell goods to them, those planters were some of the most significant people in town—even if they rarely visited. Cotton factors, with their businesses located in a single neighborhood near the river, helped make Memphis a place that served their interest in making money and spending it.[30] Many planters expected factors to keep up with the latest fashions and to know which were the best goods. When Whitmore asked his factor for a "well selected" silk vest, he was asking the factor to do the selecting. When factor J. W. Champion sent Lewis Clarke a new sewing machine, he said he could have bought a cheaper one, but "I sent you such a one as I would select for myself."[31] A New York merchant wrote a wealthy man in central Mississippi to recommend buggy style number 44 "for its superior comfort and elegance, besides the novelty of the style. Buggies such as I sold you, are now nearly out of date."[32]

This personal relationship between factor and planter distinguished upper-class spending patterns from the habits of most farmers. While farmers feared that store owners and shopkeepers might be untrustworthy creditors looking to take advantage of them, planters tended to see factors as agents, friends, and, they hoped, men of honor outside the faceless rules of the marketplace. Thus, planters seem to have felt some assurance that they could run up huge expenses without facing immediate threats of foreclosure.[33]

The planters' partially urban consciousness and intense interest in changes in cosmopolitan styles may complicate what seems one of the defining features of southern slaveowners. In his comparative study, Peter Kolchin stresses that while Russian lords lived as absentee landlords in cities with great interest in city people and goods but little interest in their serfs on rural estates, plantation owners in the South lived on their own land and took far more interest in the lives of their slaves. Southern plantation owners, according to Kolchin, had identities rooted in their experiences as masters and members of their families and local communities.[34] Could they be both cosmopolitan spenders and rural paternalists? Many no doubt saw no problem trying to be both. But the two sides of upper-class spending—the public and private sides—were sometimes so different as to be in conflict. While the public side connoted permanence and stability, the private side relied on novel experiences rooted in the urban world and on dreams of even more new experiences. A large carriage made a public statement, but imagining the ways carriage style 44 would be an improvement over style 43 or the ways a Kidderminster carpet differed from some other style was a profoundly individual experience.

Despite all of their shopping trips to cities, their use of factors to buy luxury goods, their desire to use appearances to strike the pose of elites, and their wishes as cosmopolitan individuals to know about the latest styles, antebellum planters still had reason to fear the effects of overspending. Men had a difficult time admitting to themselves or others that it was important to them to buy and own luxury goods, and William Henry Holcombe's statement of identity that the southerner is one who loves to spend money would not have rested lightly on their shoulders. Planters could never be quite sure that they could stay out of debt; much of the language of debt-free independence came from the pens of wealthy Mississippians. Even if they expected cotton factors to carry their debts for years, they could never be sure the good times would continue. Sudden changes in cotton prices, government currency and credit policies, the weather, and the financial well-being of individual factors all threatened the certainty of the independence that came with wealth.

A second reason some wealthy Mississippians worried about spending habits was less prevalent and less compelling. Some planters feared that they might become—or at least be seen as—vulgar cotton snobs. In his study of eighteenth-century Virginia, T. H. Breen has detailed the ways tobacco planters struggled to escape debt while at the same time buying more and more luxury goods from Scottish factors to prove they really belonged to the gentry.[35] The tensions generated by trying to look the part of an aristocrat without succumbing to a vulgar materialism could be even more powerful in a Mississippi society not far removed from the frontier. In 1860, Alabama writer Daniel R. Hundley identified the cotton snob as a particularly repugnant social type in the western South. After a long discussion of "The Southern Gentleman," he turned to "Cotton Snobs," who took to destructive and vicious extremes many of what Hundley considered the best sides of the South. Among them was a taste for "vulgar display," especially in clothing and carriages. Cotton Snobs traveled widely, drank heavily, gambled wildly, read almost never, and had tastes for anything they could buy from stylish cosmopolitan centers. He asked rhetorically what southerners had done "when we discard the plain but honest virtues of our sires, to embrace every hollow flam and shallow pretense newly imported from Paris or London? 'Tis time indeed Americans should learn to cease from following after strange gods, and to put more trust than they have done of late in straightforward integrity of purpose and a pure genuine morality, and less in corrupting riches and a shallow outward polish, which, like the sleek crust over the smouldering volcano, conceals ever beneath its shining exterior only stifling ashes and treacherous fires."[36] There were moral responsibilities an upper class should pursue, Hundley made clear, but too many people were trying to dress the part without knowing how to play it.

Wealthy Mississippians did not often join Hundley in writing about ostentation, but Mississippi was an object of occasional derision from other southerners. For example, J. Floyd King, a member of a wealthy family from coastal Georgia, wrote home from Mississippi in 1866 that the "Western Planters . . . impress me as being purse-proud, ill-educated, raw, drinking, gambling bravas; who, when they were rich, spent their money in negros and dissipation, and left their debts unpaid."[37] Many wealthy Mississippians may have worried that whatever their concerns about paternalism and membership in a cosmopolitan community, they were in fact just trying, like William Faulkner's Thomas Sutpen, to buy their way into respectability.

Planter Everard Green Baker repeatedly worried that spending money to enjoy himself might violate his role as head of a household of family members and slaves. On the one hand, he recognized the importance of displaying wealth and offering hospitality. Baker was pleased to be able to attend a dinner a judge gave that turned out to be "a sumptuous banquet," and he believed Christmas presents to his slaves left them "joyous & happy,—& am glad to see them enjoying themselves with such a contented hearty good will." On the other hand, he frequently fretted that his own tastes for enjoyment worked against his responsibilities. As a young plantation owner in Panola County, he pledged "to be henceforth stingy as far as unnecessary expenditures" in part because he could buy only through "hardest labor" and "greatest deprivation" of his slaves. More often, he worried that if he enjoyed himself too much or too often through "the belching of the purse" and the "pampering of different passions," he could be endangering his own independence and the futures of his children. He criticized himself for going into debt, complaining that "this credit system is so fascinating, so inclined to make a man go further than prudence would dictate." Baker's goal was to be a good paternalist without spending too much money on it, and he always worried that he could not do both.[38]

Wealthy men dealt with worries about their spending habits in part by claiming it was not they but really other members of their households who were the true consumers. Men could claim that in paying for luxuries, they were not indulging their own tastes but were indulging the weaknesses of less serious people. They could claim, with Lucy Irion Neilson, that interest in fashion was "woman-like." By laying the responsibility for luxuries on women, children, and slaves, they could more comfortably maintain their own identities as independent farmers, as controllers of their households, and perhaps as paternalists, but not as consumers.

Male newspaper editors delighted in making fun of rich women for their expensive and changing tastes. The editor of the *Lexington Union* took pleasure in portraying the flightiness of young women who made demands on their mothers.

> Fashion—1837. "Dear Mother, you must let me have fourteen yards in my frock.—Mrs. Thompson says she can't get a pair of sleeves out of less than seven. And you know, mother, that a dress would look bad with stinted sleeves. Did you see Mrs. Mixers new Dress, how awkward it looked—the sleeves all scrimped up, and she had five yards in them—you must get fourteen mother."
>
> 1838. "Oh mother, I do wish you would let me get my purple silk dress altered, those great sleeves look so awkward and bungling, I positively can't wear them, they are perfectly frightful. Tight, small sleeves look so neat and graceful."

The editor concluded, "Oh! thou fickle Goddess!"[39] Such editorial remarks suggested that the women were in charge of spending decisions—a questionable arrangement for most white Mississippians but one wealthy men could indulge. Another editor claimed that fashion was an exclusively female concern unintelligible to innocent male simpletons. "The truth is, men, as a rule, know very little about the value of female attire, except when they have to foot the bills. Cost is the standard of a woman's excellence in costume." Arguing that "women dress to provoke envy in each other," the editor said women—and he surely meant upper-class women—could size up the clothing of their peers and "reckon up the hablements of a rival in the beau monde almost to a cent. . . . She triumphs in the reflection that her splendors are genuine, and that her 'set,' sharp-eyed as a lynx, can distinguish between tweedledum and tweedledee."[40] In this passage, written early in 1866 when white Mississippians were more obsessed than ever with questions of debt, the editor suggested that women spent great time and energy worrying about their own and other women's clothing in an effort to judge who really could identify the most expensive goods. To this writer, women were the ultimate consumers who spent their time assessing whether other women were buying the goods they all assumed everyone should want.

In 1853 planter Gustavus Henry and his daughter Sue went to New Orleans and experienced both the city's attractions and what he saw as its temptations. He wrote his wife, Marion, that "Sue has been making the 'dimes fly.' I am getting very anxious to get her away from this city. There are so many things, very attractive, that a young girl or man cant stand the temptation to buy. I came here with $300, have now only $60." He contrasted the consuming tendencies of his daughter with the higher virtues his wife represented. "You do not know how your unpretending virtues loom up before me, in contrast with the heartlessness of fashionable life."[41] On the surface, Henry's statements seem to lie in the evangelical and republican traditions that feared consumption and prized modesty and thrift. Even his language that Marion Henry's "virtues loom up" linked her character to cloth-making as an essential part of household independence. But it was Henry who chose to take his daughter on a shopping trip to New Orleans, and then regretted only that she enjoyed it too much. Had he been completely committed to notions of frugal independence, he would not have taken $300 on a pleasure trip to the big city. Instead, he took pride in playing the role of the responsible male fleeing from consumer opportunities before the supposed weaknesses of his daughter brought more damage to the family.

The parents of Lettie Watkins tried hard to control her spending habits while she was away at school. Her father, Thomas, wrote from his home in Carrollton asking her to refrain from indulging herself on extravagances and once praised her for asking for a book instead of her normal requests. "You have heretofore asked for sugar toys, looking glasses, earrings, fine shoes, head dresses & oranges." Her mother added that "Your Papa says I must write he has no money to throw away." But, like Gustavus Henry, he took his daughter on a spending trip to New Orleans. When Lettie asked a friend to accompany them but that friend's father refused to allow it, she responded with a compliment to her father that must have made Thomas Watkins wince. "I do not see the use of people having money if they do not intend to enjoy it." Such a statement, very much in the tradition of William Holcombe's ideal southerner, violated everything Lettie's father had told her, but it also showed how happy she was that he was letting her go shopping in New Orleans. While he worried about the money she spent, he also had to be pleased that his daughter was bragging to her friends that she had "a *mighty* good Father."[42]

A planter in Alabama made a similar point about upper-class women and modern patterns of spending. A. L. Pickens wrote in 1850 that his wife's trunk was "filled with various articles of her wardrobe-bustles, shirts feminine . . . corsets, perhaps-stays, collars, skirts, whalebone, and other foreign importations, which I have heard, make up the composition of the modern lady."[43] The list suggested abundance, in part simply because it was long and also suggested that "foreign importations" signified modernity. Most important, the bemused tone of the letter suggests that Pickens considered his wife's elaborate array of clothing less a threat to his household's income than a mild enough burden that wealthy men could bear with a wink and a smile.

Like Thomas Watkins, Gustavus Henry, and *The Coahomian*, A. L. Pickens felt he could indulge women's tastes by claiming to be responsible enough to overlook such indulgences. Instead of posing threats to the independence of farm households, the tastes of wealthy women seemed mildly guilty pleasures, light and frivolous but rarely something wealthy men believed they needed to control. For men in such households, allowing such spending seemed part of being paternalistic heads of households.

What worried wealthy men more were the expenses associated with slaves. Spending money for the clothing, food, and housing of slaves elicited little jocular language and few hints that they should simply indulge the weaknesses of wasteful slaves. On the one hand, many large slaveowners took considerable pride in seeing themselves as kind and paternalistic figures who looked after the material needs of their slaves. An essential element of the pro-slavery argument that developed in the late antebellum period asserted that the material conditions of southern slaves were far superior to those of South American and Caribbean slaves and to many northeastern and European industrial workers.[44] On the other hand, slaveowners looked on slave clothing as a marginal expense that, if not watched carefully, could threaten their profits and possibly even their independence.

Like smaller farmers, planters relied on the language of independence when they pondered the place of goods in their own households. Like the smaller farmers, planters feared unnecessary costs and hoped sewing could hold down expenses. But the planters applied the language of debt-free independence to the clothing of their slaves. Particularly since they were substantial consumers themselves, planters viewed spending money on the goods of slaves as a minor expense to be avoided when possible. A Yazoo County planter complained of going into debt for summer clothes for his slaves. "I intended never to have done that for as long as there was a prospect of living without it."[45] Planters often paired the goal of feeding the entire household with the goal of clothing the slaves. Gustavus Henry tried to limit expenses in a year of low cotton prices by using home production to feed his family and clothe his slaves. "I will make enough of corn, pork & c to support the family. mrs. Harris has . . . made all the negro clothing nearly."[46] In 1849, a west Tennessee planter saw homemade clothing for slaves and a good supply of hogs as standard elements of a self-sufficient household. "I have now a prospect of raising Enough Hog-meat to serve my family after this year. . . . My wife has all of my negro clothes made at home. So you see we are trying to get back to the old North Carolina custom of making all we can at home."[47]

Large slaveowners tried to use slaves to sew as much clothing as possible for use in the slave quarters. Slaveowners who wrote about sewing did not use the heroic language white men used to describe white women who sewed. Instead, they simply listed the work of slaves who sewed as production in ledgers that listed the amounts of hoes rowed and cotton picked. For example, while twenty-one other slaves worked in the fields on Joseph Jayne's plantation in Rankin County, Cely was "Making Negroes Clothes."[48] Gustavus Henry described the value of his spinning wheel. "All acknowledge it is right that every family ought to make its own clothing. Charles will in this way be one of my most productive laborers and so will several of the women." Henry said that such work made all of the cotton clothing for his slaves in 1846.[49] Hinds County planter Martin Philips, whose diary entries often discussed the need to economize, simply noted in 1842 that his slaves had spun fifty-seven yards of cotton cloth.[50]

Having a loom and spinning wheel was *not* a sign of small-farming self-sufficiency. As shown in a study of 180 probate inventories of the possessions of white Mississippians in the 1840s, 1850s, and 1860s, wealthier households were far more likely than ordinary households to have equipment to make their own cloth. The wealthiest families in Table 5 were the only group in which a majority had either a spinning wheel, loom, or spinning machine. The wealthiest households owned by far the most valuable machines. Whereas the average spinning wheel—the most common piece of equipment—had a value of about four dollars, the average value of spinning ginneys, owned only by the wealthy, was fifty-five dollars. Those elaborate machines were the ones turning out inexpensive clothes for slaves.[51]

While the slaveowners did not view the slaves who sewed cloth as performing moral service to the household, they were extremely suspicious about slaves who used too many shoes and clothing. Viewing slaves as self-indulgent and wasteful, wealthy Adams County planter George Washington Sargent was exasperated by requests his slaves made for new clothes. He wrote his overseer in March not to give out summer clothes while winter clothes were still acceptable, no matter how often slaves asked for them. "I do as much for my people as any one if they think they have nothing to do but to destroy and get new Cloathes they will find themselves mistaken and the sooner they find this out the better for them and me." In one of the clearest statements possible that he did not want slaves to develop tastes for new goods, he suggested that the slaves who asked for new clothes deserved whippings instead. When it was time to give out summer clothes, Sargent, still suspicious, urged his overseer to "Make them show you first last years pants, and report to me their condition."[52] In northeastern Mississippi, Francis Leak did not threaten whippings, but he showed the same suspicion about slaves who wanted what he considered too many goods. Leak instructed his overseer "not to distribute the boots among the negroes until the ground becomes quite wet." He was adamant that the

TABLE 5. *Spinning Wheels, Looms, and Spinning Machines Owned by People of Different Levels of Wealth in Nineteenth-century Mississippi*

	Property Value			
	$0–400	*$401–1,100*	*$1,101–5,000*	*$5,001–70,000*
No. of inventories	46	46	46	42
Spinning wheels				
Number owning	10	9	12	17
Total number owned	16	10	18	43
Total value ($)	32.62	23.37	63.50	231.12
Looms				
Number owning	7	9	7	16
Total number owned	7	9	7	16
Total value ($)	44.00	54.50	54.50	111.25
Spinning machines				
Number owning	0	0	2	8
Total number owned	0	0	2	9
Total value ($)	0	0	170.00	435.00
Number owning cloth-making equipment (spinning wheels, looms, or spinning machines)	11	13	18	23
Percentage owning spinning wheels, looms, or spinning machines	24	28	39	55

Sources: Inventories of 180 estates in nineteenth-century Mississippi. Included are 47 from Amite County, 23 from Lawrence County, 4 from Quitman County, 6 from Sharkey County, and 100 from Yalobusha County. The inventories date from 1819 until 1882, with the great majority in the 1840s, 1850s, and 1860s. All of the inventories are in MDAH.

Note: Several of the people with inventories had more than one spinning wheel, loom, or spinning machine. The figures listed in the final column show the percentages of individuals who owned any cloth-making equipment.

overseer "count the boots and shoes *carefully*."[53] James Ruffin was diligent about what he considered wastefulness among slaves. Every slave was to receive the same amount of clothing, and if it wore out, Ruffin expected them to go without. The slaves who received extra shirts in the winter of 1842, for example, "are *not* to have any next winter."[54]

When slaveowners distributed goods to the slaves, the nature of the goods themselves clearly worked against the development of ideas that goods might express individuality. Most slaveowners distributed the same goods among their slaves, with no interest in catering to individual preferences. Owners cut most clothing for slaves from the same inexpensive bolt of cloth, and generally gave out the same quantities to each slave. Some described the process of distributing slaves supplies in ways that sounded more like taking care of animals. "Negroes Shod—58" was John Houston Bills's cryptic language in 1859. An overseer made the same connection in listing that his responsibilities included distributing "anything such as Clothing shoes, hats & c that is given out to the negroes, also the horses stock of all kinds."[55]

More common in owners' descriptions of slave goods were commonplace statements that everyone of the same gender and size received the same things. At the end of each year in the 1830s, each male slave on the Killona Plantation in Holmes County received two shirts, a pair of pants, a coat, a pair of socks, and a pair of shoes, while each woman received two pairs of shoes, a coat, a pair of stockings, and a handkerchief. Each received the same things, except a few women received shifts. On Charles Whitmore's plantation in 1840, every male slave received a pair of shoes, a pair of pants, a shirt, and a blanket, and each female received a pair of shoes, a shift, a dress, a blanket, and a handkerchief. All of the male slaves on the Panther Burn Plantation in Sharkey County received a hat, a shirt, and two pairs of pants, and the women received shirts and chemises. The only differences among the slaves was that some received one pair of shoes, others received two or three, and seventeen of the forty-three slaves—most likely the adult men—received a pair of boots.[56]

Descriptions of the "negro clothes" general stores and plantation merchants advertised in newspapers were uniformly utilitarian, never mentioning color, decoration, or anything new or unique. Such advertisements simply offered shoes and hats and cloth without description. Osnaburg—so-called "negro cloth"—combined durability with low cost. Such cloth made all slaves, at least at work, dress basically alike. The slaveowner in Wilkinson County who bought 200 yards of "negro clothing" in order to make two garments for each slave, male and female, had no interest in variety. In choosing cloth or clothing, slaveowners showed interest exclusively in price and durability. A south Mississippi planter ordered for his slaves winter clothes "of a material that I trust will last better than the goods sent last winter."[57]

Whether slaveowners bought slave clothing and shoes in bulk or had slaves make cloth and sew clothing from it, the effect was to produce inexpensive clothing that made most slaves dress almost alike. As former slave Pernella Anderson recalled in a WPA interview, all of the slaves she knew "wore one kind of clothes."[58] The slaves who spent their childhoods wearing ungendered canvas smocks or potato sacks with holes for heads and eating from troughs with gourds or their hands were not likely to be developing the idea that personal fulfillment came through new goods and the appearances they created.

For all of the efforts by slaveowners to limit the money they spent on supplies for slaves, most owners at the same time allowed and even encouraged slaves to earn and spend small amounts of money. The issue of slaves as consumers may seem almost ridiculous. Many slaves would have agreed with Mississippian Ike Woodward, who recalled in a WPA interview, "Course I didn' make no money workin for Mr. Conner. Money is one thing us niggers didn't see."[59] But the variety of ways Mississippi slaves made money is impressive. Most common seems to have been selling the products of their own gardens, cotton and tobacco patches, and henhouses, often to their owners. They also made money as carpenters and shoemakers as well as by carding, spinning, and selling thread, putting shingles on buildings, selling the hides of animals they had trapped, picking and selling wild grapes, blackberries, and persimmons, selling herbs and grass seed, hauling fruit and rags, making hominy, singing and playing musical instruments, opening and closing toll gates, working for wages for employers other than their owners, and simply by receiving cash gifts.[60] One young slaveholder on the frontier in 1836 wrote that her slaves seemed to share the excitement about the possibilities for profit in Mississippi. "I have not seen a single soul that is willing to leave this country. the negroes would not go back if they could. They make money every way."[61] A northern man who spent two years in Adams County made distinctions between slaves on smaller and larger plantations. On the smaller estates, slaves worked their own gardens "independent of the master," while those on larger plantations received pay for work beyond their tasks. He emphasized, "I never saw a plantation where this was not permitted to a certain extent."[62]

Almost every plantation diary and account book from the Mississippi area included at least some mention of paying cash to slaves.[63] Many cotton planters came to regard payment as part of their responsibilities, whether they were irritated by the necessity or proud of its paternalistic implications. In describing the money he received from his owner, former slave Rubin Fox suggested his owner went beyond most. "Master George was mighty good 'bout giving us money when ever we asked him for it."[64] Many slaveowners were far more cautious and gave money to their slaves during the special occasion of the Christmas season to turn something resembling payment into something intended to create or sustain loyalty. When slaveowners paid slaves at Christmas, they were usually paying for extra work. On Christmas Day in 1828, John Nevitt "gave all hands holyday until Monday next gave them their treat and paid them of all that was due them." The notion that money was due the slaves, as distinct from treats, suggests that planters viewed cash payments as part of their obligations. John Houston Bills gave out money only because his eighty slaves had come to expect it. "Christmas is anything but fun for me. I divide $150 among my slaves." The day after Christmas in 1858, the owner of a Washington County plantation "paid up my negroes for their work, except Dave and Darius. I am square with them all, with the above exceptions." The concept of being square with slaves again suggests that both slaves and slaveowners saw pay for extra work as a predictable part of their relationship.[65]

If so many slaves were making money, the question becomes what they did with it. Some saved it for long stretches, hoping to buy freedom for themselves and their families. But legislatures throughout the South were making it difficult for slaves to gain their freedom. So how did they spend their money? We might expect that slaves with small amounts of money to spend would have used it to buy basic goods to help with everyday survival. If they were like other groups of rural poor people, we might expect to find them buying tools, seed, food, and tobacco. We might expect them to buy the most basic clothing and shoes to replace or supplement the clothing supplied by their owners. We might expect that people who had little money might have bought the least expensive goods and thus goods with little variety. And we might expect that they concentrated their purchases around holiday seasons to celebrate major events in the crop year and the life cycle.

It was not easy for slaves to enjoy spending money. Like everyone except the very wealthy, they had only occasional access to peddlers and smaller general stores. Furthermore, the laws of Mississippi were strict in limiting any access slaves had to the marketplace without the consent of their owners.[66] Finally, the existence of a deeply felt racism discouraged expressions of a democracy of appearances.

On the other hand, spending money was a rare chance to use the marketplace for their own benefit. Did the opportunity to spend money allow slaves to define themselves as individuals, particularly since so much of their material lives had the opposite intent? If so, what kind of statements did they make? When they had the chance, what kind of consumers were they?

The ledger of a general store in the southwestern Tennessee town of Jackson offers a rare opportunity to address those questions. Seventy-two slaves made purchases at the Rogers and Hearn general store in 1859 and 1860, and store owners recorded their transactions in their own individual accounts. As with any case study, the existence of an exceptionally vivid example raises the question that it might be too unusual to be very useful. While the number of slaves with store accounts was out of the ordinary, it is clear that many slaves made occasional trips to stores. In Montgomery County, Alabama, planter A. H. Arrington recorded the small accounts his slaves had with Offutt's Dry Goods store. Seventeen slaves had accounts between one and seven dollars for hats and shoes.[67] A general store owner in Oxford, Mississippi, indicated that many slaves had access to goods in stores. Foster Freeland wrote his mother in Boston that his brother, another store owner in Holly Springs, sold goods to slaves every Sunday, receiving between fifteen and forty dollars every week.[68]

In the eyes of storekeepers Rogers and Hearn, the first point that distinguished slaves from free customers was their ties to their owners. For storekeepers who listed customers as Willoughby's Alf and Godwin's Willis, the process of selling goods to slaves, and expecting payment for those goods, took place within the slave system and not as a challenge to it.[69] Slaveowners knew their slaves were making purchases at Rogers and Hearn, and the store owners knew the ties between slaves and owners. So the goods of the slaves were never completely their own. Nor, significantly, were the debts. The owners owned anything on their property, including the goods of the slaves, and they were ultimately responsible for the slaves' debts. If they knew about the purchases their slaves were making and if, as we will see, they sometimes guaranteed their debts, then it is clear that they were benefiting from the part the slaves were taking in the consumer economy.

More than simply allowing their slaves access to stores or peddlers and make purchases, some slaveowners actively encouraged it. At the Newstead Plantation, the owner had his slaves "pay Greenville a visit in order to do their trading." A former slave in southern Mississippi recalled that slaves on one plantation "were given an order to a local store of from $5 to $10 each to spend as they pleased." One Mississippi planter wrote in *De Bow's Review* that he gave each of his slaves five dollars and sent them "to the county town under the charge of the overseer or driver, to spend their money." Some slaveowners oversaw the purchases of slaves in ways that reinforced planter notions of paternalism. According to one former slave, "When peddlers would come on the place we would be called to the big house to look at what they had to sell and if we had any money to buy. My marster didn't mean to have nobody cheat us." Here is a case of a slaveowner making sure that market relations worked in the favor of his slaves—and ultimately himself. Another former slave recalled that when his mother accompanied her female owner to Memphis, the owner and

TABLE 6. *Methods of Payment at Rogers and Hearn Store, Jackson, Tennessee, 1859–1860*

	Free Customers (N=192)	Slave Customers (N=72)
Paid cash in full	103	14
Signed note to pay	83	0
Paid with produce or work	3	3
Debt left unpaid	3	39
Paid by owner	0	16

Source: Rogers and Hearn Store Ledger, TSLA.

her friends "honor her. They take her down town and buy her shoes and dresses. Buy her whatever she want."[70]

The unique position of the slaves as property set them apart from other groups of the rural poor on the crucial issue of debt. As slaves, they suffered no consequences when they did not pay their bills. As Table 6 indicates, an almost amazing 55 of 72 slaves did not pay their bills at Rogers and Hearn for 1859–60 or sign notes promising to pay them. Owners paid the debts of 17 of the slaves, and 39 slaves—54 percent—simply left their bills unpaid, with no signs of promises to pay. This was not a common practice for free men and women. While 43 percent of the free customers (83 of 192) at Rogers and Hearn signed end-of-year notes promising to pay their bills and accepting the interest rates on those notes, only 3 of the 192 free customers left debts unpaid, without notes promising to pay.

Store owners apparently expected that the owners of the slaves would either pay those bills or force the slaves to pay. The effect for the slaves was to free them to make purchases without fearing the consequences. With no fear of debts, they did not face one of the most important factors that worked against consumer spending. Since a majority of the slaves paid some cash, as Table 7 shows, the store owners could apparently expect that the bills would be paid eventually. The slaveowners who paid the debts of 16 slaves best represent the efforts of some owners to use the consumer economy for paternalistic purposes. When Robert Conally went to Jackson the day after Christmas in 1859 to pay the debts of his slaves, he was not merely making sure they had clothing and hats but that they had in their lives at least a small element of choice. Such choices, he surely hoped, would buy him loyalty that mere goods could not secure.[71]

Slaves rarely used their opportunities for consumer spending to buy basic

	Number	Percentage
$0	32	44
$.01–$.99	9	13
$1.00–$5.00	15	21
$5.00–$10.00	7	9
More than $10.00	9	13
Total	72	100

Source: Rogers and Hearn Store Ledger, TSLA.

goods for everyday survival. We might expect to find them buying the most inexpensive clothing and shoes to replace or supplement the minimal clothing their owners supplied, and we might expect to find relatively little variety among their purchases. However, as Roderick McDonald found in his study of Louisiana sugar plantations, goods bought by slaves showed great variety.[72]

With just one exception, slaves bought very few inexpensive subsistence goods. By far the most common purchases were snuff and tobacco—goods most nineteenth-century Americans considered virtual necessities. The 72 slaves made 78 purchases of snuff and tobacco, almost all of them in small amounts. Tobacco was a common Christmas gift from owners but, as most records indicate, not part of the routine food supplies slaveowners distributed to slaves, so slaves often bought a dime's worth on their infrequent trips to the store. Beyond tobacco, few of their purchases could be considered subsistence goods or goods that duplicated the goods owners supplied. They bought virtually no food products—only minimal purchases of cinnamon, ginger, pepper, and candy. And even those were purchases that added flavor to their food rather than bulk. They bought no tools with the single exception of a slave who paid a nickel for a fishing line. They bought only one broom and one washboard to clean their homes or clothes and only one purchase of nails to build anything. And they bought only single purchases of liniment and camphor to keep them healthy.

A few purchases allowed slaves access to activities denied them by the normal routines of the institution of slavery. Slaves made eight purchases of candles and one bought a lantern, thus gaining the ability to do some things indoors at night and transcending the dawn-to-dusk schedule slaveowners set for them. Hearn's Bill paid a substantial amount for a banjo and also bought some violin strings. A dozen slaves bought pocket knives, which enabled them to control their material environment in ways the goods distributed by slave-owners did not allow. Davis's Tony tried to buy an expensive watch, but ultimately had to return it for a partial refund. And the slaves who bought knives, forks, spoons, plates, and bowls rejected the apathy of the slaveowners about the eating habits of slaves.

Slaves bought far more cloth and clothing than anything else at Rogers and Hearn. The three slaves who bought mirrors obviously considered their appearances important. Some clothing purchases showed that slaves used their consumer opportunities to follow cosmopolitan styles in dress. Most obvious were the eleven purchases of hoop skirts. Hoop skirts for slaves generally cost less than those whites purchased—$1.50, as opposed to about twice that much—but they nonetheless represented an important sign of a desire for luxury and perhaps display. Slaves also bought a dress pattern for $6.05 and a dress for $6.00, healthy amounts comparable to the most money virtually any whites spent on dresses at Rogers and Hearn. Perhaps the best example of an adoption of cosmopolitan styles of dress showed in a surprisingly widespread taste for silk. Four slaves bought silk fringe to attach to clothes, four bought silk belts, four others silk handkerchiefs, one a silk parasol, and another a silk cravat. Most expensive was a silk dress Eseck bought for more than ten dollars. Silk was the most expensive fabric at Rogers and Hearn, costing a dollar a yard in contrast to osnaburg and calico, the cheapest fabrics, which cost about thirteen cents a yard. For slaves to have bought silk surely suggests interest in some of the goods wealthy whites identified as valuable.

Numerous purchases for men suggested the same idea. The slaves who bought eight neckties and the silk cravat had accepted that convention of cosmopolitan culture. Four coats—two of them cashmere and an Italian coat Eseck purchased—cost between $5.50 and $11.00 and surely contrasted with anything the slaveowners might have provided. Many slaveowners in Mississippi provided no coats at all. And the two slaves who bought collars for shirts, Hunter's Willis and Hearn's Ann, were improving on the hole-for-a-head style of most slave shirts that negated the possibility of wearing neckties.

Like most farm people who shopped at general stores, slaves spent most of their money at Rogers and Hearn on cloth material for clothing, and what is most striking about that material was its variety. The most common materials, calico and so-called domestic fabric, were also the most common among whites. But Table 8 shows that slaves purchased at least twenty-five different kinds of material, and only one bought any osnaburg. Again this variety shows that slaves were using their ability to make consumer choices as ways to identify themselves as something other than workers and to reject the appearances created by slaveowners' practice of handing out the same clothes to everyone.

TABLE 8. *Fabric Purchases Made by Slaves at Rogers and Hearn Store, 1859–1860*

Type of Fabric	Number of Purchases	Type of Fabric	Number of Purchases
Calico	26	White Hose	3
Domestic	25	Alpaca	2
Ribbon	12	Jaconet	2
Silk	9	Swiss	2
Gingham	8	Robinet	2
Lawn	6	Satinet	1
Delane	6	Cambric	1
Linen	6	Casinett	1
Cottonade	5	Sholly	1
Muslin	5	Flannel	1
Linsey	4	Jeans	1
Lace	3	Osnaburg	1
Brilliant	3	Damask	1

Source: Rogers and Hearn Store Ledger, TSLA.

Like white farming women, female slaves spent a good deal of their time sewing clothing. Unlike them, they heard little praise of sewing as a great virtue. As far as evidence indicates, no one referred to a slave who made clothing as Dorcas who sewed for the poor or as an angelic figure whose hard work preserved the independence of the household. But we can assume that slaves who had the chance to sew for themselves took considerable interest in turning their clothing into something with special meaning. They turned the various pieces they bought at Rogers and Hearn into their own pieces, mixing fabrics and probably colors in ways whites in Mississippi likely did not. Cloth had long been crucial as a way of marking individuality and hierarchy in African societies. Scholars such as Robert Farris Thompson and Shane and Graham White have analyzed the tendency of slaves to use an African aesthetic that emphasized contrasting colors, irregular striped patterns, and a willingness to mix patterns and fabrics that European Americans saw as incongruous or gaudy. As the Whites conclude, the control slaves enjoyed over the making of their clothes for Sundays "allowed them the scope to fashion a distinctive appearance."[73]

Hats were another common purchase, and here again slaves showed considerable variety in their purchases. Had they merely wanted shelter from the sun,

TABLE 9. *Value of Hats Purchased by Slaves at Rogers and Hearn Store, 1859–1860*

	Number Purchased	Percentage
$.30–$.70	9	24
$.71–$1.50	16	42
$1.50–$7.00	13	34
Total	38	100

Source: Rogers and Hearn Store Ledger, TSLA.

they could have bought what store records described as a "chip hat" for thirty cents. But only five of the thirty-eight hats for which prices are clear cost less than fifty cents. Most cost between seventy-five cents and $1.50. Two women's bonnets cost $2.50 and 4.05, and one man's hat cost 3.75. Along with the prices, the variety of fabrics shows that the slaves were interested in more than basic utility. Several hats were described as soft, others as cloth, others as wool, one as cassimere. Again, it is clear that slaves made choices based on a variety of criteria—style, appearance, and social convention—and they used their choices to identify themselves as something other than workers.

A final major purchase consisted of shoes and boots. Slaves bought forty-seven pairs of shoes and ten pairs of boots in 1859 and 1860. Here it is more difficult to deduce any signs of desires for special luxury or appearance. Slaves generally wore the cheapest shoes slaveowners could buy, often with soles of cardboard and no differentiation between left and right. In the WPA interviews, former slaves recalled them as the most uncomfortable, most hated part of their clothing. Thus slaves around Jackson seized the opportunity to improve first on the comfort of their shoes. It was especially important that they were able to choose shoes that fit. Their store-bought shoes and boots were clearly of a quality superior to those owners supplied them. The shoes the slaves bought generally cost between $1.50 and $2.00, with shoes for children costing less. Boots carried the healthy price of $4.00 or $5.00. At least a few slaves were concerned not just about the comfort of their shoes but about appearance and style. Sam bought what were identified as "fine boots" for the high price of $6.00. Nely purchased a pair of "guitar shoes." And unlike the cheapest shoes that the slaveowners bought, the slaves distinguished between shoes for men and women.

Many people have traditionally grouped their few consumer purchases around holidays. Here again, slaves did not resemble other poor rural workers. Many slaveowners distributed money among their slaves around Christmas—a

TABLE 10. *Visits by Slaves to Rogers and Hearn Store, March 1859–February 1860*

Month	Number of Visits	Month	Number of Visits
March 1859	18	September 1859	32
April 1859	55	October 1859	32
May 1859	33	November 1859	21
June 1859	30	December 1859	28
July 1859	28	January 1860	5
August 1859	30	February 1860	2

Source: Rogers and Hearn Store Ledger, TSLA.

Note: Total number of slaves in tally was 75.

tradition that continued well into the free labor period—and it is clear that many slaves made their purchases then. But slaves did not visit Rogers and Hearn more frequently in December than in other months. As Table 10 shows, slaves went to the store all year, with the exception of January and February, possibly because winter weather made travel more difficult. From April through December, slaves made about the same number of trips to the store.

The slaves who shopped at Rogers and Hearn conformed to none of the characteristics of the spending habits of most rural poor people. They were unconcerned about debt, they did not concentrate their purchases around holiday celebrations, and they bought a wide variety of goods that were not solely for subsistence. They lived in a peculiar institution in which consumer purchases, though not often possible, had few of the dangerous consequences or negative connotations that they carried for most rural poor people.

What, if any, of the American dreams of consumer spending did slaves find attractive? The dreams of abundance and democracy seem largely irrelevant to opportunities slaves might have had. Elizabeth Fox-Genovese argues that many slaves took pride in having clothes and homes that were superior in quality to those of lower-class whites and that "many slave women, like many slave-holding women, took seriously the discriminations that fashion encoded" and tried upon emancipation to dress as stylishly as their incomes allowed.[74] But it is hard to imagine that slaves placed great value in emulating wealthy whites. While some of the slaves who shopped at Rogers and Hearn certainly found attractive the goods of wealthy whites and hoped to buy silk or neckties that would resemble them, the possibility of a symbolic democracy with the wealthy does not seem to fit into the opportunities slaves had. More important was the element of choice in shopping and possibly in thinking about shopping. The chance to shop offered slaves a rare occasion to exercise choice over their own identities. Within those choices, and the longing that probably accompanied them, slaves seem to have had opportunities for romantic imagination.

The best evidence that slaves might have shared some of the romantic aspects of the consumer lies in the goods they bought at Rogers and Hearn, their variety, their nonutilitarian quality, and their touches of the luxurious and fantastic. Those choices reveal too many individualistic statements not to have included important elements of personal identification and excitement. Slaves had freedom to make few choices in antebellum Mississippi, and we can assume that they relished any chance to bring into their lives choice, novelty, and realization of romantic longings. The shopping experience itself may well have been as important as the use or display of goods.

WPA interviews with former slaves in Mississippi included language that suggested the importance of individual choice in the experience of shopping. Prince Johnson recalled that slaves "could use the money we made for anything we pleased." Josie Martin said that with money she made selling eggs, "we was allowed to spend for what soever we wanted." The slaves who worked with Pet Franks made money selling vegetables from their own gardens. Franks recalled that "When de boats went down to Mobile we could sen' down for anything us want to buy. One time I had $10.00 saved up an' I bought lots o' pretties wid it."[75] In each of the recollections, the language of choice stressed the ability to complete decisions without owners' involvement; Franks's mention of buying "pretties" has a romantic air of enjoying the purchase of inessential goods.

The existence of consumer choices in the lives of slaves raises the question of what the slaveowners gained by letting their slaves make purchases. If slaves used their occasional visits to stores to overturn some features of the appearance of being slaves, why did slaveowners not just allow it but even encourage it and pay for it? The easy answer, partly true, is that allowing slaves to make purchases was one of many strategies owners used to encourage slaves to be content enough to keep working and resist thoughts of revolt or escape. The complicating factor, however, is the issue of the choices involved in consumer purchases. It is easy to see why slaveowners wanted slaves to have relatively comfortable homes and relatively plentiful food. But while the ideal of paternalism stressed material security, it in no way stressed choice. The logic of paternalism led owners to extend their influence as far as possible into the lives of slaves. If slaveowners claimed to be upholding the best humane traditions *not* governed by the marketplace, why did they encourage slaves to shop?

Allowing slaves to be consumers was one way slaveowners dealt with the tensions between their images of themselves as being responsible, debt-fearing masters of self-sufficient plantations while also being fun-loving, free-spending members of cosmopolitan communities. In an atmosphere in which the wealthy bought consumer goods in large numbers but raised numerous objections to what such goods represented, luxury goods took on the frivolous quality of guilty pleasures. Buying goods for pleasure seemed indulgences enjoyed by those without responsibilities or self-control. Thus, slaveowners could tolerate and even encourage slaves to taste the occasional pleasures of consumer spending because they liked to consider those pleasures to be a bit childish. They often warned themselves of the consequences of self-indulgence, but they could see self-indulgence among slaves as one of the many weaknesses of character that marked slaves as needing their supervision.

By allowing slaves to make money and encouraging them to spend it, slaveowners could have things both ways. They could keep intact all of the meanings about power relations that the drastic differences in their goods reflected, especially in the clothing that served as the uniforms of slaves' conditions. At the same time, they could pride themselves in a paternalism that came in allowing the supposedly weak-willed to indulge their weaknesses.

CHAPTER THREE

You Don't Want Nothing

GOODS, PLANTATION LABOR, AND

THE MEANINGS OF FREEDOM,

1865 – 1920s

In a 1901 essay on the postbellum economy, Mississippian Alfred Holt Stone scolded workers for their spending habits. "Experience has taught no lesson more severely than that the average Negro will throw away—and I use that term advisedly—whatever money comes into his hands." At the end of the cotton-picking season, "the Delta Negro, especially when in the presence of his brother from less favoured section, is as free a spender as the world affords."[1] Emancipation raised new questions. For newly free men and women, would spending money and choosing and enjoying goods be a significant part of the new meaning of freedom? Would they try to turn the rare pleasures that shopping had been under slavery into part of a new definition of Americanism, much as many immigrants to America found new freedoms in urban stores? Or would freedpeople develop their own notions of land and independence, with the inherent fear of the debts and dependence goods could bring? And what of the landowners? Would landowners who had taken some pride in the ability of slaves to make occasional purchases change their thinking and their language after emancipation? For all involved, how did questions of goods and shopping figure in redefining the meaning of freedom?

Groups in power can use goods to extract labor from poor people in two ways. One is to keep the poor on such a narrow margin that they have to depend on the dominant group for their survival. The other, the defining approach of a consumer economy, is to entice the poor to work through the promise of material comforts. It was once common for scholars to view the second approach as important in the process by which postbellum landowners gained control over labor. Many historians, arguing that landowners and merchants locked workers into debts in a state of peonage or near-peonage, suggested that it was in the interests of landowners to encourage workers to run up expenses so high that the workers could not escape their contracts. But many recent scholars have argued that debt did not often force agricultural workers into situations resembling peonage. The power of debt is beyond question, but the picture is now more of workers with no collateral, moving from debt to debt, instead of a picture of debt tying workers to specific creditors for years or decades.[2] This new picture suggests that keepers of plantation commissaries and general stores had little economic incentive to encourage farm workers to spend large amounts of money as part of their goal to control their labor. If they could expect labor only from farm workers who owed them large debts, they would have had incentive to encourage workers to become consumers on a large scale. Without that incentive, the economic picture is less clear, and cultural questions are uncertain as well.

It is very clear that white landowners in Mississippi continued to see blacks as wasteful consumers. Their common complaint was that African Americans were such free spenders that they were better off without cash. Very soon after emancipation and continuing well into the twentieth century, many white Mississippians—landowners, employers, store owners, politicians, and others— said that if African Americans had the chance, they would literally spend themselves into starvation. The long-held views that African Americans would not work without coercion and had overpowering tastes for physical pleasure quickly combined into a largely new idea that the free market was leading to their demise. One landowner in northeastern Mississippi made the argument about black retrogression into a picture of consuming self-indulgence. Late in 1865 Samuel Agnew described a man named Archie as "an idle and trifling negroe. . . . [U]nless he mends his ways there is nothing ahead of him but starvation except he can gain a subsistence by stealing." Planter and merchant John Houston Bills said 1867 was a fine year for those who would work; "the freedmen however do not feel the necessity of it an[d] are lazy indolent improvident Creatures, Winter shortly to be upon us and not one of them provided with suitable clothing shoes, and even houses to live in[.] no care for the future." Later he made the same statement—in some ways a lament—that the freedpeople, "poor Creatures, they must suffer for want of food and raiment, they are wholly improvident and unsuited for their situation, freedom is anything but a blessing to them." A Lowndes County planter argued that sharecropping was far superior to paying wages to workers because "the negro, being thriftless and improvident, will by no other system have so much at the end of the year." Western Tennessee planter and merchant Robert Cartmell said in 1880 that some African American workers had managed "for the first time in 2 or 3 years have had a cent over." But, he said, "So soon as they get some money, gives them *fits*." G. P. Collins, a large planter in the Delta agreed, concluding in a significant phrase that "on the whole their enforced economy will do them good."[3]

Throughout the period that sharecropping dominated labor relations, land-owners agreed that African Americans spent money as soon as they got it and were better off living on narrow margins. The idea that they had the paternalistic responsibility, in the language of G. P. Collins, to enforce economy continued with great strength through the end of the sharecropping period. An Arkansas planter made the same point in the 1920s, saying the typical farm worker "is wild for money, but when he gets it, it is not worth five cents on the dollar to buy his needs. That is for waste, his needs are bought on credit." A large landowner told John Dollard in the 1930s that "the Negros will not save, and that they always spend all of what they get," and late in the 1930s the huge Delta and Pine Land Company tried to limit the access workers had to many goods, especially automobiles.[4]

Government officials were quick to use this image as a cause of the problems African Americans faced. In 1913 Henry A. Turner made a report to the federal government about labor conditions in LeFlore County. This nonsoutherner wrote in much the same vein as Mississippi planters that "after a Negro gets his settlement at Christmas he will not do a stroke of work until his money is all gone. . . . This is apt to be along in January or February for they soon spend their money." In a 1929 report to the State Board of Health, Coahoma County health workers blamed a high rate of pellagra on the spending habits of tenant farmers. Sounding very much like planters in the immediate postbellum period, they claimed the high death rate "is due to a faulty diet and is especially hard to combat among the negro tenants who are prone to spend all cash allowed them on their crops on such things as cars, tires, and gasoline."[5]

Delta author David Cohn provides the longest description by a white observer of the spending habits of African Americans. "The cropper," he wrote, "sees but little cash during the cultivating and growing season." But at the end of the year, spending habits changed dramatically.

Now that he has money in hand he goes on a spending spree. The little country grocery stores which summerlong have had in stores only the most utilitarian foods such as beans, fat meat, flour, lard, and coffee, now flaunt on their shelves the unaccustomed luxuries of dried figs and raisins, apples, and oranges, lemons and grapes, and tinned California fruit. The dry-goods stores, which have sold only work clothes and cheap cotton dresses, now display wondrous suits for men dyed strange shades and richly adorned with multicolored buttons. "Sunday" shoes, too, are now to be worn every day. Rayon socks and rayon neckties are bright with shine, dripping color. Caps will be worn, jauntily backwards, and there are shotgun shells for rabbit-hunting.

For the women there are dresses of fairy-like splendor woven of the mist ingeniously mixed with satin, billowing with ruffles, bouffant with lace, smart with pink and blue marabou, and all for less than five dollars. Admirable dresses for walking in the rain across muddy fields to visit neighbors; superbly smart when worn with long white kid gloves to stand long hours in hot dusty streets, waiting for the circus parade. Underwear, too—Negroes in their conservatism still wear it—of maize and purple rayon embroidered with magenta roses. Shiny panties are only seventy-five cents, and that is merely the garnered sweat of ten hours-work with a hoe in the hot sun magically crystallized into silver. Love flourishes, beauty burns, and "us sho gwine have us a good time while us can." So, with the buying of this and that with the garnering of trinkets and bright trash, the stores are crowded and the money is spent.[6]

The length and detail of this flowery passage suggest Cohn was trying awfully hard to make his point. Such depictions served the purpose of saying that since African Americans could not handle money, they were better off without it. Conflicts over material goods and confusion about their meanings began immediately after emancipation. In 1867 former slaveowner Adelaide Stuart was shocked when her cook, dressing for a dance, asked the woman of the house "to lend a white waist for the occasion! I fully expected a scene, but Mrs G, smiling very blandly told Yellow rose she didn't think they were of the same size & so could not oblige her. Not long afterwards it was my turn, she walked into my room one morning & requested the loan of a net for the back of her hair. I had taked the cue from Mrs G. & so was polite but thought I to myself, Ye days of Emancipation, is this only the beginning of your evils?"[7] Many white Mississippians met freedpeople's demands for the symbols of equality with resentment and resistance. An editorial in the *Vicksburg Times* in 1866 addressed the explicitly political meanings of freedpeople's clothing. It called on landowners to cut off wages of former slaves not only to force them to work but also to remind them of their proper social positions. "The day of flaunting in finery has gone by, to return no more—instead of sporting a stovepipe hat, gloves and cane, Sambo must content himself with the axe and

Abroms New City Store in Rosedale, Mississippi, 1939. Such stores tried to benefit from the idea that African Americans were compulsive spenders. (Photo by Marion Post Wolcott; courtesy Library of Congress)

plow, and Miss Dinah instead of flourishing in hoopskirts and high-heeled boots—instead of flaunting of sun-shades and fancy hats and feathers, will be content to take up a hoe and go to work."[8] And the much discussed figure of the undeserving legislator newly dressed in ill-fitting suits fits clearly into the notion of freedpeople who were not working, were wasting money, and were trying to be something they were not and should not become.

Exactly how freedpeople received their clothing was a point of some debate in the years immediately after emancipation. A survey of more than 2,300 labor contracts registered with the Freedmen's Bureau in Mississippi showed how quickly the antebellum system of furnishing clothing changed. Freedpeople entered the marketplace for clothing very quickly after emancipation. In the large majority of Mississippi contracts in 1865, landowners supplied clothing to workers. In the summer and fall of 1865, 92 percent of the 1,621 contracts in Mississippi included clothing as part of the payment landowners owed their workers. But contracts from December 1865 through 1866 and 1867 were very different, including clothing only 27 percent of the time.[9] Necessitating that freedpersons find ways to clothe themselves, this change became part of liberating but also a very threatening part of the meaning of freedom.

The contracts in 1865 showed a desire by employers to continue the material meanings of slavery. Some stated specifically that landowners should furnish clothing "such as was provided for them in each instance before the late re-bellion." In August of 1865 Thomas Topp and Henry signed a contract "to continue the same rules as heretofore as regards medical treatment, hours of work, food and clothing," along with paying Henry the value of one-fifth of the year's crop. J. Butcher agreed only to provide Freeman and his family "such clothing as has already been furnished."[10]

In both quality and amount, the clothing landowners provided workers closely resembled clothing slaveowners provided slaves. Clothing for freedpeople typically consisted of two pairs of pants and two shirts for men, two frocks for women. Giving out new clothing on a seasonal basis had been common-place under slavery, and in freedom winter and summer clothing continued to mean the clothing best suited for working outdoors. Many contracts included shoes, but few included hats or jackets. Even the contract that included the most clothing any landowner paid his workers shows the limits of those pay-ments. L. P. King paid the men in Gates London's family "one good linsey or kersey sound jacket, one pair of linsey or kersey pants, two pair each of cot-ton pants, 3 osnaburg shirts each, & 1 substantial pair of shoes each," and paid every woman "2 cotton frocks & 2 chemises, one pair each of good substantial shoes."[11] The fact that even this exceptional contract supplied workers with such spartan clothing shows that the landowners were continuing the ante-bellum practice of clothing workers in the uniforms of their conditions. None of the contracts included descriptions of clothing that might be considered luxurious, or decorative, or even special.

Another sign of continuity with slavery in the 1865 contracts was the ability for laborers to weave clothing from cotton. Numerous contracts specified that landowners would pay their workers with cotton and the right to use it. In 1865 Caroline Gordon agreed "to furnish Sams wife with wheel card and cotton to make clothes for herself and two children and loom to weave the same." Mary King paid Jacob and his family with "a good pair of winter shoes" and "time given to them to spin and manufacture their own clothing."[12] The two dresses John Gregory paid Mary Jane Tucker in 1866 were made of the homespun cotton fabric that prior to the Civil War had clothed far more slaves than nonslaves.[13]

Beginning in December 1865, most landowners stopped supplying clothing and the cotton with which to make it. In January 1867 Joseph Brooks signed a contract saying he "shall not use cotton for beds, pillows and comforts or for wearing, and spinning, or any other purpose."[14] The most important reason landowners stopped supplying clothing would seem to be that landowners in late 1865 and 1866 had serious shortages of cash and wanted to minimize purchases of any kind. As Gerald Jaynes has explained, it was the lack of cash that determined the ways landowners paid their workers, and "The Long Pay" became a dominant part of the rhythm of their lives.[15] With landowners choosing to give up their old interest in clothing their workers, the process of the experience of clothing themselves now fell far more than ever before on the freedpersons.

All signs suggest that the freedpeople wanted this new freedom. The contracts themselves were largely silent on the issue of what the freedpeople wanted, except one in August 1865 that paid the former slaves with food, housing, and medicine but stated that the "freedmen prefer and agree to furnish their clothing."[16] Jaynes's argument that freedpeople wanted the economic freedom that went with cash payments suggests they would have rejected the dependence that came with having landowners make purchases for them.[17] The best evidence that freedpeople wanted the freedom to buy their own goods lay in the numerous references in the WPA slave narratives to the exhilaration that accompanied former slaves' first experiences of buying clothing. One recalled that her "greatest pleasure was independence—make my money, go and spend it as I see fit." Hattie Jefferson made her first two dollars by picking cotton. "I bought myself a new dress with part uf dat money." Lewis Jefferson received a dollar for helping to spin cloth. "Dat was big money fur me an' I bought myself a hat wid dat money."[18]

If freedpeople had the freedom to buy goods for themselves and, like many poor working people, had the freedom to walk the line between occasional pleasure and devastating debts, we must examine their place in plantation commissaries and general stores. Freedpeople did not spend their money wildly, as so many white Mississippians argued, but instead stood at the margins of the consumer economy. They enjoyed its pleasures occasionally but for the most part feared its effects. Plantation stores were new establishments that turned the antebellum practice of furnishing goods to slaves into a business practice, while general stores were older institutions that had to learn how to deal with freedpeople. Accounts at both stores reflect both the high debts and the very limited luxury purchasing of the freedpersons.

For all the power they held over land, credit, and the law, large landowners in Mississippi always felt it a struggle to keep their farm laborers at work. As Michael Wayne shows of the postwar Natchez region, the free labor system necessitated more negotiation and sheer irritation than large landowners felt was befitting men with traditions that demanded command. To them, the market offered too many chances for workers to assert their power through trickery, argument, or flight.[19] At John Petty Moore's plantation near Helena, Arkansas, tenants made their deals in January and stayed in debt until the end of the year when some paid their accounts in full. Moore recorded not only their accounts, but his frequent anger and distrust. Jonathan Jones had a 1903 account for $44.15, but, according to Moore, "the rascal run off-gone." Another tenant, Hugh Wilson, was "a rotten scoundrel." H. H. Lunsford had a debt of $50.00, but he "did not pay—he is a rascal, a lean beast."[20] Leroy Percy, despite owning a huge operation in the Delta, made a point of displaying the power the plantation had over tenants. In 1906 Percy wrote a manager, "I don't think it's a good idea to let Aaron Fuller get his supplies anywhere except at the store. The fact of it is, it will lessen your control over him, and it puts notions in the heads of the other negroes." Percy continued in a way that showed his refusal to bargain with workers. "If this does not suit him, I would not take him. He has nothin and he is in no position to dictate terms."[21] Working as a clerk in a Delta plantation store, C. C. Barbour used similar language in the 1880s to justify the use of violence against an African American debtor who challenged his author- ity. When the man refused to pay, Barbour swung at him with brass knuckles in front of a large crowd of farm workers and ended the dispute by pulling a pistol. Barbour told a co-worker, "I have got to finish him *now* or else we will have trouble all the fall when setting with the negroes."[22] Plantation stores were thus tools that landowners used less for selling goods than for maintaining power relations.

Searching for the day-to-day accounts of the transition to freedom in the stores shows above all that freedpeople were slow to spend their small amounts of money. Workers on the Montezuma Jones plantation in Bolivar, Tennessee, had some experience as slaves in earning money and spending it. In the 1850s Jones kept accounts with his slaves, with payments to them and debts due from them. In 1856, thirty slaves earned between one and three dollars. Extra shoes were their most common expense, and the accounts were extremely small. After emancipation, their accounts changed dramatically. First, the account notations now granted them surnames. Houston and Alfred became Houston Jones and Alfred Jones. Second, notations identified them with the designation of "negro." Third was the notation "Dr," meaning the individuals were debtors to Montezuma Jones. Such a combination signified that both skin color and indebtedness were to be central to the identities of African Americans after emancipation.[23]

A feeling of liberation no doubt came with these new identities, in which freedpeople faced a range of possibilities they had never known. Account nota- tions indicate arguments that were unlikely under slavery. In December 1866 the plantation owner claimed to have advanced Lewis Jones $50, but "Lewis claims to have used himself only $25." I. Bent Walker's bill for 1865 was never settled because "He claims all pd." The freedom of the debtor to argue—the freedom not to have one's economic identity as defined as fully as under slavery—had powerful dangers as well as new opportunities. In less than a year the debts of the workers jumped from one or two dollars to amounts large enough to threaten the independence of the freedpeople. In 1856 Lewis had a debt of $4.00. But in January 1866 Lewis Jones owed his former owner $230.24. In 1856 Alfred owed his owner for a hat and a pair of shoes, but at the end of 1865 Alfred Jones owed $100.62. Such debts escalated quickly. At the end of 1865 Major Jones owed $53.57 and Crocket owed $74.50, but by 1870 each had debts close to $200.[24]

The purchases the freedmen made from their former owner were all for subsistence goods—meal, bacon, molasses, tobacco, shoes, one overcoat.[25] It is not surprising that Montezuma Jones stocked no luxury items at his plantation in 1865 and 1866; he was simply continuing the antebellum practice of supplying basic goods and, not incidentally, probably had little cash for new purchases anyway. But the effects of these credit arrangements had significant consequences. Freedmen and women who were in debt for subsistence goods had little or no ability to buy anything they might have considered luxuries.

At the Lewis plantation known as the Hermitage in Greene County, Alabama, freedpersons showed the same tendencies to amass large debts and to buy almost nothing but subsistence goods. Of thirty-one freedmen who had debts with M. F. Lewis in 1873, fifteen had debts over $100, and one had a debt of almost $400.[26] With accounts averaging about $50 a year, customers at the Ivey F. Lewis plantation store near Demopolis, Alabama, in the 1870s and 1880s bought very little more than meat, corn, meal, tobacco, seed, and bagging. A few bought shoes and small quantities of inexpensive cloth, either stripes or osnaburg at twenty cents a yard or kersey at thirty-five cents. The Lewis storehouse was obviously well stocked, because Calvin Eidson bought a pocketknife, some buckets, and a set of plates, and a few customers bought hats.[27] The availability of such goods renders more meaningful the fact that so few customers bought them. Had such stores stocked only food and farming goods, we might assume that freedpeople went elsewhere to buy their more interesting or personal or luxurious goods, but it seems far more likely that subsistence goods were the only purchases they made.

At a fourth plantation, located at an unspecified site in Mississippi, freedpeople showed the same tendency to buy only subsistence goods. Former slaves identified in the ledger only as Charles, Frank, Lucy, Scipio, and Bill made purchases in 1866 that left them with year-end bills worth between twenty-eight and eighty-two dollars. They bought meat, flour, and meal. Two purchased whiskey, and most bought essential goods like boards, rails, and cotton seed. What they did not buy was anything that seemed to express individuality, luxury, or the pursuit of pleasure.[28]

Workers at Arthur and Fannie Rice's plantation in Oktibbeha County also moved from receiving small payments under slavery to building substantial debts shortly after emancipation. Many of the forty-four slaves received tiny payments in cash or wheat for their eggs and chickens. More surprisingly, men received between five and ten dollars each on April 28, 1865, in "money pade out to the servants out of the prosedes of the crop made on the plantation in 1864."[29] Many of the same workers, now identified with the last name Rice, had debts between fifty and one hundred dollars by 1868. None had any cash until November, but most were able to pay their accounts by early January with either cash or cotton. The majority bought simple goods like boots, cloth, pants, tobacco, meat, and farm goods such as mule feed. Only one, Nat Ross, bought anything one could consider a luxury item, a suit for twenty-three dollars.[30]

Plantation stores offered the least chance for the fun and potential romance of consumer spending. Indeed, some plantation owners did not consider their establishments to be stores. In two cases before the Mississippi Supreme Court in the 1890s, landowners who sold goods only to their workers claimed they were not storekeepers and thus should not pay the taxes to which stores were subject. A. H. Pattison, for example, sold twenty-four varieties of food, tobacco, soap, and clothing to her tenants. She did not believe her smokehouse constituted a store and asked exemption from paying taxes. The lawyer in the case of *James Alcorn v. State of Mississippi* likewise claimed that even an establishment that employed several clerks and supplied goods to over 500 workers on Alcorn's large plantation was not a store because it supplied goods only to Alcorn's tenants.[31] The significance of their arguments is considerable for analyzing the limits of the consumer opportunities agricultural workers had. Since landowners who sold goods to their workers considered themselves suppliers of goods and not storekeepers, they had no interest in keeping up with changes in styles of goods or in advertising their goods along the lines of modern stores.

The records of a small cotton farmer in western Tennessee illustrate the point clearly. Hamilton Parks kept small accounts with workers Sam Parks and Sam Pass, both of whom bought bacon, beef, salt, tobacco, shoes, and small tools from their employer. Hamilton Parks probably never considered himself a creditor, although he lent his workers sums of cash up to seventy-five cents, nor did he see himself as a storekeeper. Quite likely he supplied his workers from the same room and smokehouse he used for himself. Not seeing their workers as shoppers, such an employer did not try to encourage them to spend more and certainly not to enjoy the experience.[32]

It is not the minor point it might seem that such agricultural workers took little part in the experience of shopping—an experience poor people in American cities were enjoying. In cities in the late nineteenth century, rich and poor shared the experienced of wandering department store aisles, even if they did not share the ability to buy what they saw there. Urban shopping could be absolutely liberating for middle-class women and recent European immigrants and especially immigrant children.[33] Whereas the urban department store impressed shoppers with the size and grandeur of the experience of shopping, plantation stores were small establishments dwarfed in size and significance by the cotton gins that typically stood beside and towered over them.

Whatever array of goods the Mississippi plantation stores carried, workers often had little access to them. By the twentieth century, some large plantations maintained separate stores for cash and credit transactions, and the separation dramatized the bleak experiences of those without cash. The Mississippi Delta Planting Company was a rambling operation consisting of eleven plantations in Bolivar County. Its cash store was a large operation with three clerks and a stock, according to a government report in 1913, "superior to many of the better stores in larger towns." But most of the workers operated under the share system and rarely had the chance to make purchases at the cash store. Instead, they could buy goods only at the "time store," which had "a plain stock, nothing fancy is carried. A great pile of fat salt pork in slabs awaiting the knife (noe other meats), packages of flour, corn meal, sugar, cans of beans, corn, etc. and other staple articles constitute the stock. Shoes are carried, but no other clothing."[34] Workers who received their goods from such a store, or who obtained them from a landowner's smokehouse, did not even see goods in stores for the majority of the year and certainly had few opportunities to develop romantic notions about goods and shopping.

For farm workers, the business of getting their few goods carried countless signs of their lack of power. It was difficult to develop an air of intrigue about goods when the landowners, as former sharecropper Sylvester Baldwin recalled in a 1970 interview, "would issue you out what they wanted you to have." Methods of payment prevented them from enjoying a sense of freedom in shopping, since they could not be certain how much they were paying for goods when they received them as advances on a future crop. Mattie J. Cooks remembered the furnishing system as being intentionally mysterious. "You see, the reason they [sharecroppers] couldn't understand it was they [landowners] wouldn't furnish folk money to get groceries. They just write em an order. Give em so many pounds of fatback and gallons of molasses. And every time you wouldn't know what they cost." Receipts could have recorded the purchases and taken the mystery out of the transactions, but receipts were rare. Many former sharecroppers considered it laughable to have expected shopkeepers or landowners to have given them receipts. Responding to that question in an interview, Josephine Beard asked, "What kind of receipts? (laughter) What sorta receipts, brother? What sorta receipts? (laughter)." Another recalled, "Naw, my daddy didn't have no receipts."[35]

As if to symbolize how the sharecropping system worked against the possible development of a consumer ethic among black Mississippians, the book in which transactions at plantation stores were recorded was sometimes called the limit book. The contemporary contrast to the limit book would be the credit card, which in name and function suggests that spending should always be possible.[36]

If plantation stores did not encourage consuming habits among black farm workers, what of the general stores that were so important in the postbellum South? Very few stores made explicit appeals to African Americans as potential customers. Just before Christmas in 1865, an advertisement in the *Oxford Falcon* urged, "Young folks, old folks, big folks, little folks, white folks, black folks will not forget to call at Rueff's Confectionary where they will find every variety of toys, Christmas presents, cakes, candies, etc."[37] With few such exceptions, stores in the postbellum South did not advertise in ways that reached out to African Americans as potential customers.

General stores were not settings for racial equality. One might expect that the logic of the marketplace would have worked against racial discrimination, but store owners made clear distinctions between black and white customers. At least into the 1930s and possibly later, many store owners identified black customers by writing "col" in their ledgers.[38] The ledgers do not indicate that those African American customers faced different prices or interest rates than whites. But the fact that they were identified as different from white customers indicates that buying goods did not offer the freedom from their past that shopping and buying offered to other American workers in the late nineteenth century.

Despite the freedom African Americans had to shop in them, the stores remained largely the preserve of white men, whose presence for leisure as well as purchasing goods made African Americans conspicuous outsiders. Few African Americans found jobs as store clerks,[39] and the crowds of white men often made black men nervous. Ned Cobb's description of the possibility of facing harassment every time he went to a general store, and William Faulkner's story of Lucas Beauchamp, who had to walk a gauntlet of disapproving white men to do his shopping, suggest that tension and suspicion, rather than a sense of freedom, characterized most trips to the stores. The recollection of a Holmes County man shows the combined sense of the possibilities for a sense of freedom and male camaraderie with the ever-present fear of powerlessness. Chalmers Archer quoted the reminiscence of his Uncle Nick that "the store was a place where races mixed well, considering that it was during the early 1900s." African Americans, he recalled, spent only a few cents at such stores and always had to look out for trouble. "I remember that there was more familiarity and friendliness at the store than anywhere else during those times of Jim Crow laws and strict customs that worked so well to separate the black and white races. But, invariably, some white boy, usually in the company of five or six of his friends, would approach me with a push or shove or come across with an off-color, racist remark. I would simply proceed to knock his block off. Most of the time I lost the fight because the whole gang jumped me." When Charles Evers recalled growing up in Scott County in the 1920s, he thought only of the conflict and oppression. He and his brother Medgar always hated having to go to the store because "Soon as we'd go in the white men standing around there would start picking on us and trying to make us dance. 'Dance, nigger!' The owner of the store was worst of them all." Such stories reached into more recent Mississippi. Clifton Taulbert remembered that he always felt like a powerless outsider when he went into a white-owned store in 1950s Glen Allan. Before the "supermarket concept" of shopping reached his town, the young Taulbert had to ask a tyrannical teenage clerk named Billy Roy to serve him. Once, when Taulbert received the wrong coffee and had to return it, "Billy Roy's acne got bigger and blood rushed to his already red face. 'Boy can't you read? Why didn't you ask for the right kind in the beginning?' he yelled." Taulbert drew a political lesson from the story. "Most of us lived on the edge of segregation, in this society created so that even a sixteen-year-old white kid could take advantage of a position of power."[40]

African American customers made far fewer purchases at general stores than white customers. In three stores that made distinctions between African American and white customers, the white customers went to the store more often and bought far more goods. Of the thirteen customers listed as "col" at the Collier General Store in Charlotte, Tennessee, in 1890 and 1891, six had expenses of a dollar or less, and only four had expenses of over four dollars. Only one paid as much as the typical white customer. At Henderson's Store in Preston, Mississippi, in 1902, fifteen of the thirty-one customers listed as "col" had accounts worth less than a dollar and a half, and thirteen visited the store three or fewer times in a year. In 1869 and 1870, the African American customers at S. G. Burney's General Store in Oxford had accounts averaging eighteen dollars, less than half the average value of the accounts of white customers, and most of those customers visited the store only one or two times.[41]

Very few of the purchases in general store ledgers seem to indicate any sign of the romantic potential of consumer culture. General stores had far larger inventories than most plantation stores and offered more choices in quality, but

African American customers still bought little more than subsistence goods. Among the 128 customers at S. G. Burney's General Store, 13 were identified as "col." Their purchases showed few signs of using consumer goods to pursue novelty. Two bought axes. Eleven of the thirteen bought shoes and boots. Only Wilober Daniel showed any taste for novelty. Among his purchases were a wool shawl, a vest, a box of shirt collars, two pairs of stockings, and two hand-kerchiefs. The rest, with the exception of one who bought a spelling book, bought basic goods—inexpensive shirts, pants, and shoes.[42] Thirty years later the African American customers at Henderson's Store bought little more. Most had no purchases that cost more than a dollar, and the most frequent purchase was tobacco. Of the larger purchases, most common again were shoes, and here black customers made the choice to economize. All but one chose shoes worth between $1.00 and $1.50, while most white customers bought shoes worth over $3.00. Only two bought suits. The other customer who bought goods beyond a level of subsistence was Smith Roberts, who one day bought a pair of white gloves along with ten yards of black satin, some black cloth, and black ribbon. At the same time, he was buying six coffin tacks and screws, so it seems that the most elaborate goods any African American customer made at Henderson's Store went to bury the dead.[43]

White customers had considerably more cash than African Americans, and they settled their accounts far more frequently. At the Burney Store, only 10 percent of the white customers left their debts unpaid at the end of the year, while three of the thirteen black customers did the same. Five of the 115 white customers paid their bills at least in part with labor, while five of the African American customers—38 percent—worked for Burney to pay their debts. At the Collier Store, 28 percent of the whites but 85 percent of the African Americans left their debts unpaid at the end of the year. Sixty-eight percent of the African American customers at Henderson's Store did not settle their debts at the end of 1902. Far more than the white customers, African Americans had to fear the consequences of debt with every purchase.[44]

Further isolating African Americans from the process of spending and shopping was the fact that so few of them were involved in selling goods. With virtually no access to credit, African Americans were slow to become store owners. Some of the first African American businesses such as joint stock companies and insurance companies were ventures in which numerous poor people contributed tiny sums to share the benefits of businesses outside the control of large landowners.[45] The businesses individual African Americans were able to start tended either to sell food or to depend on skills developed as slaves. In 1883 African Americans in Mississippi owned at least sixteen grocer-ies, five restaurants, and seven saloons and liquor stores. These stores were spread widely throughout the state, with no particular concentration of black-owned businesses. Some built on individual skills to open fifteen blacksmith shops, four shoe shops, and four barber shops. Black Mississippians owned nineteen general stores in 1883, a number that might seem substantial except in comparison to the 2,229 general stores owned by whites.[46] Significantly, only two black-owned general stores in 1883 were located in the Delta, where white landowners wanted as much labor and as little African American independence as possible. With so few of their own stores, African Americans who bought goods did so at white men's places, often with their names on white men's books.[47]

Thirty years later, the trends toward segregation were complete, and black Mississippians responded by building more of their own institutions to serve black customers. In some areas such as Farish Street in Jackson and Mobile Street in Hattiesburg, African Americans formed their own districts for doing business and enjoying themselves. African American customers chose to stay in their own neighborhoods to do business with black barbers, hairdressers, dressmakers, and owners of so-called "eating houses." African Americans developed a number of professionals—preachers, funeral home directors, lawyers, teachers—who found a substantial niche serving the black population. But the state still had few African Americans who sold new clothing, furniture, automobiles, or other substantial consumer goods. In the black majority town of Clarksdale, African Americans owned virtually all of the businesses—including fourteen eating houses—in a three-street area, but they owned none of the town's eleven clothing stores, sixteen dry goods stores, or sixteen general merchandise stores. Thus, the experience of shopping meant leaving the friendship and support of the local neighborhood to go into territory owned by white Mississippians and governed by their rules.[48]

One way to circumvent the tensions and fears of visiting white-owned stores was by shopping through the mail. Shopping in catalogs and ordering goods from Chicago mail-order houses like Montgomery Ward and Sears Roebuck allowed black farm workers some relief from both the debts of plantation stores and the potential indignities of shopping in racist settings.[49] Such shopping revealed the potential meaninglessness of racial distinctions in the marketplace, because the Chicago businesses treated orders without writing "col" in the margin and without asking certain customers to go to the back door. Photographs taken by Marion Post Wolcott in the 1930s in the Delta dramatize the potential offered by mail-order shopping. On Good Hope Plantation in Mileston, two boys lingered over a catalog, while a third did school work, perhaps with the suggestion that consumption and education offered two ways out of the agricultural system that dominated the lives of their parents. In another

Among the businesses on North Washington Street in Vicksburg, Mississippi, in 1936 were the Savoy Barber Shop, the Brother-in-Law Barber Shop, the S. A. Bingham Barber Shop, and a Bargain Store. Most businesses owned by African Americans sold services or used goods rather than new consumer products. (Photo by Walker Evans; courtesy Library of Congress)

photograph, a young woman on the porch in Washington County closed her eyes in an inscrutable expression while a catalog lay in her lap. Was she dreaming? Was she grimacing in pain? For many farm workers, the opportunities for mail-order shopping could not have been extensive, simply because so many of them had little cash for most of the year.

Debt was one of the two economic realities that helped determine the perspective African Americans developed toward goods in the years after emancipation. The other was the hope of owning land. Both forces worked to limit consumer spending, one through force and the other through incentive. The respectable line among black political and religious leaders in Mississippi held that hard work and rigorous thrift would help poor people escape landless poverty and dependence. For example, AME minister Jonathan J. Morant, born in the 1860s in Mississippi, wrote in his autobiography that he learned early in life that "labor without the sense of thrift amounts to nothing but being a slave to an employer." After he made his first money, "I took every dollar I had and purchased teams, farming tools and then paid for six months' supplies for

Good Hope Plantation, Mileston, Mississippi, 1939. Two children look through a mail-order catalog. (Photo by Marion Post Wolcott; courtesy Library of Congress)

the family." Money, he claimed, "helps when one is willing to use it for a good cause. Otherwise it is trash."[50]

Until the second decade of the twentieth century, the goal of owning land was not a foolish hope. With the availability of land, especially in the Delta counties, the number of black Mississippians who owned land slowly increased to 15 percent by 1910—the highest that figure ever reached. Sydney Nathans writes even that African Americans who were interviewed in the 1980s recalled the period from the 1880s until 1914 as a "heyday for blacks" in the Delta.[51]

As long as that possibility remained, many African Americans had reason to avoid both debts and the consumer goods that increased them. A series of interviews of African Americans in rural Mississippi in the 1970s showed the strength of these beliefs in a form of self-denial that had turned necessity into a moral virtue. Former sharecroppers recalled that while they and their families had chafed under the necessity to do without comforts, they did not share the desire for nearly constant new experiences that consumer goods could bring. The search for independence had come to outweigh the taste and desire for most goods. Former sharecropper Nettie Bell thought she and her husband could have gotten credit, but they were reluctant to use it. "You know I was always like this. If I didn't have, I would do without. If my money give out, I

A woman with a mail-order catalog on the Aldridge Plantation, Washington County, Mississippi, 1937. (Photo by Dorothea Lange; courtesy Library of Congress)

would make out without it. . . . I was always taught by my mother that if you ain't got, you try to make out if you can." Artley Blanchard made the same point, recalling that "you had to do without ah lot. Couldn't do no better. you had to do without (pause) make out. You have to make out on different thangs that you, you know don't want nothing." William Carr repeated the point. "Some winters couldn't even buy winter clothes to put on the family. Just whatever we could scrape up and patch and do around." Those interviews include repeated descriptions of the virtues of saving money. One said his father had the money to buy land because "well, he just saved it. Just worked hard and saved it." Amy Jane Bafford said her husband "jest know how to manage. And so we always had plenty common food and plenty clothes. They might not have been what the children would like to had all the time, but they didn't have to go cold." That picture of self-restraint contrasted with her description of her father, who "jest seem like he jest gets things we jest really didn't need. . . . So, all that would be on the bill in the fall."[52]

Living on narrow margins, fearing the mysterious power of debt, and moving from place to place almost every year, agricultural laborers typically accumulated only a few material goods. Mississippi home economist Dorothy Dickins evoked a spartan image of a tenant dwelling in 1928. "The average home has only the furniture they cannot do without, such as beds, chairs (usually not more than four, possibly a dresser and wash-stand, more often a dresser than a wash-stand)." David Cohn, despite his interest in the spending habits of sharecroppers, emphasized how few possessions a typical family had as they arrived at a plantation to start a new season. "They own some pots & pans, two cane-back chairs, a Bible and a mail-order catalogue, colored photographs of themselves, a rickety bed, a few 'crazy' quilts and a rooster." By mentioning a catalog, Cohn showed that the sharecroppers knew about and hoped for better things, but his picture was one of scarcity. He concluded, "They stand in all the clothes that they have."[53] A WPA study in 1934 indicated that most black workers in the agricultural South had few choices or comforts in their clothing. Tenants made clothing purchases only once a year, at the end of the crop season. "If the tenant has made no profit on his operations or if he is unable to obtain further advance credit, his last year's wardrobe must suffice. Clothing purchased is of the coarsest, crudest character—denim overalls for the male members and cheap cotton goods for the female members. Brogan shoes, no socks, and homemade underwear, if any are the rule."[54]

If poverty and fear of debt led black Mississippians to economic caution and sparse material conditions, should we assume that wealthy Mississippians were simply wrong when they said African Americans spent money quickly? It would be easy simply to dismiss the statements of the whites as lies they told to justify their control of a system that denied African Americans access to cash for most of the year.

Most of the whites who claimed that African Americans were free spenders said simply that sharecroppers spent money as soon as they got it. Sharecroppers themselves named and interpreted their spending habits differently. Discussing their childhood experiences, former sharecroppers discussed the yearly time their families made purchases in relation to the Christmas season and not simply as the time when accounts were settled. As such, it was a ritual activity that carried meanings extending well beyond the simple purchasing of supplies. One recalled "Christmas money for to go to town and get clothes for Christmas." Another said that after he wore out a pair of shoes, he went barefoot "till next Christmas." Emily Carouthers recalled that when she was growing up outside Buena Vista, "We didn't know what it wuz going to town, only Christ-

Workers moving between Clarksdale and Greenville in 1938. The transient nature of the lives of farm laborers discouraged them from accumulating goods (Photo by Dorothea Lange; courtesy Library of Congress)

mas times, once a year. . . . We got dry goods. We'd set there and they would get some shoes and bring em for us to try em on to see if they would fit."[55]

Rituals often allow people to relieve the pressures that build up within the structures of their everyday lives.[56] The basic economic structure for rural African Americans consisted of the necessity for hard and steady labor with the hope for eventual land ownership, and a denial of the comforts and pleasures available in consumer goods. The brief, ritualized consumer pleasures available once a year offered a denial of that structure. Christmas spending offered leisure and a limited form of self-indulgence. Those indulgences had to be small ones—a stick of candy, good tobacco, and hardly ever an expensive suit. These opportunities allowed not a ritual overturning of the structure of everyday life in Mississippi, but only an inversion of the few features of their economic lives they could control.

In the tendency to spend and enjoy their money only on ritual occasions, black Mississippians conformed to a holiday schedule that gave group or family life a significance that outweighed the desires of the individual. Scholars who have analyzed the spending habits of other ethnic groups have discussed the ways in which periodic ritualized purchases served to reinforce family or religious traditions. Andrew Heinze, for example, writes in *Adapting to Abundance* that eastern European Jews traditionally spent most of their money not on everyday pleasures but on communal holiday celebrations. Poor people throughout much of the world concentrate much of their spending around holidays, when they serve food and drink to their friends and families, put on their best clothing, and decorate their homes and communities.[57]

For generations, the Christmas season had been a central holiday in both the material and ritual lives of African Americans. As slaves, Christmas had been the time for substantial parties, with drinking and eating and several days of unabashed leisure allowing a rare escape from hard work and scarce food supplies.[58] But it had also been the time when most slaveowners distributed shoes and clothing to the slaves. Those who paid slaves small amounts of cash frequently made those payments at Christmas as well. Thus African Americans had by the time of emancipation come to view Christmas as a time for a combination of material accumulation, sensual gratification, and holiday from labor.[59] After emancipation, it was the one time when most could spend substantial periods of time in the towns, away from both the fields and their everyday responsibilities.

It seems likely, to summarize, that black Mississippians did indeed change their spending habits in December. But those changes, far from proving the harshly paternalistic assessments of large landowners, constituted a ritualized release from the economic behavior necessitated by a system controlled by white landowners who believed "their enforced economy will do them good." This system of enforced economy, spartan and infrequent spending, and ritualized spending around Christmas began to decline when chances for buying land decreased, when the decline of sharecropping brought on more labor for cash, when more wage work outside of agriculture became available, and, eventually, when migration to the cities became common. At the same time, the white Mississippians' argument about the weakness of African American character shifted to the figure of the welfare Cadillac—a modern construct that includes many of the traditional notions about African American self-indulgence without the corresponding ideas about the paternalistic obligations of the upper class.

CHAPTER FOUR

New Stores and
New Shoppers,
1880–1930

While so many black Mississippians remained in a system that tried to define them as both nonconsumers and wasteful spenders, increasing numbers of white Mississippians were changing the ways they bought and thought about goods. Edward Ayers has described the 1890s as a turning point in the development of a marketplace for goods in the South, as a powerful national mass production and distribution system made more goods available, a rapidly growing railroad system took them into once remote areas, and cash payments allowed more southerners to buy them.[1] While it is always difficult to deduce precise moments of change in the history of consumer behavior, it is clear that some new directions emerged around the turn of the century in the economy, in advertising, and in the nature of store life. In substantial ways, store owners were finally able to achieve more of what they had wanted all along, emphasizing the special attractions of their goods, attracting more women into the stores, encouraging more customers to pay with cash, and making shopping more fun. Mississippi remained an agricultural population until recently, and it remains a poor state today, but growing numbers of Mississippians were taking on some of the habits of and adopting a fascination with consumer culture.

Two crucial changes in the Mississippi economy in the early twentieth century altered the place of the store in people's lives. One was the rapid decline in the proportion of farm people who owned their own farms. Just as black farmers saw their chances to own land fade from view, many white farmers and their children were losing their dream of independence and becoming tenants. The white tenant population more than doubled between 1900 and 1930 and by the latter year made up 27.8 percent of the state's white population.[2] Those tenants faced many of the same obstacles to spending as the African American tenants discussed in the previous chapter. Although whites generally did not work on the same huge plantations with all-powerful company stores and assuredly never had to go to the back door of stores, they were far from modern consumers. Even as many white farm owners started to buy more consumer products, white tenants kept the interiors of their homes as sparse as ever. State home economist Dorothy Dickins found in a 1942 survey that 10 percent of the white sharecroppers owned ice boxes or refrigerators and 14 percent had radios, while farm owners had at least three times as many of each item.[3]

The other economic change was the rising number of people who worked for cash outside agriculture. The agricultural cycle that paid farm people only at the end of the year had long encouraged and almost forced large numbers of farm people to economize. The percentage of the Mississippi population defined by the U.S. Census as rural decreased from 97 in 1880 to 86.6 in 1920 and 83.1 in 1930. For the first time in the state's history, the number of people living and working on farms decreased in the period from 1910 to 1920, and it increased only slightly during the 1920s. Most significantly, the number of people earning wages increased from 5,827 in 1880 to 57,560 by 1920, and total wages in that period went from slightly over $1 million to $51 million.[4]

Moving away from the farm did not necessarily turn farm people into active consumers. The most important industry around the turn of the century, the timber industry, did only a little to turn Mississippians into cash-spending pleasure seekers. On the one hand, lumber work offered more freedom to spend money than sharecropping because it put more cash in the hands of its workers, and it paid them more often than once a year. In the late 1800s, workers received about a dollar a day and usually received their pay at the end of the month.[5] On the other hand, lumber workers faced many of the same limits as sharecroppers. They received much of their pay through stores owned by the lumber companies. Stores in tiny communities with lumber camps or turpentine works appeared rapidly around the turn of the century. In timber areas such as Sunflower County in the Delta and Greene County in the Piney Woods, most of the communities with stores also had businesses in lumber, turpentine, or saw milling. In the 1880s, none of the communities in those sparsely populated counties had lumber operations, but by 1905 Sunflower County had fifteen communities and Greene County had twelve communities that had both stores and lumber works. Such small, new communities often consisted of groups of men working exclusively in lumber. For example, Rounsaville in Greene County had a general store and turpentine factory and no other businesses to serve its fifty people. Bexley, with twenty-five people, had only a lumber mill and a general store. Leaf served its 450 people with a general store, a lumber mill, and the Leaf Mercantile Company.[6]

Living in largely male communities, working hard, and then moving on to the next lumber camp, timber workers who received and spent their money at small company stores were unlikely to shop often or to take much excitement from their shopping. Many companies began to adopt the practices large land-owners used with sharecroppers, by paying employees with special tickets or tokens they could spend only at company stores and making few cash payments except around Christmas.[7] The men who worked for the R. F. Learned Lumber Company in the 1920s paid their bills at company stores with more cash than sharecroppers were able to pay, but, like sharecroppers, they made the great majority of purchases for basic goods—sausage, coffee, eggs, tobacco, and dry goods like shoes, boots, and gloves.[8]

Having spent the early years of her adult life in lumber camps in the 1890s and early 1900s, Mary Hamilton described in her autobiography a life that offered few chances to become a consumer. Above all, life as a lumber camp cook and the wife of an ambitious lumber worker was transient, and the family traveled light. Floods and frequent movement made it difficult to keep any of their goods. Her family left many of their goods behind as they started over time after time. Before one of many trips, "We sold out the most of our things again, packed our trunks with what was left, clothes and bedding, took our boy Ozzie, and started." Living in tents, shacks, dormitories, and other temporary quarters, the family had little space to accumulate goods.[9]

Hamilton illustrated the tensions between her ultimate goal of household independence and occasional possibilities for men to save money. A would-be agrarian even as she moved from camp to camp, she wanted to minimize expenses to afford the little house and farm she pictured as the keys to the good life. But with money and access to goods coming sporadically and with little control over the spending, she recalled that camp life was "always either a feast or a famine." Good times often led to what she considered reckless pleasure. "I am thinking, as I write, of those wasteful days. The candy we gave away to the Negroes working for us. . . . I don't even remember what we spent the money for, but I know if I had it now in these hard times I could live high on it two or three years."[10] In sum, Hamilton showed that even though she and her family made money more often than most farming people, industrial work did little to turn her into a consumer.

Other forms of industry on the rise in Mississippi employed white workers almost exclusively and, beginning in the early 1900s, employed more women than men. Textile mills, garment factories, and other forms of industry continued the southern concentration on low-skill, low-wage labor, but they paid cash far more frequently than farm work and timber labor, and it was cash payments that allowed and encouraged new spending habits among working people. In several studies in the 1930s, Dorothy Dickins examined the incomes and expenditures of Mississippi's textile and garment workers, almost all of them female, to compare them to farm households. Industrial workers bought more goods than farm people, whether they owned their farms or worked for the owners. Farm people in the South had long claimed that their ability to make some of their own goods was part of what defined them as southerners and free people. The differences, however, were striking. In 1941, 68 percent of the garment working women had bought at least three pairs of shoes, but only 8 percent of the farming women had done so. Sixty-one percent of the garment-working women but only a third of the farming women had bought rayon dresses.[11] Textile mill workers were much more likely than farm families to have electric lights. Factory workers also had more contact with mass culture, owning radios and going to movies far more frequently than farm families.[12]

The families who worked in factories paid cash for goods much more often than farm owners or farm laborers. Families that included women working in textile or garment factories had more than twice as much cash income than farming families. Industrial workers with reasonably steady paychecks could experiment with a form of credit few farmers had ever imagined—installment buying. Of the mill village families Dickins studied in the late 1930s, 73 percent were buying goods on installment plans, but just 8 percent of the full-time farmers used that form of credit.[13]

One of the clearest changes in the early twentieth century was the rise of new varieties of stores that sold to people whose lives did not follow the traditional rhythms of agriculture. Types of stores appeared after 1910 and into the 1920s that had not existed forty years earlier.

The most dramatic additions to the shopping landscape were establishments that sold automobiles and automobile parts. In 1910 43 businesses sold automobiles in Mississippi; by 1929, cars and trucks were sold at 455 stores in over a hundred Mississippi towns and cities, including two towns of less than 100 people.[14] Some of the new dealers combined the new business with their older livery stables, but most were younger men, many of whom came from Michigan. They offered more than a smooth transition from horse to horseless carriage.[15]

As the central objects in the emergence of consumer culture, automobiles also offered privacy, speed, excitement, and frequent changes of style. Cars offered the possibility for people to shed their identities quickly and take on new ones. The first cars were so novel that they helped encourage the fascination with novelty so significant to consumer culture. In 1909 a south Mississippi newspaper reported, " 'Horseless carriages' are becoming all the rage in Summit. This week [three men] have received elegant and substantial new auto buggies, and now the honk, honk of the horns of these and other autos are familiar sounds on our street."[16]

Automobile lovers saw the car as the key to breaking down the isolation of rural people. In 1916 the editor of the *Greenwood Commonwealth* breathlessly claimed, "The auto has opened up a new life and a new world to the country people. . . . It has brought the church and the theatre and the lecture and picture show right to the man who lives in the country." It took farm families, he claimed, "to the front door of the shopping centers, it brings them every fine thing which a town may enjoy."[17] In fact, more industrial workers than farm people bought cars, but the image of the declining isolation of rural areas was important.[18] As a Monroe County native recalled of his family's purchase of a Ford Model T in 1926, "When a family buys their first automobile, you can wager your bottom dollar that everyone wants to go on a trip."[19]

Perhaps as significant as car dealerships, new stores emerged that operated differently from general stores and plantation stores. Establishments that sold smaller dry goods changed the way shoppers paid for goods. Most grocery stores continued to offer store credit in the 1920s, and the large majority of furniture stores and automobile dealers offered forms of credit. But two-thirds of the dry goods stores, along with virtually all variety and five and ten cent stores, operated on a cash-only basis.[20] Perhaps most illustrative were institutions calling themselves cash stores. Already present in the late 1800s, their number grew to thirty-seven by 1925. Stores like Simmons' Cash Store in Duncan and the Lambert Cash Store operated on the cash basis that merchants had been wanting to achieve since early in Mississippi history. A Mississippi chain of grocery stores called Jitney Jungles began a cash-only policy after World War I, complete with an emphasis on self-service. Cash stores were located throughout the state, even in tiny towns like Jaw, Rienzi, and Lumberton. A related new establishment was the five and ten cent store. By 1929, Mississippi had 126 variety stores, five and ten stores, and to-a-dollar stores. All but five operated on a cash-only basis, selling the sorts of smaller items men had traditionally bought on credit on trips to general stores. Twenty-four of the variety stores belonged to national chains and thus had few links to the traditional practices of general stores that had emphasized store credit, male recreation, and personal relationships.[21]

The second change in how Mississippians paid for their goods involved installment buying. Farm people had long lived on credit, but store credit worked according to the rhythms of the farm year. Believing or at least hoping

The Hoffman 5 and 10 Cent Store in Greenville, Mississippi, 1905.
(Mississippi Department of Archives and History)

they would pay their store bills at the end of every year, farming people had good reason to limit their expenses to keep those bills low. Mail-order catalogs helped initiate rural people into installment buying, as they mailed orders and partial payments to mail-order houses in Chicago and New York.[22] Installment credit required frequent—often monthly—cash payments and had the effect of encouraging purchases of more expensive goods.[23]

In 1929 Mississippi had fifty department stores, twelve of which belonged to national chains.[24] Such stores came to dominate the shopping opportunities of Mississippians and overwhelm the pages of local newspapers. As historians of urban department stores have detailed, customers felt a new freedom when they could walk among goods, going from department to department, rather than shopping in the traditional method in which goods lay out of customers' reach in areas controlled by a clerk. Dramatizing the excitement possible in shopping, the department store stressed a new relationship between shopper and goods. The businessman who named the Help Yourself Store in Meridian was advertising the difference between his establishment and stores where Mississippians had shopped in the past.[25] As William Leach stresses in his analysis of modern stores, department stores also celebrated the romance of goods by decorating front windows and placing new emphasis on store decor and color to create as much mystery and intrigue as possible.[26]

In 1929 Mississippi had 133 ready-to-wear clothing stores.[27] These offered

Kew Mercantile in Wiggins, Mississippi, advertised the differences among its departments. (Ann Rayburn Collection, Special Collections, University of Mississippi Library)

many women their first opportunities to buy clothing itself rather than material from which to sew clothing. At ready-to-wear stores, they could find clothes that conformed to seasonal changes in style, and they likely found some freedom from the need to think of sewing as their duty.

The combined effects of the automobile dealers, the cash stores and five and dime stores, and the ready-to-wear clothing stores and department stores opened new opportunities for shopping outside the yearly agricultural cycle of credit and debt. They stressed the importance of paying cash, even for small goods, or paying in monthly installments. They offered Mississippians access to the latest clothing, latest technological innovations, and the ultimate consumer product—the automobile. The new stores displayed goods in intriguing ways and promised a kind of frequent novelty previously unavailable to most Mississippians.

Ultimately more important than the new types of stores were the new practices store owners began to use in the early 1900s. Store owners had never felt satisfied to sell bulk supplies and cloth to farm men at a slow pace in a predictable environment. They had long hoped to sell more expensive goods and to receive cash throughout the year. Most had always thought they should profit from their connections to cosmopolitan centers rather than simply serve a local farming economy.

The Woolworth store in Laurel, Mississippi, was far larger than most stores had been in the 1800s. (Ann Rayburn Collection, Special Collections, University of Mississippi Library)

Around the turn of the century store owners began to experiment with ways to make shopping more exciting. Beyond simply advertising low prices, they now offered sales that promised nearly carnivalesque shopping events that would attract large crowds and turn shopping into entertainment. In 1906 the Potts Store in Kosciusko advertised a sale of cloth goods ranging from towels, sheets, tablecloths, and bedspreads to corsets, hose, hats, and handkerchiefs to skirts and dresses to lace embroidery. Advertisements trumpeted the two-day event as a "White Carnival," featuring "the Greatest display of White Goods ever shown in this section of Mississippi." The sale "should appeal to everyone" and "fill the store with eager buyers." Store owners hoped a new millinery department could attract women shoppers who might have been accustomed to shopping only in millinery stores. Most significantly, the Potts Store tried to bring women together with men and children into a large crowd and exciting consumer experience it called the "Big White Show."[28]

Garry's Store in the same town was even more elaborate in planning a sale that would "go down in history as the greatest sale known throughout our state." Advertisements announced: "United States Weather Bureau Warning!! A Tornado In prices of Merchandise will sweep the city of Kosciusko and vicinity." The store promised a "mammoth" dry goods sale that would be "a Carnival Indeed." To enhance the carnival side of the event, Garry placed a red canvas tent in front of the store and promised to pay railroad fare to people from out of town. Probably coincidentally, the advertisement for the 1906 event was located next to an advertisement for the Great Wallace Shows, a circus promising the "Greatest, Grandest, Purest and Fairest Amusement Enterprise in the World."[29]

A store in Greenville tried to bring together the theme of the carnival with the illusion of unlimited abundance. Significantly called The Fair, the store put out a large black tent and invited shoppers to "10 of the Biggest Sales Days known in the History of Mississippi." The event, store owners hoped, would be "Colossal! Mighty! Stupendous!" Along with $85,000 worth of dry goods, The Fair hoped parents would bring their children to a "gala" opening day in which employees would throw free clothing and straw hats from the top of the building. As in the other sales, the store advertised that prices would be so low that it would be exciting to take advantage of them. Thus, it was great fun to overturn the expectations of everyday life by leaving at home norms of quiet frugality, face-to-face relationships, and relative predictability. Going to the store, such advertisements promised, should be a dizzying experience.[30]

The notion that shopping was exciting showed in other changes in advertising. The clearest differences were the growing reliance on brand names and the increasing use of drawings of men and women in the advertisements. Mass distribution and an expanding railroad system brought to the stores not only new goods but new meanings as well. Susan Strasser has detailed the crucial changes in the early twentieth century from a system in which customers bought unmarked goods from large boxes and barrels to a marketing system based on special packaging with brand names and advertising on individually wrapped boxes or bags.[31] Name brands emerged as a dominant and largely new feature of advertising goods in the early twentieth century. Whereas earlier advertisements had touted either the low price of goods or their origins in cosmopolitan centers of fashion, newspaper advertisements in the early decades of the century suggested that almost all goods changed with new styles. Hardly ever mentioning the point of origin of goods, new advertisements mentioned brand names and assumed their audiences would know or learn their meanings. Thus store owners asked shoppers to identify themselves with the products of American corporations, offering goods that had little direct connection to European or northeastern fashion centers. Advertisements continued to stress that goods were modern and up to date, but by replacing London and Paris with the names of American companies, they suggested that more consumers could afford to be modern. Seward and Company said the sure way for men to "Dress Well, Look Distinguished, Be Contented" was to wear "the smart new Spring models of famous Snellenburg Clothes."[32] Simon Loeb's Department Store in Columbus advertised that it sold Waldorf, Astor, and Bannister shoes.[33] Ben Swanson's Mississippi Shoe Store sold Johnson and Murphy Shoes, "the best and highest grade of mens shoes."[34]

Commerce Street, West Point, Mississippi, 1907. Large crowds sometimes filled the downtown areas of small towns. (Mississippi Department of Archives and History)

Arrow collars, High Art suits, and Johnson and Murphy shoes gave consumers a new language. Only the wealthy had such a language in the mid-1800s, but twentieth-century store owners hoped brand-name goods would be points of possible conversations. As one store owner suggested in 1916, "Men who have worn a High-Art Suit will tell you of their wearing qualities."[35] Most clearly, Ford, Overland, Chevrolet, Maxwell, Chandler, Buick, and the rest could not be separated from their brand names. There were no automobiles without brand names, and those names made enormous differences in choosing, displaying, enjoying, and discussing cars.

The other dramatic change in newspaper advertising was the use of drawings of people enjoying new clothes, or a new automobile, or other new goods. Most advertising illustrations in the nineteenth century, as Warren Susman has argued, emphasized the utility of items by depicting them simply, without backgrounds and without people using them. Putting people into the pictures suggested that goods could change the people themselves by making them the smiling contented figures they saw in the newspapers or catalogs. Pictures urged potential shoppers to dream and to imagine how new goods could transform them into new people.[36]

The first drawings of people in the early 1900s tended to portray male figures wearing suits, coats, and shoes. They looked satisfied, well off, and heavily dressed, especially for the Mississippi climate. Often well-dressed men talked to each other in scenes that suggested they might be discussing their good taste in clothing. Other drawings portrayed serious and confident professional men. The drawings suggest the men belong to a group secure in their own identities. What the men did *not* resemble were farmers; overalls did not make an appearance. Thus the advertisements offered to transform rural and town men into people who could enjoy themselves like urban professionals.

In the 1920s and 1930s, drawings of women first appeared and then almost replaced drawings of men in clothing advertisements. As Roland Marchand writes in his history of the advertising profession, by the 1920s, "women were viewed as virtually the sole buyers of 'style goods.' "[37] Women in the drawings of clothing tended to be younger than the men who dominated earlier advertising, and they wore lighter clothes that reflected ease and pleasure more than work or after-work conversations. The drawings suggest Hollywood poses, moments that seemed to catch women artfully off balance. Marchand also notes that such drawings tended to suggest a degree of unreality in the way they portrayed women as incredibly tall, thin, and barely balanced on the ground.[38] They looked very much unlike farm women. By the 1920s, such women consistently advertised specific clothing in most Mississippi newspapers. By the 1930s, Reed's Department Store in Tupelo typically pictured "Hollywood Creations by Justine," which, Reed's stressed, were advertised in *Vogue*.[39]

The new advertisements that dramatized what modern and stylish, ready-made, brand-name clothing could do for women were one of several signs of the increasing importance women played in the stores. Store owners had been inviting women to shop since the antebellum period; by the early 1900s they were finally achieving some success. Women shoppers for the first time started shopping at Jitney Jungle groceries in the 1920s, attracted both by low prices and the ability to serve themselves. According to a descendent of the founder, in that decade "Jitney shopping became a social ritual, for which ladies bought cotton frocks, which were actually called 'jitney dresses.' "[40] Some stores adopted unusual advertising strategies to attract more women, offering college scholarships to women customers or hiring women to display products. Most significantly, stores began to employ women as clerks. South Mississippi native Julia Arledge Thigpen remembered that women, first employed as clerks around 1900, had a real influence on the life of the store. "Once women were employed by one store in town, the women patrons liked to trade with them so much better than with the men, that soon all the stores would begin to hire women." [41]

By the early 1900s, the figure of the overworked female clerk was common. The editor of the *Clarksdale Banner* asked Christmas shoppers to visit the stores early to spare the women who had to "answer tirelessly and cheerily the thousand and one queries which bubble from the lips of bargain seekers."[42] The diary of a dime store clerk in Aberdeen shows how important such employees were becoming. When Virginia Howell took her job at age sixteen, she was one of at least three young women working in the store in the Christmas season. She frequently saw men and women of her age in the store and seemed to have had an especially good time selling them small goods, especially candy. For such employees, the connections between making money and spending it were clear. On her first day on the job, Howell sold thirteen dollars worth of goods and recorded, "I sure feel proud of my first earned dollar, and I guess I will spend it for Xmas presents."[43]

As the statistics cited in Chapter One reveal, women shopped in increasing numbers in the 1880s and 1890s. The language newspapers used in the early 1900s suggested they were finally becoming frequent shoppers. Advertisements noted particular parts of stores where women did most of the shopping. For example, a large store in Aberdeen advertised, "Ladies go to Seward & Co. for your skirts. . . . Ladies, you can get any kind of Hand Bag you want at Seward & Co's. . . . Go to Seward & Co and see that line of Ladies' belts from 10 c to 1.00."[44] A store in Brookhaven advertised a sale as "the Housekeeper's Chance to help the family purse by a substantial saving in the cost of goods."[45] In Laurel, L. Fine advertised that "every woman in this vicinity should come to our store and buy one or more of our $3.00 sample skirts."[46]

While women gained more access to traditionally male shopping areas, they lost the only stores that had catered only to women. The millinery shop, the one traditionally all-female store, declined in number from eighty-seven shops in 1883, to fifty-three in 1929, to just fourteen in 1948.[47] Many larger stores for the first time created millinery departments to attract women who had long been buying their hats in all-female establishments. For example, Hicks Mercantile Store in Laurel brought "an experienced trimmer from St. Louis" to take charge of its new millinery department. She was "ready to show you a very high grade line of Hats, Trimmings, Etc."[48]

Dividing large stores into departments was an essential element in encouraging women to become shoppers. Having female clerks selling items women used was crucial to ending the male domination of the space full of men behind the counter, on the porch, or selling and enjoying alcohol in the back. Moreover, having stores large enough to walk from department to department to shop gave women a freedom they had not enjoyed when they had to brave the overwhelming male presence to enter the old general store.

At the same time women were starting to come into stores in large numbers, store owners took steps to make Christmas a major shopping event. Women were vitally important as Christmas shoppers, and newspaper reports routinely discussed throngs of women shoppers. In Clarksdale, the newspaper suggested that "if you want to see the prettiest girls and the handsomest matrons in the world, anchor yourself on Delta Avenue one of these afternoons and watch the Christmas shoppers go by."[49] In Aberdeen, Virginia Howell worked until almost midnight on December 23, 1916, a day when Santa Claus visited the store and she "never saw such a crowd in all my life."[50] The notion that stores were for all people—at least all white people—came to fruition when store owners tried to include children as shoppers. In the late 1800s and especially the early 1900s, store owners began putting Christmas displays in their windows and placing special Christmas advertisements in newspapers. Only then did they start encouraging children to mail their gift wishes to Santa Claus. It was a great bonanza for stores when newspapers began to print children's letters asking for specific name-brand goods. The stores continued to sell small novelties to make children happy at Christmas, but they offered far more toys and for the first time used Santa Claus to suggest children should ask for and expect presents in large quantities. In 1903, for example, Galbraith's Cash Store in Hattiesburg advertised itself as Santa Claus's headquarters.[51] In 1936 Penny's in Tupelo set up a new section called Toyland that promised a "Carnival of Joy! Bushels of Toys for Girls and Boys."[52]

Perhaps as important, stores began in the early 1900s to encourage customers to buy Christmas presents for adults. Some listed possible gifts for men and women, and many offered to help people choose gifts. That offer seems particularly important since few adults traditionally received gifts, so storekeepers were increasing their roles as teachers of fashion and consumption. In 1906 a jeweler in Columbus set up "large and beautiful holiday displays" and offered to deliver presents on Christmas morning.[53] G. D. Hall's clothing store in Iuka suggested sweaters, ties, silk hose, and the like as gifts men and women should buy for each other.[54] By 1936, McGaughey's in Tupelo was urging men to "make shopping a pleasure" and advertised its first annual showing of "Gorgeous Christmas Lingerie."[55]

Of course, Christmas had long had a carnivalesque, sensory side of eating heavily, eating sweets, setting off fireworks, and allowing children and at one time slaves liberties they did not normally have. White and black men had once viewed Christmas as a time to crowd the towns and join the drunkenness in the stores or streets. In the emerging consumer culture, Christmas meant more gifts and more expenses. It thus meant that more white southerners were finding the indulgence of spending money and enjoying goods more acceptable. But they did so in a much quieter family setting. Domestication, Christianization, and commercialization, in Leigh Eric Schmidt's analysis, were the main elements in the coming of the modern Christmas.[56] Together, the three developments reduced downtown male drunkenness, encouraged family members of all ages to spend more money to give gifts to each other, and kept the holiday in the family. By de-emphasizing the impermanent, carnivalesque, and sensory sides of the holiday in favor of the exchange of durable goods within the family, commercialization and domestication vastly reduced the distance between the home and the store.

The simple conclusion is that growing numbers of people in Mississippi, especially white women, started visiting stores more often, buying more goods, paying with less store credit and more cash and more installment credit, and looking forward to buying goods as an exciting and romantic experience. Some stores in Mississippi were taking on some features of the grand palaces for selling that had revolutionized the experience of buying goods in northeastern and European cities. It would thus be easy to stress how much had changed by the 1920s and 1930s. For example, when an exhibit at the Yazoo County Fair in 1936 treated visitors to the "unique sight of a woman spinning from a wonderful old spinning machine,"[57] she seemed to symbolize the end of a perspective on goods too old to survive except in memory.

Despite all of the changes, vital features of Mississippi tradition remained clear in the 1920s and 1930s. The state ranked last in the country in the percentage of its people with radios and telephones in their homes, last in the proportion of people with motor vehicle registrations and homes wired for electricity. In 1937, less than one percent of the farms in the state had electricity. The state ranked last in the country in per capita wealth, with less than half the national average. Even more dramatically, Mississippi was last in the country in per capita retail sales, with a figure 34 percent of the national average.[58]

Back on the farm, many patterns continued, even if growing numbers of farming families were driving to town to buy more goods than they had in the 1800s. In an elaborate study of farm-owning families in 1942, Dorothy Dickins found that the clothing of white men cost about 50 percent more than the clothing of white women. Men paid more for jackets and sweaters, while women continued to make many of their cotton dresses, slips, and nightgowns from inexpensive material. Women also continued to sew far more clothes for other women than for men. As Dickins realized, this imbalance ran counter to a national trend. Americans began to spend more money on clothing for women than for men around 1910, and by the 1920s and 1930s they were spending 50 percent more for women's clothing than men's.[59]

The most significant continuity was that African Americans still had not become significant figures in the stores. Custom required black Mississippians to go to the back door and denied them the freedom to try on clothes; agricultural poverty and the tenant system limited their chances to be consumers.

The boyhood recollections of Cecil Cook, a white man who grew up in Columbus in the second decade of the twentieth century, dramatize how the arrival of department stores did not seem to offer new opportunities for black Mississippians. Writing almost as a geographer, Cook described the very different shopping experiences available as one moved down Main Street. First was Commerce Avenue, "an affluent shopping address" where one could shop at several general stores and hardware stores and two newer department stores. In advertising "We sell everything but whiskey," the department stores announced that domestication had joined consumer culture to create stores unlike the sleepy old general stores that served as establishments for male recreation.

Moving west a block to Mobile Avenue, one found "dozens of bargain-merchandise stores, owned and operated for the most part by first-generation Jews." This was the shopping spot for the working men and women who had just moved away from the farms. As Cook recalled, "On Saturday afternoons, Mobile Avenue was the most crowded place in town," with discount stores "patronized by customers mainly from the plantations, cotton factories, and sawmills." One more intersection farther west was Catfish Alley, which had a different clientele and offered a very different array of goods. "It was a narrow street with dilapidated, down-at-the-heels restaurants, poolhalls, soft drink parlors, and dirty little meat and fish markets and grocery stores." As Cook remembered it, the progression of shopping areas moved from solid purchases of durable goods to inexpensive goods to passing pleasures for the senses. He characterized Catfish Alley as " 'nigger heaven' for the town and plantation Negroes. The smell of overfried catfish and the hickory smoke smell of the barbecued porkchops usually permeated the air in the area."[60]

Cook's comparison suggests two significant points. First, it shows that the coming of the department store did little to include African Americans in the experience of shopping.[61] In the period from 1910 to 1920 in a fairly large town, shopping was racially segregated. Even the growing number of inexpensive stores that served people who had never done much shopping did not offer goods to black customers. Second, in suggesting that whites shopped mostly for durable goods while African Americans spent their money on fried and barbecued food, Cook kept alive the old idea that black men and women wasted their money on passing physical pleasures. In Cook's portrayal, far more white Mississippians than ever were becoming modern consumers, but blacks remained indulgent and perhaps reckless pleasure seekers.

Cook recalled an African American house servant, Uncle Eli, in a way that suggested he thought the older man was easily satisfied with the pleasures of strong tastes. On trips to town, Eli liked to pay fifteen cents for some cheese, a can of sardines, and "a big cold drink," along with some free crackers. "Parisians may have had their Maxim's but Uncle Eli would have chosen Saturday in Columbus with sardines and cheese." In his descriptions of Columbus and Uncle Eli, Cook continued ideas that had been common in nineteenth-century Mississippi. Choices about durable goods helped define freedom for most whites, but African American, according to him, seemed happy enough with the occasional pleasure.

Uncle Eli, significantly, had his own interpretation of the meaning of Saturdays in downtown Columbus. Cook divided the experiences along Main Street into three geographic and social categories, but Eli "told me one time that all you got to do is to take a look at the people on Main Street on a Saturday afternoon. You will see blacks and tans and whites and not-so-whites and a lot of dirties. You will see overalls and homemade percale dresses and brogan shoes and just a few fine cut people with suits and dresses from Memphis and Birmingham." Eli thus interpreted Saturday shopping as cutting across social boundaries rather than reinforcing them. Mississippians have debated that difference in their words and actions throughout the twentieth century.[62]

CHAPTER FIVE

Gladys Smith, Dorothy Dickins, and Consumer Ideals for Women, 1920s–1950s

A young Gladys Smith, according to her biographer, was "a consumer and a half, and had been since her earliest days back in the country on Burk's Farm where Lily Mae Irwin had watched her and her sister Clettes go in and out of the Irwin store 'sixty times a day' buying one item at a time, clearly enjoying purchasing almost as much as the purchase. Down the years Gladys had clung stubbornly to that notion of hers that life's pleasures were not only meant for the rich."[1]

That description goes a long way toward defining the ideal twentieth-century consumer, but it may seem a surprising description of a poor teenager in rural Mississippi in the 1920s. Born in 1912 and raised in Lee County, Gladys was one of four children of Bob Smith—a white man, failed sharecropper, occasional moonshiner and worker at odd jobs—and his religious and invalid wife Doll Smith. The family never had much money, and they moved every year or two of Gladys's childhood. Gladys must have heard the traditional lessons about the dangers of consumer goods. As part of a large farming family, she must have heard that buying goods caused debts that threatened the financial independence of the family or hindered their efforts to gain that independence. As a young woman, she must have heard about her duty to sew as much clothing as possible. And as an evangelical, she must have heard that consumer goods posed the threat of indulgence—a term religious folk used to suggest the enjoyment of passing, selfish pleasures at the expense of higher virtues.

She must have heard those lessons, yet from an early age Gladys Smith was dreaming all of the dreams of the American consumer. She wanted a great variety of goods. She fit the notion of a democracy of goods with her belief that goods should not be just for the wealthy. Her unending trips to the store made her almost a penultimate shopper for pleasure. Finally, in seeing the trip as more important than the products she took home, Smith had the romantic, unquenchable thirst for new experiences promised by the progression from one product to the next and then the next.

Who might have taught the young Gladys Smith to be such a consumer? Did the state of Mississippi encourage women to make such a break from the past? Through the work of its agricultural extension service, the state was trying to set standards. Extension service reports combined survey data written in scientific language with suggestions about how to modernize rural life. Did the state encourage families to appreciate consumer goods and to make money to buy them? Or did the state encourage a safety-first approach that emphasized making goods at home?

Throughout rural parts of the country, home demonstration extension agents in the early twentieth century encouraged women on farms to do more of the shopping for their families, to learn to use new labor-saving devices, and to adopt middle-class standards of consumption. The general philosophy of home demonstration workers suggested that more women would choose to stay on the farm if they could look and work more like women in the cities. In some areas, they had a difficult time balancing lessons about smart shopping with lessons about making things at home.[2] In a few areas, such as eastern Tennessee, agents did not choose to encourage black women to become more involved in shopping until the women themselves demanded more programs about consumer issues.[3]

The clearest lessons that home demonstration workers in the Mississippi agricultural extension service tried to teach women and girls lay solidly in the traditions of white farm women in the South. Since sewing added to the independence of the household, satisfied a Protestant work ethic, and bound women together in respect for particularly female experiences, extension service workers who addressed how women could improve rural home life naturally turned to sewing.

Home economist Dorothy Dickins was Mississippi's leading extension service worker and writer on issues involving the home. Born in 1898 and raised in the Mississippi Delta, Dickins was a bit older than Gladys Smith and far wealthier. After receiving a master's degree in home economics at Columbia, she returned to Mississippi for a job as lunchroom supervisor at a school in Jackson before gaining a position in 1925 with the still-new home economics division of the state extension service.[4] From 1927 through the 1950s, Dickins authored numerous publications for the Mississippi Agricultural Experiment Station. Her first report embodied a thoroughly traditional perspective that viewed consumer goods as threats to the independence of the household. Beginning with the question of why people in a state with an excellent climate and soil should ever go hungry or dress in rags, she concluded that they needed to make more of their goods at home. From that agrarian premise, she labored to show how inexpensive home production of goods, especially clothing, could contribute to the financial success of every household.[5]

In significant ways, Dickins and the other leaders of home demonstration work in Mississippi represented the traditional belief that women should make goods and not buy them. Authors of extension service publications repeatedly described how much clothing Mississippi women made under their direction and how much money they saved by doing it. For example, women in 1928 made 1,098 hats at a saving calculated at $940.[6] Dickins calculated in 1940 that a woman in a typical family in rural Mississippi could save $26.93 by sewing clothes rather than buying them.[7] She always stressed the vital role farm women played in home production, especially sewing. "The sewing machine," she claimed, "is to the clothing budget what the milk cow, the garden, and the orchard are to the food budget."[8]

Dickins's level of interest in the issue showed in the energy and detail with which she addressed it. In a garment-by-garment study of ninety-nine rural families in 1928 and 1929, she showed that families had more than five times as many ready-made clothes as homemade clothes, with the poorest groups having the lowest percentage of ready-made clothes. Women in ninety-eight of the ninety-nine households sewed some clothes for their families. More than half of the families bought some of their clothing from mail-order catalogs, but "the ordinary articles were, for the most part, bought in small centers near home." Far from being isolated from mass culture, about half of these women took at least one fashion magazine, and many "obtained the fashion sheets distributed free at dry good stores."[9] Dickins chose not to condemn fashion magazines or mail-order catalogs, but even if her argument against ready-made clothing stressed economics rather than tradition or morality, it reinforced traditional notions about the duties of women.

Other home demonstration writers in Mississippi made unequivocally moralistic statements of the need for white farm women to sew as many household goods as they could. In an introduction to a long and detailed description of different stitches, one manual for white 4-H Club girls claimed, "The only way the phrase, 'the homemade look,' can be redeemed from disfavor is by using the correct finish with the right style and material."[10] Numerous publications went

Quilters in a home near Pace, Mississippi, 1939. Home demonstration workers would have admired this example of home production. (Photo by Russell Lee; courtesy Library of Congress)

into great detail about how to make particular stitches, how to repair clothes, and, beginning in 1920, how to use sewing machines.[11] Such advice represented an example of the state acting as a mother, trying to teach lessons mothers had traditionally taught. The very phrase "home demonstration" work had a parental quality of teaching lessons about home life. Demonstration agent Mary Cresswell used the language of the nineteenth-century parent when she reminded rural Mississippi women that "being well dressed does not necessarily mean expensively or elaborately dressed. . . . A homemade frock, carefully planned, fitted, and finished, often has a style and an individuality not to be found in a much more expensive ready-made garment."[12]

Home demonstration workers showed their most moralistic sides when they addressed the popular topic of shopping. Home economists argued that shopping posed a great threat to the incomes and independence of rural families if women did not shop in proper ways. Advice to shoppers had the unchanging themes of caution and thrift. Anne Jordan, author of several reports on clothing and home interiors, made the point as simply as possible. Addressing a bulletin to "those dwellers in small houses, who would like to make their homes as attractive and homelike as possible with limited funds," she gave advice about how to shop for furniture. "Avoid anything which strikes you as elaborate in a furniture store. If a rug, or piece of furniture stands out in a shop, you may be certain it will be too conspicuous in your home."[13] Above all, she could have been addressing Gladys Smith directly when she said, "Avoid novelties."[14] In 1927 Jordan offered a set of guidelines for teenagers who were shopping for clothing.

> Strive To:
> Make the money you have to spend go as far as possible.
> Avoid extravagant clothing. Dress appropriately for the occasion.
> Purchase as few garments as you can get along with comfortably.
> Learn to shop intelligently. Study materials, compare quality and cost.
> Recognize expensive but poorly finished novelties.[15]

Ten years later, another clothing guide for 4-H Club girls began with a similar warning against fashion. Mary Cresswell cautioned that "the real artist in dress does not slavishly conform to extremes in style."[16]

Such advice closely resembled the advice nineteenth-century parents wrote in countless letters to their daughters, especially those away at school. This language, which condemned extravagance and indulgence, remained in extension service terms like extremes in style, novelty, slavish conformity, and, again, extravagance. In fact, Jordan made that point explicitly in advising parents how to dress their children. "A child over-dressed, in extravagant, fussy, or faddish clothing is apt to think too much about clothes and to become snobbish and affected."[17]

For at least a hundred years rural Mississippians had been telling themselves and each other to concentrate less time and energy on cash crops and more on goods to eat and use at home. This had often taken the form of jeremiads southern leaders made to the moral ideal of debt-free independence while they pursued quick wealth. In the extension service publications of the 1920s and 1930s, this discussion had become primarily an issue for women. Extension work for men tried to teach better ways to participate in the cash economy. When their publications discussed the need for diversified agriculture, they were searching for new cash crops, not for ways to achieve self-sufficiency.[18]

A series of questionnaires Dickins administered in the 1930s confirmed that rural men still did far more shopping than women and continued to spend far more on their clothing than women. To challenge that tradition, then, was to advocate something new that past rural mothers had not taught. Increasingly in the late 1930s and 1940s, Dickins argued that women should become much more involved in families' shopping and financial planning. In her 1940 publication, "What the Farm Woman Can Do to Improve the Economic Status of Her Family," she worried that women with little shopping experience tended to buy goods on credit without knowing the lower cash price.[19] Arguing that cost-efficient shopping was a necessity for farm women of the future, Dickins urged that literacy and training in mathematics were becoming more important for rural girls than boys. If women became more efficient shoppers, she argued, men should give up their dominance over shopping.

The critique of male shopping points out some of the ambiguities in how Dickins and other Mississippi extension workers thought about consumer issues. If they urged sewing and thrift on one hand, they did not at the same time condemn modern fashion. One sign of the ambiguity in the goals of the extension leaders lay in the goals of sewing and thrift. For all that Dickins advanced some traditional expectations for women, they had far more confidence in the possibilities of consumer culture than Mississippi farm women had in previous generations. For all that they used language that feared style and the money that could buy it, they rarely used the traditional moralistic language about duty or women's work. They almost always used the language of economic efficiency, and they described their goals not as the old objective of debt-free independence but as a murky but significant concept Dickins called "better living."[20] That concept primarily meant simple health and comfort, but it also included significant elements of consumer culture.

In a 1942 report, "Improving Levels of Living of Tenant Families," Dickins used consumer goods as the standard for gauging how well different economic strategies were working. Compared to tenants, she found, owners of farms owned far more radios and refrigerators. The significance lay in the assumption that such consumer comforts were so obviously desirable that they could serve as tests of economic success or failure. In a conclusion about how tenants could improve their economic conditions, Dickins instructed that tenants should develop "a feeling of need by the members of a family for improved standards of living. To really want a high level of living is the first step in securing it." If radios and refrigerators were part of her definition of a "high level of living," Dickins was ultimately urging poor people in Mississippi to develop tastes for modern consumer goods.[21]

One of the most intriguing and ambiguous reports was an exhaustive 1942 account of the clothing worn by 759 white farm families. Dickins and co-author Alice Bowie broke down the clothing worn by white males and females of different age groups, detailing the number of different articles of clothing, how many of those articles were home-made and ready-made, and how much they cost. The goal of the study was especially intriguing. The authors argued that farm groups themselves set the standard for appearance that other farm families should understand in order to know how to dress. A "satisfactory wardrobe" consisted of clothing that allowed people to fit in with members of their community and social class. "Having clothes like most other people who attend the same social events is essential to an adequate, satisfying clothing supply. Thus, clothing fulfills a social need and clothing plans for farm people should be based on clothing used by a representative group of socially active farm families."[22] Here the state was again acting as mother, telling rural Mississippians how to clothe themselves. But this was a modern rural mother more interested in keeping up appearances than keeping out of debt. The idea that clothing fulfills a "social need" was part of a twentieth-century notion that people need to keep up appearances in a society where people really do not know each other.

For white farming women in Mississippi, the lessons the state taught were not clear. Dress as style-conscious urban women dress, but do not spend much money to do it. Learn to shop more often, but shop in order to economize. L. A. Olson boasted that because of the work of home demonstration agents, "thousands of rural girls have become so skilled in selecting and making their own clothing that one frequently hears the observation that country girls now go as well dressed as town and city girls."[23] The goal was to find ways to fit into consumer culture without being able to afford it. For all that the extension service writers encouraged economizing and rejected the romantic, unsatisfiable ideal of the modern consumer, they also upheld the important modern consumer notion of the democracy of appearances, at least for women who were white.

The ambiguities in the perspective of state authorities like Dorothy Dickins become more apparent when one compares demonstration lessons for white women to the lessons they tried to teach African American women. Those lessons were clear. African American women should economize, avoid extravagance, and be content with few goods. Extension workers encouraged black women to shape clothing out of sugar, flour, and feed sacks. Year after year in the 1920s and 1930s, Negro Extension agents—both whites and African Americans themselves—urged African American women to make clothing without spending money. The yearly report of the extension service in 1930 cheered that African Americans had used sugar and flour sacks to make "more than 50,000 useful garments for families."[24] Another report in 1932 detailed that African American women working in department programs had made from such material 9,925 quilts, 9,017 dresses, 7,362 articles of underwear, and "132,000 other articles such as boys' and men's shirts, overalls, pillow cases, curtains and towels." To celebrate such achievements in frugality, participants in clothing

A woman in Hinds County, Mississippi, hoes a field, wearing clothing made from a fertilizer sack. (Photo by Dorothea Lange; courtesy Library of Congress)

programs, as well as the twenty-two African American home demonstration workers, put on dresses made of sacks and paraded down Capitol Street to the capitol building in Jackson.[25] Extension publications mentioned this practice among white Mississippians only twice. But those statements were brief and never suggested the practice held the key to solving the economic problems of white farm families. There were no parades of sack-wearing white women.[26]

If the state's perspective on the place of white women in the consumer society was ambiguous, its perspective on the place of black women could not be more clear. They should not be part of it, and they were better off surviving frugally outside the consumer economy. In 1924, early in the history of the state's home demonstration work, director R. S. Wilson mentioned, "It is extremely interesting to see the products made by the negro women from absolute waste materials. Rags from worn out garments, for instance, are cleaned and made into useful and attractive rugs." The writer was also impressed by purses made from old inner tubes and baskets made from snuff boxes.[27] This has the sound of progressive-era settlement school workers who were intrigued by the colorful ways the poor survived their poverty and tried to encourage them to continue. It sounds a great deal like the cultural work David Whisnant describes in *All That Is Native and Fine*, in which good-hearted reformers encouraged poor people in Appalachia to hold on to practices that protected the poor from the damage they felt mass culture was doing.[28] By 1925, Wilson was not merely intrigued by the efforts of African American women to recycle old products, he was instructing agents to teach the practice.[29]

Even when the extension service encouraged African American women to spend money, it was ultimately trying to teach them limits. A project in the late 1920s gave a dollar to each teenage member of African American 4-H Clubs with instructions to buy all of the material they needed to make a dress. To clinch the point that this trip to town was teaching a lesson in restraint contained by the boundaries of the state's economic traditions, the shopping girls were to make their trip wearing dresses made entirely of cotton.[30]

Dorothy Dickins took a fairly complex and not entirely moralistic approach to the spending habits of black Mississippians. She argued that since landowners allowed tenants few opportunities to grow food for themselves, tenants had to spend a greater percentage of their scarce cash on food than farm owners did.[31] Thus, she did not hold tenants themselves completely to blame for their low levels of home production. She also reasoned that since many tenants moved from house to house every year, they had little incentive to spend money on their homes. The most important aspect of the perspective Dickins had on the material lives of tenant farmers was simply that she took the subject seriously enough to study it in intricate detail. She was troubled by African Americans' lack of physical comforts and especially by the lack of variety in their food. Above all, she was troubled by the poor health she attributed to their diet and lack of material goods, and she did not simply tell tenants to struggle through economic difficulties by economizing.

Despite the relative subtlety of her perspective, Dickins agreed with the traditional upper-class criticism that African Americans tended to waste their money. Arguing that too many families wasted money on tobacco, she singled out "one negro family on the poorer soil area with four children, aged seven years, four years, three years, and three months, [who] reported spending $7.50 in cash during 1934 for food and $5.00 for snuff. . . . Another negro family consisting of a young man and wife reported $20 for snuff, $5 for chewing tobacco and $24.50 for food."[32] Dickins also made the old planters' point that black Mississippians spent money as soon as they got it. She complained of African Americans that "the majority have not yet adopted the slogan coined by Negro Extension Workers, 'Take what you have and make what you can out of it.'"[33]

Efforts to keep African Americans outside the consumer economy had deep roots in Mississippi history. Slaveowners had limited the slaves' access to money and stores, and landowners had claimed since emancipation that African Americans spent their money too quickly and were better off without it. Thus, Dickins was using the language of the longtime economic interests of the planter elite and the cultural contentions that accompanied them. But this criticism had a modern side as well as a planter-dominated traditional side. As Dickins and the other extension workers were writing, they recognized that African Americans were leaving the farms for new, often unsteady employment in towns and cities. By 1940, they could see that increasing numbers of African Americans would be receiving money from federal programs. Both of those changes meant that African Americans would be receiving money outside the old constraints of planter domination, the long pay, and the plantation store.

Ideas of the free-spending black man originated with the planter class and served its purposes, but they spread far beyond their initial economic and cultural context. Perhaps the idea of the self-indulgent, free-spending poor was most popular to people who were part of the consumer society, or, in the case of early twentieth-century Mississippi, becoming part of it. Extension writers who said white Mississippians should enjoy their access to consumer goods as long as they shopped efficiently found in the idea of the free-spending poor black man the perfect rationale for claiming African Americans were irresponsible people who did not deserve full access to goods and stores. That argument had a clear gender dimension. Dorothy Dickins was troubled to find that even more black men than white men did all of the shopping for their families and argued that their families suffered from the lack of a mother's more prudent approach to shopping. In describing how the African American spent money too freely, she used the masculine pronoun in complaining, "If the negro makes more than his expenses, it is generally spent by February."[34]

Identifying black men as wasteful consumers may have been the easiest way for extension service writers to reconcile the tension between their fears about spending money and their appreciation of the democracy of appearances. White Americans had long attributed to African Americans their fears about their own most indulgent sides.[35] If African Americans represented the bad consumers, whites could be the good shoppers. By claiming that African Americans were wasteful consumers while whites properly trained in home demonstration work could enjoy the benefits of consumer goods without the supposedly wasteful, financially dangerous, self-indulgent sides of mass culture, extension writers could urge southern white women to become more involved in the task but not the joy of shopping. On an everyday level, they could encourage white women to shop without the threat of rubbing elbows with black men. On a more symbolic level, they could claim that skillful shopping represented a new way to uphold the special moral virtues of white women.

Finally, we return to Gladys Smith. Studying the ideals that people like Dorothy Dickins tried to set for rural women helps explain the meaning of those trips Gladys took to the store. Who taught Gladys Smith? It certainly was not a home demonstration worker employed by the state. Whatever the ambiguities in the lessons the state extension service tried to teach, Gladys Smith was a rebel. Mississippi state officials in the 1920s and 1930s never encouraged poor teenage farm girls to indulge themselves in shopping as Gladys did. Never did they suggest that the store should become the center of anyone's life. Gladys's tastes for shopping dramatize how poor people could use consumer spending as a way to reject dominant cultural expectations.[36]

By becoming an American consumer, Gladys was enjoying herself in ways that neither her own southern cultural traditions nor a new state agency encouraged or even tolerated. It may have been a small rebellion, but it was a powerful one she most likely communicated to her son. That son, Elvis Presley, learned the lessons of self-indulgence and self-assertion, took great pleasure in flaunting the conventions of southern society by adopting mannerisms long associated with black southerners, and became one of the most outlandish consumers of his day. For Gladys and son, shopping was a form of self-assertion that represented an escape from the conventions of life for poor farm people. It is well known that Elvis Presley, for all of his rebellions against American conventions, never rebelled against his mother. Perhaps one reason is that within the context of early twentieth-century Mississippi, his mother was a rebel herself.

If Dorothy Dickins did not teach lessons to Gladys Smith, perhaps people like Gladys and her son ultimately helped people like Dickins to change their minds. People who in the 1920s and 1930s spoke up for thrift, caution, home manufacturing, and self-restraint were by mid-century giving up their old arguments for household self-sufficiency. Dickins noticed that spending habits were changing, and in general she welcomed them and encouraged more. Women were doing more of the shopping, and they were shopping more often.[37] All rural shoppers, male and female, black and white, traveled more frequently beyond crossroads markets to shop in larger stores in towns and cities.[38] She recorded profound increases in the number of farm-owning families who owned important household goods. In a 1948 study, she found that electric lights, refrigerators, and indoor plumbing, all rare on farms in the mid-1930s, were fast becoming commonplace for farm owners. Radios were nearly universal for rural people, white and black, farm owner and tenant.[39] After decades of studying household behavior of rural Mississippians, she concluded in 1950 that "thirty years ago one could readily distinguish between a Southern rural and urban family, but this is usually not now the case. The food, clothing, and the family dwellings of rural families are becoming more like that of town families."[40]

In fact, Dickins finally decided to reject the ambiguities of her earlier approach and embrace the teaching of consumption as the main goal of her discipline. She worried that conditions on the poorest cotton farms had taught too many people to expect poverty and to survive on as little as possible.[41] Excessive thrift, she feared, would have disastrous consequences as poor Mississippians moved into jobs off the farm. Without the incentive of pursuing new goods, the poor would not develop the work habits necessary for employment in an uncertain nonagricultural economy. In a direct repudiation of the lessons earlier home economists had offered the poor, especially poor African Americans, she argued in 1948 that "members of low-consumption families must have more direct contact with higher consumption levels. They must desire goods and services that only higher incomes can produce. It may be that home economists of the South should give more emphasis in their teaching programs to stepping up the next level of consumption; perhaps less emphasis on managing what one has. Home economists might well teach, 'Decide what you want and then plan to earn income to get it,' rather than 'Take what you have and make what you want out of it.' "[42] In the last bulletin of her long career, Dickins encouraged farm families in 1963 to go into debt because wise use of credit could "bring about larger and more profitable farms as well as higher levels of living."[43] For this longtime spokesperson for thrift and debt-free independence to urge farm families to go into debt shows how dramatically Mississippi's economy and culture had changed. Dickins never wrote about the virtues of blue suede or gold lamé, but by the 1950s and 1960s, her perspective was less like a traditional farm woman and more like that of Gladys Smith Presley and her son.

CHAPTER SIX

Goods, Migration, and the Blues, 1920s–1950s

Not many African Americans rushed to embrace the message the government of Mississippi offered them to "Take what you have and make do." But did they share with Gladys Smith the idea that they could use consumer goods to redefine themselves and reject what people in power expected of them? Walls, Mississippi, native Minnie McCoy, better known as Memphis Minnie, raised the issues in 1941 when she recorded "Me and My Chauffeur Blues."

> Won't you be my chauffeur: I want someone to drive me downtown.
> Baby drives so easy: I can't turn him around.
> But I don't want him to be riding these girls: to be riding these girls around
> You know I'm going to steal me a pistol: shoot my chauffeur down
> Well I must buy him: a brand new V-eight, a brand new V-eight Ford
> And he won't need no passengers: I will be his load.[1]

What did a southern black woman mean when she used the metaphor of a chauffeur, a symbol of luxury for some and subservience for others? Why did she think a V-8 Ford—again a symbol of luxury for some—would keep a man satisfied and faithful? And why were relations between Minnie and her chauffeur so tense that she threatened to shoot him down?

African Americans of the blues musicians' generation faced a dramatic decline in their chances to buy new land, a decline in agricultural labor, and a resulting change in the nature of their economic insecurity. In the second quarter of the twentieth century, young black Mississippians faced the necessity of looking harder and going farther away from home to find work. Moving from plantation to plantation had long been common, but sharecroppers on the move typically shifted locations at most once a year, and many who moved remained in their home counties. Far more frequently in the twentieth century, young adults had to scramble for a living by moving seasonally from farm labor to temporary labor in town and cities and then back again. Survival required repeated migration, not simply one great and final move from the Mississippi Delta to Chicago. The better-known migration to northern cities usually took place after several economically driven moves within the South. Men, especially younger men, moved more often than women, attracted by the various forms of physical labor. Women had narrower options, usually involving jobs as cooks and maids.[2]

Particularly important for consumer spending were the ways the decline of agricultural labor affected family life and gender relations. For agricultural families, even under conditions as oppressive as sharecropping, a large family was an asset. On this laborers and landowners agreed. Owners of plantations gave clear advantage to large families who worked together, very aware of the benefits large numbers of children provided at cotton-picking season. A 1936 WPA report on the cotton belt found that "large families have been encouraged by the plantation system because cotton production creates heavy demands for labor in the spring and fall over and above the demands of normal crop operation. . . . Hence, large tenant families have been, at least until recently, an economic asset to both landlord and tenant."[3] Couples responded appropriately. Many Mississippi blues singers grew up in such sizeable farm families. Charley Patton was one of twelve children, Minnie McCoy was one of thirteen, Bill Broonzy one of twenty-one.[4]

As black Mississippians increasingly worked irregular jobs as individuals and rarely worked as family units, the individual rather than the household became the primary component of the economy. Of course, former farm workers did not lose interest in spouses and children because of economic changes, but the decline in the economic benefits of a big family rendered many rootless men and women more rootless and insecure than ever.[5]

African Americans made two primary responses to those changes, and consumer goods were important to both. The elderly, whose words appear in hundreds of interviews the WPA conducted with former slaves in the 1930s, scoffed at the young for their frequent movement, their selfishness and greed, and their growing taste for consumer goods. The older generation grew up with the hope of owning land and the accompanying necessity for self-denial. But the young and mobile, represented by blues singers like Memphis Minnie (born in 1897), embraced many of the new opportunities for pleasure that consumer culture offered. The younger generation had few hopes of owning land but felt far more comfortable pursuing a consumer's version of the American Dream.

Elderly men and women consistently denounced the young for their immorality, especially their greed and lack of concern for their families. Consumer goods played an important part in what they saw as the sins of the young. The elderly men and women argued that living away from farms made the young mindless of responsibilities of men and women to each other, of the young to the old, and in general of people to each other. As former slave Tanner Thomas said when criticizing young people in the 1930s, "God intended for every man in the world to have a living and to live for each other but too many of 'em livin' for themselves." This kind of individualism—this "living for themselves"— meant failing to live up to previous expectations men and women had for each other. Alice Johnson condemned economic difficulties for producing the kind of strained and competitive relationships so many blues singers described. "I stayed with both of my husbands till they died. I ain't bothered 'bout another one. Times is so hard no man can take care of a woman now. Come time to pay rent, 'What you waiting for me to pay rent? You been payin' it, ain't you?' Come time to buy clothes, 'What you waitin' for me to buy clothes for? Where you gittin' 'um frum before you mai'd me?' "[6]

Working or looking for work off the farm naturally meant that young people had to pay for almost everything they used. The elderly were troubled by the necessity to buy everything and to do all of their business in cash or credit rather than trade in goods. As Jack Temple Kirby has argued, living out of bags was one of the major developments in the modern South. Former slave Lillie Williams echoed this claim, complaining, "There is something wrong about the way we are doing somehow. It is from hand to mouth. We buys too many paper sacks."[7] In a harsh critique of young Mississippians, former slave Isaac Stier said that pursuing independence was the best way to avoid ambition, luxury, and debt. "None of 'em is sati'fied wid plain livin. Ebber body wants de moon wid a fence around hit. Dey wants a car en fine clothes . . . in dis day en time dey ain't no satisfaction wid life. Folks is seekin what dey kaint find. De thing to find is peace en simple things. It aint de thing dat costs money what gibs de most happiness."[8]

Many of the elderly men and women thought young blacks were trying to live like wealthy whites. From childhood they had associated luxury goods with wealthy whites, and they believed that behind the greed of young blacks lay the sin of envy. One claimed that the morals of the young were declining because "they do like they see the white girls and boys doin'." William Henry Rooks lamented that "Folks gone scottch crazy over money, money! Both is changing.

The white folks, I'm speaking about, the white folks has changed and course the colored folks keeping up wid them." A third considered "young folks wasteful— both black and white. White folks setting the pace for us colored folks. It's mighty fast and mighty hard."[9] The elderly men and women in the 1930s repeatedly lashed out at young blacks for their tastes for consumer goods and the luxury, self-indulgence, and frivolity they represented. The automobile Memphis Minnie found so appealing was a particular reason for disgust. "Seems like dis young bunch awful no 'count er bustin' up and down de road day and night in de cars, er burnin' de gasoline when dey outer be studyin' 'bout makin' ah livin'." Another worried, "Seems like we all gone money crazy. Automobiles and silk stockings done ruined us all."[10]

To African Americans raised in the generation of high hopes for owning land, the actions pursued by the young and far less hopeful generation represented moral decline. Once, they said, people had worked as families, but now they worked and played as individuals. People had once denied themselves consumer pleasures for the greater goods of independence and family security, but now they pursued immediate pleasures just as whites did. Blues singers belonged to a new generation, and they had a different opinion. The young black men and women represented by the blues singers saw goods as important elements in gaining self-esteem, respect in the black community, and romantic success.

Blues performers were marginal characters in southern society, moving quickly from town to town, welcomed in some places and shunned in others. In their economic lives, they faced extreme examples of the challenges faced by most blacks of their generation. Mississippi blues was the music of the generation of young men and women who experienced the most dramatic shift from agricultural to nonagricultural labor. The first recorded blues music was recorded primarily by men and women born between 1890 and 1910.[11] Almost all blues musicians in Mississippi grew up in farm families, and most at some point worked on farms.[12] Many went back and forth between music and farming. Some, such as Mississippi John Hurt, played music for a few years and then returned full time to agriculture.[13]

In their lives as musicians, blues men and women understood and could sing about the scrambling, insecure economic lives most African Americans struggled to endure and overcome. Young, poor, and mobile, they traveled from the countryside to towns and cities and back again looking hard for ways to make money. Playing music was another way to make money, and bluesmen and women consistently combined music with driving tractors, working on railroads, levees, and in lumber camps, delivering laundry, washing dishes and cars, selling whiskey, boxing, almost anything to make a few dollars.

TABLE 11. *Nonmusical Work Performed by Blues Musicians, 1910–1949*

Will Batts	Worked for lumber company
Eddie Boyd	Chauffeur
Big Bill Broonzy	Coal mining; railroad construction; preaching
Robert Burse	Deliveryman for laundry
Gus Cannon	Plumber's assistant; gardener
Arthur Crudup (Big Boy)	Worked on levees and in lumber camps
Willie Dixon	Boxing
Sleepy John Estes	Railroad construction
Lil Green	Waitress
Son House	Worked in steel plant and on railroads
Skip James	Preaching
Floyd Jones	Filed saws; drove mule teams
Charley Jordan	Bootlegging
Furry Lewis	Worked in garage and in Memphis sanitation department
Albert Luandrew (Sunnyland Slim)	Sold whiskey; cook, chauffeur, muleskinner; worked in turpentine, logging camps, railroad construction, road construction
Eurreal Montgomery (Little Brother)	Worked in lumber camp
Charley Patton	Worked in sawmill
Yank Rachell	Worked on railroad
Will Shade	Worked on river boat
Allen Shaw	Worked at cotton gin
Johnny Shines	Dishwasher
Frank Stokes	Blacksmith
Roosevelt Sykes	Worked in sawmills, turpentine camps, on levees
Muddy Waters	Bootlegging; ran club
Booker White	Construction, boxing, baseball; worked in lumber camp
Joe Williams	Railroad construction, levee work
Sonny Boy Williamson (Rice Miller)	Preaching

Sources: Harris, *Blues Who's Who*; numerous interviews in *Living Blues*; Charters, *The Country Blues*; Charters, *Sweet as the Showers of Rain*; Barlow, *"Looking Up at Down"*; Neff and Connor, *Blues*; Palmer, *Deep Blues*; Shaw, *Honkers and Shouters*.

For many blues musicians, the crucial theme of rambling meant a chaotic and largely unplanned life on the road. When Robert Jr. Lockwood told an interviewer, "Musicians don't have a destination. I might go anyplace," he spoke for the plight and also the sense of freedom of countless young black men of his generation. Blues musicians had a clear economic purpose when they had what Robert Johnson called "Rambling on My Mind."[14]

In this insecure economic environment, payment came at irregular intervals. Musicians often went weeks without decent pay, but they also had occasional opportunities for small windfalls that occurred when they played the right music for the right crowd. Most performances made them only a dollar or two, along with the possibility of a meal and a better chance of a drink. But sometimes blues performers made what Hammie Nixon described as "right smart money." Muddy Waters recalled how performing compared favorably to farm labor. "I used to make two-fifty on Saturday night at a frolic or supper with my guitar, and you couldn't make but three-seventy-five for five days' work on a plantation." Johnny Shines recalled that saw mills or stores hired him and Robert Johnson to play "for four dollars a night and all we could drink. Different guys'd give us a quarter to play this piece or that piece, so we'd end up with twenty-five or thirty dollars."[15] Most musicians saw playing the blues as a far preferable way to make a living than farm labor. As James "Son Ford" Thomas recalled, the arrival of his first guitar from the Sears and Roebuck catalog changed his life. "After I got my guitar I wouldn't pick no more cotton."[16]

The travels of the blues musicians repeatedly carried them to the settings where black Mississippians either got their money or spent it. Numerous bluesmen performed in traveling medicine shows, serving as attractions to precede a hard sell.[17] Blues men and women often played on paydays for workers, whether playing at cotton harvests, the conclusion of cotton chopping, or at the paydays of highway, railroad, and levee crews.[18]

Rambling often and scrambling for cash, enjoying occasional windfalls and suffering more frequent insecurity, living outside an agricultural system that encouraged self-denial and family labor, blues men and women offered a new perspective on the relationship between economics and family life. The most famous reason for the blues was the unfaithfulness of women or men. Songs combined romantic laments with financial tensions, as singers bemoaned not merely the lover who left them but especially the one who took all their money. Other songs celebrated not just the good-hearted or sexually exciting man or woman, but the lover who was free with money or at least did not steal it.

Blues singers often claimed they deserved far better from women or men. After all, some singers argued, they had tried to give them as much money as their faithless partners demanded. As Furry Lewis sang, "Give my woman so many dollars; it broke her apron strings / All she give me was trouble: I'm troubled all the time." Johnny Young had a hit with his first song, "Money-Taking Woman." Joe McCoy had the same lament in 1929, "Well look here mama: see what you done / Took all my money: put me on a bum."[19] Memphis Minnie wrote some of the most vivid and tough-minded songs about economic conflict between the sexes. In a song in 1940, she told a man, "I ain't going to give you my money: and don't know what it's all about / Soon as I get cold in hand: you be ready to kick me out." Money was power, and Minnie wanted as much power as she could get.[20]

This context of serious and often desperate economic tensions between the sexes helps clarify the attitudes the blues singers had about consumer goods. With the decline of agricultural labor and the increasing pursuit of irregular jobs outside agriculture, goods became crucial as a way of attracting mates. Memphis Slim made clear the connection between romantic attraction, economic power, and modern forms of consumer spending in a song full of sexual metaphors. "If you be my customer," he promised a woman, "I'll let you have it on an easy plan."[21]

In *Advertising the American Dream*, Roland Marchand analyzes the parables advertisers preached to the masses in the 1920s. One of the most important was the "Parable of the First Impression." In a society in which people were moving frequently and dealing with new people, advertisers told their audience that they had to make the proper initial impression to land a job or to get a promotion or to attract a man or woman. As Marchand argues, this message characterized much of twentieth-century popular culture, with its stress on personality, image, and appearance.[22] Blues songs dramatized the parable. Appearances mattered to musicians who were almost constantly on the move, trying to impress different people, both audiences of many kinds and passing acquaintances as well. For the larger African American population in Mississippi, appearances mattered more than ever before, and for some of the same reasons. The share-cropping system had created a kind of egalitarianism of poor appearances, in which people identified with each other in the poor material conditions that symbolized both the plight of debt but also the hope for independence. Without the hope for owning land, young African Americans were giving up the negative connotations goods had once carried. To earn the respect of other young people, the new generation wanted to prove they could succeed in spite of the obstacles, and goods were an important part of that proof.

When blues singers mentioned consumer goods, they most often sang about clothing, jewelry, and automobiles. All were conspicuous goods, and all could be expensive. Clothing signified two important things about romantic commitment or the lack of it. First, in a time when frequent mobility strained relations

A juke joint on Saturday night, outside Clarksdale, Mississippi, 1939.
(Photo by Marion Post Wolcott; courtesy Library of Congress)

between the sexes, taking one's clothes was the clearest sign of leaving. Many poor Mississippians had so few possessions that moving their clothing was the clearest sign they were moving to a new town or, most clearly in the blues, a new woman or man. The location of their clothes signified where they intended to stay, at least for a while. Big Bill Broonzy told a woman how to prepare for his departure. "Now pack up my clothes: shove into your door / I'm leaving this morning mama: I won't be back no more." In "Please Don't Act That Way," Tommie Bradley complained that after a woman had left him, his "clothes look lonesome: hanging out on the line."[23]

More important, clothing reflected an individual's success or failure under new economic conditions and helped attract men or women. For young adults, stylish and store-bought clothing no longer signified debt and dependence. To them, poor clothing was demeaning. A standard blues line wondered if a match box could hold one's clothes. But when times were good, blues singers suggested that people should buy and wear stylish or even luxurious clothing. Blues men and women themselves took considerable interest in what they wore. Big Bill Broonzy described well-dressed blues men as mysterious urban individuals who only "came out at night" and did not know or care how cotton was grown. "They went out and dressed up every night and some of them had three or four women. . . . These are the men that wear ten-dollar Stetson hats and twenty-dollar gold pieces at their watch and diamonds in their teeth and on their fingers." Several friends pointed out how well Memphis Minnie dressed. One recalled that she "would wear nice dresses, suits, eh, ladies suits, high heel shoes, and she had bracelets, she wore a bracelet around each wrist, made out of silver dollars, and then she had a set of earrings with two silver dimes on the earrings. That was her trademark, there: Money? Yeah, she was all right." Publicity photographs typically showed bluesmen in suits that were a far cry from the garb of their agricultural past.[24]

Blues musicians wanted fine clothes to enhance their status in the black community. Above all, they enjoyed giving stylish clothing as a present. The ability to buy clothing for a woman or man was part of the economic tension between the sexes that was so common in blues lyrics, but it went beyond the mere essentials of men and women helping each other survive. The bluesmen held out to women the possibility of dressing more luxuriously than they ever had, and they took revenge on women who deprived them of that chance. Some said simply, "I'll give you money: to buy you shoes and clothes: But you was evil: threw me out of doors." Many went on to specify the kind of clothes a faithful woman might deserve. Washboard Sam sang to a "Sophisticated Mama," criticizing her taste for "high-price dresses: and mmm steaks every day" and made clear that she would not get them. Sonny Boy Williamson paired dresses with an especially valuable object in warning a woman, "I ain't going to buy you no more pretty dresses: I ain't going to even buy you no diamond rings." In another song, Williamson asked Santa Claus to bring a woman several presents he could not afford to buy her. Included in the list was "one of these coats: I mean with that long fur hanging down."[25] A fur coat was one of the most expensive pieces of clothing available; for Williamson to have seen it as an ideal gift suggests that his generation had traveled a long way from the self-denial demanded by sharecropping.

Many blues songs discussed what jewelry, earrings, and even gold teeth said about gender relations. Blues singers shared the value most of American culture placed in diamonds, both because they were expensive and because they signified a special degree of commitment between the sexes. For Little Brother Montgomery, diamonds were an important accessory for a young woman. "The woman I love: she only sixteen years of age / And she's a full grown woman: but she just got childish ways / She got a head full of diamonds." Most bluesmen said they could not trust women who wore diamonds. Mississippi

John Hurt sang of taking drastic action against a woman who took his and then did him wrong.

> Bought my gal: a great big diamond ring
> Come right back home: and caught her shaking that thing.

Hurt continued that he

> Took my gun: And I broke the barrel down
> Put my baby: six feet under the ground.

In "Low Down Ways," Sonny Boy Williamson discovered that a woman did not deserve his gifts. "I was going down to the jewelry store: and I was going to buy you a diamond ring / But now you won't treat me nice: and I ain't going to buy you a doggone thing."[26]

Discussions of automobiles made the connections between impressive consumer goods and sexual attraction most dramatically. Cadillacs, Hudsons, Fords, and Chevrolets appeared throughout the blues, as scholar Paul Oliver has noted, providing opportunities for some particularly erotic metaphors.[27] Automobiles were powerful, they could be good-looking and temperamental, and they had a delicate and intricate array of parts. In each of these ways, they were subjects men chose to serve as sexual metaphors. But automobiles were not simply metaphors; they were rare luxury goods men used to attract women. Walter Roland offered an intriguing comparison of cars and women, suggesting again that blues musicians shared the distinctions most Americans were making between impressive and exciting goods and those that served utilitarian functions. "These here women what called theirselves a Cadillac: ought to be a T Model Ford / You know they got the shape all right: but they don't carry no load."[28]

In "Terraplane Blues," Robert Johnson found in an automobile inspiration for some of his most sexually charged lyrics. Johnson begins mournfully, fearing that in his absence another man is using his car to attract a particular woman. "Well I feel so lonesome: you hear me when I moan / Who's been driving my terraplane for you: since I've been gone." Then the metaphor shifts to compare the woman to the car itself. The woman, in the singer's absence, lacks proper sexual stimulation, as when an automobile lacks power. "I said I flashed your lights mama: your horn won't even blow / Got a short in this connection: hoo well babe and it's way down below." He suggests aggressive measures to correct the problem. "I'm going heist your hood mama: I'm bound to check your oil." The following lines suggest not just frustration but also a determination to restore the car and the sexual relationship to working order. The car lacks energy, with a battery too weak to blow the horn but just strong

Robinson Motor Company, Clarksdale, Mississippi, 1939. Automobiles offered new opportunities in the 1930s. (Photo by Marion Post Wolcott; courtesy Library of Congress)

enough to flash its headlights; the woman in the metaphor thus seems to have some desire in her eyes but not enough strength in her body. "Now you know the coils ain't even buzzing: little generation won't get the spark / motor's in bad condition: you get to have these batteries charged." Johnson worries that his inattention is responsible for the car's condition and, metaphorically, for the woman's lack of sexual energy. The conclusion dramatizes the connections between the terraplane and sexual excitement. Johnson boasts that he will heat up the lifeless car and, metaphorically, satisfy a woman's newly stimulated desire. "I'm going to get deep down in this connection: keep on tangling with your wires / and when I mash down on your little starter: then your spark plug will give me fire." The final metaphor associates an important consumer product with his own sexual pleasure. By repairing the car, his ultimate goal is to "give *me* fire."[29]

Johnson sang that, at its best, the terraplane could go one hundred miles an hour. Speed was important, both as a sign of physical power and also as a way to escape problems and indignities of many kinds. Sonny Boy Williamson sang of telling a woman that he planned to buy her a Chevrolet. She wanted instead not merely a Ford but specifically a "V-Eight Ford." "She say she wanted something would beat us all on the road." Walter Davis promised a woman, "I will pour in the high-powered gasoline: and see how fast we can ride."[30] According to Neil McMillen, a Jim Crow custom dictated that no automobile driven by a black Mississippian should pass an automobile driven by a white for fear that it would stir up dust on the latter. For young men and women raised in such an environment, the allure of speed as a sign of assertiveness must have been enormous. A fast car could blow dust all over white Mississippians and then, in an economy that no longer kept them dependent on those whites, outrace the possible consequences.[31] It could also get them out of trouble. Robert Jr. Lockwood recalled that a favorite 1939 Pontiac had six cylinders "but it had been all psyched up. It was super fast, used to have it on the polices in Mississippi."[32]

To attract women or men and gain respect from young African Americans, blues singers said it was necessary to display their goods. As Honeyboy Edwards said in a telling reminiscence of early days on the blues circuit, "I met a lot of pretty girls. Made a lot of money, too, but I spent it as fast as I got it. Cadillacs and clothes—you got to make a good appearance." The automobile was in this regard the ultimate consumer item. It was extremely public and announced to the world, but especially to the black community, that the individual had money and the freedom that went with it. Memphis Minnie showed the significance of the public character of an automobile and the freedom it brought when she sang, "I tell the whole round world: I ain't going to walk no more / I got a Cadillac Eight: take me anywhere I want to go." Sonny Boy Williamson had big plans to buy a new V-8 Ford and visit a woman. "Well when my baby come out and see me: I know she's going to jump and shout / Well well well if that don't draw a crowd: ooo people going to know what all this racket about."[33]

Placing value in cars, jewelry, and clothing, Mississippi blues musicians were becoming consumers. Occasional references to the array of new electrical gadgets and conveniences of the twentieth century revealed their hopes for the pleasures and comforts those goods promised. Robert Johnson made good use of the metaphor of the phonograph. As in "Terraplane Blues," Johnson used the metaphor to discuss both sexual excitement and sexual conflict. On one hand, "We played it on the sofa now: we played it side the wall," but on the other hand, the woman "have broke my winding chain." Sonny Boy Williamson wanted to give a woman two other electrical conveniences to secure her affection. He asked Santa Claus "to bring my baby one of these radios: and two or three of them little electric fans." Bill Jazz Gillum wished a woman had shown him more respect after he gave her a refrigerator. He bought her a Frigidaire, but, as his luck would have it, she now "let the serviceman: take you everywhere." Perhaps devices to keep things cold did not work well as blues metaphors. Hattie Hart used the metaphor of "a range in my kitchen" to warn a man not to get overheated in chasing her.[34] Blues singers showed no nostalgia for older material goods—none of the longing, for instance, for the old home place or simple ways that filled the lyrics of so many country songs. The old home place held no special charms; if modern goods could make life more comfortable and exciting, then the blues singers wanted as many as they could get.

The message blues songs offered about the virtues of consumer goods becomes most clear when compared to the reluctance of previous generations to embrace the consumer society. As long as poor people maintained realistic hopes of escaping debt and owning land, they viewed material goods with suspicion rooted in both Protestant self-denial and the unity of a large family. On rare occasions blues singers showed respect for this older approach to economic life. When Sleepy John Estes sang that the cry of "Need more: it has hung a many men," he recognized the dangers of the modern ethic in which more and more desires become needs.[35] But the great majority of blues lyrics suggested a new intrigue about buying goods. When Memphis Minnie sang, "I'm gonna buy my baby a brand new V-Eight, brand new V-Eight Ford," she showed a pleasure not merely in owning goods but in buying them. If they no longer had a steady place in the southern economy as laborers, they now claimed their place in the broader American economy as consumers.[36]

Contemporary Americans often view Mississippi blues musicians as dusty, rural, tortured artists who represented almost the antithesis of things connected to modern markets, mass media, and consumer culture. In fact, much of the blues represented the cultural creations of people coming to terms with new possibilities, many of them associated with mobility and urban life.

The lyrics of the blues and the lives of blues musicians dramatize the importance of migration to cities, first Memphis and then especially Chicago. Increasingly in the early twentieth century, rapid movement to northern cities gave a new character to the lives of African Americans, whether they stayed in Mississippi and heard and read about city life or if they left to try it themselves. As Neil McMillen has noted, more African Americans from Mississippi lived in Chicago in 1930 than any other American city, including the cities in Mississippi.[37] Black Mississippians were very aware of that city as a center for the distribution of goods and the excitement they could bring. Several blues musicians, including Muddy Waters, ordered their guitars from the Sears and Roebuck catalog, and we can assume they perused parts of the catalog other than the music section.[38]

Chicago was the home of both the *Chicago Defender* and the Associated Negro Press service. Along with personal conversation, the *Defender* was the most crucial medium in informing rural African Americans about possibilities in the city. The ANP offered daily stories about African American urban life. Both ran society pages featuring large pictures of well-dressed women, next to stories describing extremely stylish events for African Americans in Chicago. Consuelo Young Megahy, in her column "Highlights in the Social Whirl," detailed an event in which "many a fine crepe, linen, shantung, gabardine, palm beach and seer-sucker went to sea in fine, picturesque fashion aboard the SS Roosevelt, Friday night . . . on the occasion of the Kappa Alpha Psi sixth annual Lake Michigan boat cruise." Dramatizing how the combination of economic opportunity and interests in fashion could serve as clear alternatives to life in the rural South were two stories placed side by side in the *Defender* in 1938. One described a lynching in Rolling Fork, Mississippi. The other pictured the graduating class of the Poro College of Beauty Culture in Chicago.[39]

When Mississippians arrived in cities like Chicago, they could experiment with consumer goods and popular culture in ways unavailable in most of Mississippi. Shopping offered freedoms of many kinds. Questions of where to shop, what to buy, how to dress, how to decorate, what to see, and what to drive acquired new meanings outside the debts, forced economy, and blatant racism of rural Mississippi. As Lizabeth Cohen has argued, African Americans in Chicago were willing to seize the chances for those freedoms more quickly and openly than other ethnic groups who migrated to the city in the early twentieth century.

African Americans in northern cities tried first, like other ethnic groups, to set up their own stores as a way both to build their own economy and sustain their culture. Perhaps the most famous of these efforts were successful cosmetics companies such as Nile Queen Cosmetics and Rose-Meta Cosmetics in Chicago. Madame C. J. Walker's Manufacturing Company and Annie Pope Turnbo-Malone's St. Louis-based Poro program had offices and beauty schools throughout the Midwest. It would be a mistake to see the goal of such as establishments as reflecting a desire to assimilate into middle-class, white-skinned society by straightening hair and bleaching skin. The experience of consuming by its nature allows and encourages individuals to remake themselves and try new experiences and identities. Such firms appealed to people willing to overturn the limits and expectations they had learned in the South. In fact, at least two of the most important figures had roots in the Deep South. Rose Morgan started Rose-Meta years after her sharecropping father had brought his family of nine from Mississippi, and Madame C. J. Walker was raised in what a publicist called "a cabin of ex-slaves in Delta, Louisiana."[40] Their establishments became laboratories for experimenting with identities, all in a black-owned, black-controlled environment.[41]

The great majority of black-owned businesses in Chicago faced serious obstacles, primarily the shortage of capital, and the goal of establishing an African American economy never succeeded. But African Americans in Chicago discovered a new place for themselves in the urban economy by patronizing chain stores and purchasing name-brand goods. While other immigrants preferred the personalism and familiarity of shopping at their own establishments, African Americans found that buying name-brand goods protected them from potentially dishonest practices involved in selling bulk goods. Black customers preferred chain stores for the same reason and because they could pressure national establishments to hire black employees. As Cohen concludes, "With strict limitations on where blacks could live and work in Chicago, consumption became a major avenue through which they could assert their independence."[42]

More than a simple escape from the limits imposed by life in Mississippi, urban opportunities for consumption encouraged African Americans to reject the appearances Mississippi landlords and employers had long expected of them. As James Grossman argues, black leaders from the Urban League to Ida B. Wells-Barnett to the *Defender* urged new arrivals to the city to leave behind the head rags, overalls, and work aprons that had long signified dependence and servility. Freedom, they urged, meant reshaping both identities and the appearances that went with them. An Urban League flyer attempted to educate newly arriving migrants about American citizenship by asking them to pledge not to wear "dust caps, bungalow aprons, house clothing and bedroom shoes out of doors."[43]

As urban African Americans began to buy more nationally advertised goods, the advertising industry took notice. In an interesting twist, when advertisers confronted the old notion that blacks were naturally indulgent spenders, some—though certainly not all—embraced the idea as an appealing feature of a potential new market. Others tried to find ways to stress the dignity available in consumer culture. Among the latter, an important figure in making Chicago a center for a mass culture for and by African Americans was Claude A. Barnett, who founded the Associated Negro Press in 1919. Barnett worked growing up as a servant in the home of Richard W. Sears of Sears and Roebuck and apparently learned there the importance of advertising and national marketing. After going south for a Tuskegee education, Barnett established a Chicago advertising agency with the slogan "I Reach the Negro."[44] Along the way he helped organize Nile Queen Cosmetics, one of the many companies making beauty products for African American women. A 1919 advertising pamphlet for Nile Queen made a direct call for people of African descent to pursue the good life available through modern products. The pamphlet pictured "Kleopatra, Queen of the Nile, The World's famous Brown Beauty," and told women shoppers, "Women everywhere want to be beautiful. The lowly, uncivilized savage maiden way

An elderly couple in Madison County, Tennessee, in 1910 had the appearance that reformers in Chicago tried to teach new arrivals to the city to give up.
(Looking Back at Tennessee Collection, Tennessee State Library and Archive)

down in the jungles of Africa who tattoos her skin, files her teeth, and sticks rings through her nose, has the same motive as the classiest, most polished example of the modern feminine style and daintiness, who spends many hours in following the latest methods in Beauty Culture. Both want to look well in the eyes of the world in general and of some one man in particular."[45] Barnett emphasized that African Americans should buy from their own firms, or at least try to buy from companies that hired black employees. His advertisement for the Kashmir Chemical Company suggested that buying cosmetics was a way for women to do their part in advancing the cause of African Americans. "*Kashmir Is A Colored Concern*. We are looking out for our *Race*. You must not fail us. *You!*"[46]

As it became clear that the all-black economy was not going to succeed, Barnett made urgent efforts to open the market of African American consumers to national companies. By the 1930s, he was sending African American newspapers to white-owned companies and advertising firms to convince them to advertise to black customers. But he worried that their tepid interest might be part of an old problem. "Whether the advertisers see in the strengthening of Negro newspapers a stimulus to Negro growth and prosperity and do not want to encourage it, I do not know."[47] Barnett and others interested in expanding the opportunities for African Americans to be consumers faced the dilemma of offering them as a good market without suggesting they were the undisciplined and undignified free spenders southern whites had long considered them.

That dilemma shows clearly in a book by Paul Edwards, a friend of Barnett, professor of economics, and former baking powder salesman. Published in 1932 in an early contribution to the growing field of market research, *The Southern Urban Negro as a Consumer* tried to dispel two misconceptions about African Americans in the urban South. One was that because of low incomes, "the Southern urban Negro presents a market limited for the most part to cheap grades of merchandise."[48] The other was the notion that African Americans were wasteful spenders who wished to imitate wealthy whites. "We are told in all seriousness that the Negro wears nothing but Florsheim shoes and Stetson hats, and that he wears better clothing in proportion to his income than the white man." In a work full of statistics, Edwards tried to disprove both notions with a careful list of the features of African American shoppers. Both men and women, he said, were careful shoppers who were among the first to take part in sales. African Americans shopped in as many stores as possible and did not limit their patronage to "small, unattractive stores . . . which so universally feature congested, unorganized displays of cheap, unbranded merchandise." They had considerable interest in name brands and responded positively to advertising. Finally, African Americans were drawn to stores and advertisements that did not insult their dignity. He documented shoppers who stopped going to stores that put up whites-only signs at their water fountains and showed that African Americans rarely bought goods that used racist advertisements. As a call for advertisers to address black customers with more dignity, Edwards's book, like Barnett's work, was ultimately a call for full inclusion in consumer culture.[49]

Many advertisers, less concerned with the complexities that worried Barnett and Edwards, said explicitly that African Americans were free and perhaps hedonistic spenders who constituted a large market with great potential. In 1949, an article in *All American News* happily claimed, "This Black Market is a Spending Market which means a buying market. *Less* of the American Negro's family money goes for housing, savings, education, etc. More, proportionately, is spent for consumer goods, cosmetics, food and beverages, entertainment and clothes. The American Negro wants to live well. . . . He is breaking away from the mule and the cotton field."[50] An advertising journal ended an article eight years later with the same conclusion. "What it comes to is this: The urban Negro spends his money freely on luxury consumer goods."[51] A New York firm that described itself as the first "Negro marketing and public relations counsel" stressed in 1964, "There *is* a difference between the white and Negro consumer. . . . Urban Negro families continue to spend a higher percentage of their incomes for personal care, food, clothing, alcoholic beverages and household furnishings, than do average white urban families."[52]

All three of the groups that discussed blacks' new spending habits—the blues musicians, the proponents like Barnett and the *Chicago Defender* of the promise of urban life, and the advertisers who used language like "The $30 Billion Negro"—believed urban settings offered new freedoms for African Americans from the South. But there were differences in how the three groups defined freedom. Advertisers wanting to benefit from what they hoped were the indulgent and sensual natures of African Americans believed that a unique feature of blacks' character made them especially willing participants in American abundance. These advertisers believed their efforts could bring the dream of American abundance to people too long forgotten by American businesses. Leaders of African American consumer behavior like Paul Edwards and Claude Barnett focused more on the dream of democracy. They came closest to notions of cultural assimilation by envisioning a society where buying and enjoying goods could eliminate old social distinctions rooted in the South. The efforts of Barnett to support things like Nile Queen Cosmetics show they did not see consumer goods as leading to a culture that would completely deny a distinctively African American past. The men and women of the blues appreciated the hope of abundance, saw choice as a substantial freedom unavailable to farm workers, and believed goods could be part of a new dignity available to mobile, urbanizing people. Above all, by connecting goods to new women, new men, and new excitement, the blues upheld the romantic possibilities of consumer culture.

A pair of stories by contemporary children's novelist Mildred D. Taylor, a Mississippi native whose family left the South for Toledo when she was a child in the 1940s, help summarize the ways shopping and goods marked the differences between life in rural Mississippi and in northern cities. Like much literature for children, "The Friendship" and "The Gold Cadillac" derive their drama from a contrast between plot events and the values readers are assumed to have. From the conclusions of both stories, Taylor expects modern readers to believe that everyone should be able to purchase and enjoy the goods they can afford. For her, access to goods marked a great divide between North and South, a divide that has much to do with the meaning of freedom.

Set in Mississippi in 1933, "The Friendship" dramatizes two of the apparent irrationalities that racism brought to issues of shopping, goods, and human relations. First was the issue of the respect or disrespect expressed in the names people called each other. An elderly black man named Mr. Tom Bee calls the white store owner John Wallace by his first name despite numerous objections. Second was the disinterest of store owners in the potential of African Americans as customers. When a group of black children enter Wallace's store, his sons do not wish to serve them despite their obvious fascination with "shiny new things." The Wallaces belittle the smallest child for being dirty and threaten to cut off his hand. Then they refuse to serve Mr. Tom Bee, telling him, "I ain't got all day to fool with you," and concluding, "You already got plenty-a charges, Tom. You don't need no sardines. Ya' stinkin' of fish as it is."[53]

To the child narrator, the solution to the first irrationality is simple. People should address each other as equals. That call for respect in stores, as we will see, became one demand of protestors who used boycotts in the civil rights era. The second solution was more complex. She assumes that people should have the freedom to buy what they can afford and should expect storekeepers to encourage them to do so. An additional feature of the story brings the point to the level of children. Mr. Tom Bee buys candy for all of the children, including a white boy whose presence suggests a hope that the next generation might improve on the race relations of the past. The candy appeals to the children's fascination with new purchases and suggests the potential for a coming democracy of goods. The story ends, however, with the hopes for such a democracy dashed when Wallace shoots Mr. Tom Bee for again calling him "John."

If "The Friendship" shows the limits African Americans in Mississippi faced in trying to derive dignity from goods and shopping, "The Gold Cadillac" dramatizes the differences between the possibilities in the South and the urban North. The story begins in post–World War II Toledo and includes the first trip to Mississippi by the child narrator, Lois.

Conflicts typical in the blues dominate the book. Lois's father wants to impress everyone, especially his wife, with a new Cadillac. He is the new ur-banite who takes pride in new, name-brand goods. Taylor dwells on excess. "It was all gold inside. Gold leather seats. Gold carpeting. Gold dashboard. It was like no car we had owned before."[54] But Lois's mother is not impressed. She refuses to ride in it and reminds him they were saving to buy a home. Drama-tizing the conflict, she walks to church to avoid riding in the car.

Reversing the typical blues story, the family heads south to visit relatives, and the movement unifies the family instead of breaking it up. The father decides to drive the Cadillac to Mississippi with the pride of someone whose car shows he has overcome the limits imposed by southern poverty and racism. "I got that

Cadillac because I liked it and because it meant something to me that somebody like me from Mississippi could go and buy it. It's my car, I paid for it, and I'm driving it south." Relatives point out the danger of a black man heading south in a gold Cadillac, but Lois's mother surprises everyone by saying the whole family will go with him so "we can watch out for each other."[55] The car has brought them together instead of breaking them apart. But on the trip, the children see signs of segregation for the first time and wonder why the police stop the Cadillac as they cross the Mississippi state line. Lois's father spends several hours with the police, pays a fine, and only continues the trip after leaving the Cadillac with relatives in Memphis. Thus the car endangers the family after all, at least in Mississippi.

The story ends with a mixed conclusion. The father, happy to end divisiveness within his family and threats from white Mississippians, sells the gold Cadillac when he returns to Toledo. He tells the children, "We've got more money towards our new house now and we're all together. I figure that makes us the richest folks in the world." The conclusion that Mother knows best and family security is all-important might seem a blandly conventional moral for a children's story. But the narrator is not so sure. "I thought often of that Cadillac. We had had the Cadillac only a little more than a month, but I wouldn't soon forget its splendor or how I'd felt riding around inside it."[56] Thus even though she paired that memory with the impact of the trip to Mississippi, she was still fascinated by the gold Cadillac. Her Mississippi-born parents had learned to distrust such a luxury out of a fear for their safety and security, but the child growing up in the northern city sees fewer reasons to set limits.

CHAPTER SEVEN

Percy, Wright, Faulkner, and Welty

MONTGOMERY WARD SNOPES AND THE INTELLECTUAL CHALLENGES OF CONSUMPTION

Mississippi's greatest writers, William Faulkner, William Alexander Percy, Richard Wright, and Eudora Welty, dealt with goods, stores, and advertising as new forces that threatened to overturn Mississippi traditions, for good or bad. As the economy of Mississippi began to change, and as the broader United States economy changed more dramatically in the first half of the twentieth century, Mississippi's writers asked what goods meant to themselves and their characters. The writers addressed all four of the consumer's definitions of the American Dream—the dreams of abundance, democracy, freedom of choice, and the romance of novelty. It was the fourth that most Mississippi writers found especially fascinating, because most of them tried so hard to figure out the importance of the past. With few exceptions, goods seemed things from outside the state, offering identities the writers found either fearful or subversive or liberating.

It may be surprising that the two writers, one conservative and one radical, with the least in common found it easiest to condemn consumer culture. The conservative argued that the ideal stood in the way of meaningful traditions. For the radical, it stood in the way of constructing a meaningful future.

Will Percy was the conservative. Heir to Delta wealth and self-conscious elitism, Percy articulated the conservative perspective with particular clarity by discussing its decline and impending death. In *Lanterns on the Levee* (1941), he depicted the rise of the consumer as one of the many signs of the inevitable decline of humane values and the growth of empty forms of democracy. Percy had a unique perspective among aristocrats because he did not celebrate the glories of a luxurious past when people truly understood how to use goods to convey leadership and hospitality and to enjoy graceful ease. He had no interest in crying over mansions burned or hoop skirts no longer worn. (By contrast, fellow Delta author Stark Young recorded with wistful reverence the story of an uncle, supposedly the second-wealthiest planter in the antebellum South, who lost his house and most of his wealth in the Civil War. The old planter destroyed the walls of the mansion but left the columns. "To this day, they stand there, the four white columns of white stuccoed brick with their marble steps. He wanted them left for his children and their children to remember what had been.")[1] The Greenville of the Percy family's past, on the other hand, never had "those roomy old residences, full of fine woodwork and furniture and drapery" that had graced Natchez and Charleston. At one point, he doubted whether any twosome "ever looked less aristocratic" than he and his grandfather, the latter "in his neat but well-worn and out-of-style sack suit, I barefooted and hatless." A favorite aunt could make calls on Virginia high society "from her mule-drawn, ancient vehicle in a homemade print dress" without attracting derision.

To Percy, what mattered instead of goods were timeless virtues of manners, charm, kindness, good conversation, respect for intellect and imagination, and a paternalistic care for the poor and supposedly weak. He believed that his family and their kind concentrated "not on those virtues which make surviving possible, but on those which make it worth while."[2]

Like many social critics, Percy was more specific about what was worse in the present than what was valuable about the past. Most Americans in the twentieth century, he believed, were too concerned with physical comfort and appearances. Anyone could take on the look of the elite without knowing the values people with power should inherit; his father's rival, James K. Vardaman, was "immaculately overdressed." He hoped to the point of belief that rich southerners had once possessed essential qualities that transcended appearances. But the wealthy in Greenville in the 1930s were dedicated not to the pursuit of timeless virtues but to economic progress and the immediate and passing pleasures available for purchase. He complained bitterly about the prominence of nightly mass entertainment that came with railroads and then the trucks and buses and telephones and electric lights. "The river town has a White Way, picture shows, many radios, a Chamber of Commerce, and numerous service clubs. We have gone forward, our progress is ever so evident." The movies put on display the silly frolicking of an urban upper class, and the radio numbed the mind through thoughtless repetition. He sneered at the overconcentration on appearances in modern America in one memorable passage: "I'm unhappily convinced that our exteriors have increased in importance while our interiors have deteriorated: it is a good paint job, but the lighting and sanitation are execrable. A good world, I acknowledge, an excellent world, but poor in spirit and common as hell. Vulgarity, a contagious disease like the itch, unlike it is not a disease of the surface, but eats to the marrow."[3]

If the wealthy were losing old understandings of things that mattered more than appearances and economic gain, what of the rest of society? Will Percy had no patience for the notion that consumer culture offered new dignity to the poor. Freedoms, yes, but those freedoms represented no progress or dignity. Like so many conservatives before him, Percy thought the poor were better off enjoying contented leisure than pursuing better-paying work. He believed African Americans had a great talent for enjoying time away from work—a talent only possible in an economic system where the poor had security but few options. Sharecropping, for him, kept alive the ability of earlier labor systems to provide workers a contented subsistence without tempting them with higher ambitions or exhausting them through constant toil. "Our plantation system seems to me to offer as humane, just, self-respecting, and cheerful a method of earning a living as human beings are likely to devise. I watch the limber-jointed, oily-black, well-fed, decently clothed peasants on Trail Lake and feel sorry for the telephone girls, the clerks in chain stores, the office help, the unskilled laborers everywhere—not only for their poor and fixed wage but for their slave routine, their joyless habits of work, and their insecurity."[4] That the sharecroppers were *well* fed but only *decently* clothed shows what he found most important for workers.

The radical Mississippian was Richard Wright. With a childhood devoid of the novel stimulations that the consumer society tries to recapture and without respect for the virtues of independent farm life, Wright described in *Black Boy* his futile effort to take satisfaction in the choices available in stores. When he was able to make some money, "the boys would now examine some new article of clothing I had bought; none of us allowed a week to pass without buying something new." Wright ultimately used such stories to display the hollowness of the small victories available to all people whose daily lives were "bound up with trivial objectives."[5]

He used the same adjective in one of the harshest condemnations of consumer culture written by an American. Early in *American Hunger*, Wright described his disappointment with the empty pleasures pursued by two white waitresses in Chicago. He had hoped life outside the South offered the possibility for new forms of freedom, but "all their lives they had done nothing but strive for petty goals, the trivial prizes of American life." He listed those trivial prizes, believing it was "the daily values that give meaning to life" that "stood between me and those white girls with whom I worked. Their constant outward-looking, their mania for radios, cars, and a thousand other trinkets that made them dream and fix their lives upon the trash of life, made impossible for them to learn a language which could have taught them to speak of what was in their or others' hearts. The words of their souls were the syllables of popular songs."[6]

Wright criticized consumer culture on two closely related levels. On the individual level, Wright sought a self-understanding he believed most people lacked and did not even want. The goal he set for himself—and wanted for all individuals—was a combination of education and self-analysis that could bring out the potential for creativity and self-expression. The "outward-looking" nature of consumer culture, the desire to identify the self through new things, prohibited even the beginning of that introspection.

On the level of the group, Wright as a committed radical believed that the American fascination with goods hindered the development of a revolutionary working class. Those goods served the hegemonic purpose of encouraging popular support for capitalism, diverting the attention of workers and the unemployed from their lack of real power over their lives. Instead, most Americans had "a lust for trash" and "the basest goals in the world." In his lament, Wright did not merely agonize over the empty goals of the dominant white culture. He seemed even more troubled that American capitalism and consumer culture had convinced a great many African Americans of the essential worth of those goals. They too, he believed, were consumers, or at least they wanted to be. "The most valued pleasure of the people I knew," he wrote of his acquaintances in Chicago, "was a car." The Chicago-based fascination with the new things and new identities available through name brands and chain stores seemed to Wright a great failure of African American culture. A revolution would come, he said, not from those who tried but could not share in those pleasures but from "those who do not dream of the prizes that the nation holds forth."[7] Only then would blacks and whites struggle together as fellow workers, because only then could they identify themselves with something other than the search for immediate pleasure.

Wright gives his most subtle and ultimately devastating treatment of consumer issues in the short story "Long Black Song." Beginning with the title, he places the main character, Sarah, in a long African American tradition that consumer culture challenges in a sudden, violent way. She and her husband Silas have the old American goal of independent family farming. In an impassioned description of his life, Silas cries, "Fer ten years Ah slaved mah life out t git mah farm free."[8] He has a patriarchal ideal, and Sarah, defined throughout the story as a wife and especially a mother, struggles to limit her expectations to fit into the traditional place of a woman in a farm family. It is a salesman who brings a shock to both the relative calm and painful limits of farm poverty. At first remarkably appealing, the white salesman is young and apparently innocent. Sarah thinks several times that the salesman "was just like a little boy. Jus like a chile."[9] In his youthfulness, the salesman embodies the emphasis consumer culture places on novelty, with its essential freshness and innocence. The salesman offers Sarah a combination clock and record player. The childish innocence of the salesman is even more pronounced in the record player. The clock means nothing to Sarah, but the device is appealing simply in its appearance. "She bent forward, looking. Lawd, but its pretty! . . . The gilt of the corners sparkled. The color in the wood glowed softly. It reminded her of the light she saw sometimes in the baby's eyes. Slowly she slid a finger over a beveled edge; she wanted to take the box into her arms and kiss it."[10]

Like many consumer goods, the device offers Sarah a connection not only to novelty and youth but to her own culture. The Long Black Song the salesman plays is not a new Tin Pan Alley song but a spiritual, "When the Roll Is Called Up Yonder." Experiencing the power and beauty of church music in her home almost overpowers Sarah. "She leaned back against a post, trembling, feeling the rise and fall of days and nights, of summer and winter; surging, ebbing, leaping about her, beyond her, far out over the fields to where earth and sky lay folded in darkness. She wanted to lie down and sleep or else leap up and shout."[11]

The promise of combining the best of novelty and tradition proves too good to be true. In a quick drama of seduction and violation, the salesman first tries to convince Sarah she can enjoy the device without consequences. He begins, "It won't cost you anything just to look,"[12] and continues with an offer for her to pay just five dollars down and five dollars a month. Then he rapes her and she, powerless in her society, cannot resist. What came into her home with the apparently innocent goal of easing the problems of home life under poverty ultimately destroys that life.

When Silas returns and discovers the salesman has been inside the house, he accuses Sarah of infidelity and forces her to leave. The next day he kills the salesman, and Sarah watches as a group of white men kill Silas and burn the house. It is a story of race, rape, and the tensions in family life on the economic margins of a violent society. The fact that an appealing salesman with an appealing product turns out to be a rapist brings to life Wright's perspective that the consumer economy could undermine the chances African Americans have for freedom, however they defined it.

For all of their differences, Richard Wright and Will Percy shared the belief that America was selling its soul for meaningless and temporary pleasures. For

Percy, that soul lay in the past of the South and western civilization. For Wright, it lay in the possibilities of a future international working class. But both thought too much immediate enjoyment and too many consumer pleasures stood in the way of higher values and had ultimately destructive consequences.

Unlike Percy and Wright, William Faulkner falls into no clear categories. Faulkner might seem just another ascetic critic of consumer culture. His greediest characters were among his most despicable, and he had Gavin Stevens make a conventional critique of the ways American men in the twentieth century misused their abundance. "The American really loves nothing but his automobile: not his wife his child nor even his bank-account first (in fact he doesn't love that bank-account nearly as much as foreigners like to think because he will spend about any or all of it for almost anything provided it is valueless enough) but his motor-car. Because the automobile has become our national sex symbol."[13] By condemning the practice of spending on anything without value and by linking that practice to automobiles and the pursuit of sexual pleasure, Faulkner might seem to have been just another critic of the fun morality of twentieth-century America. Finally, Faulkner would seem to have had little patience for the ways consumer culture tends to deny both pain and the past, for without pain and the past, he would not have had much to write about.

But instead of portraying consumers in a consistently negative light, Faulkner dramatized the tensions of people in conflict with themselves, and his critique of twentieth-century America becomes clear only within those conflicts. He used automobiles with great purpose in his last two works. In *The Mansion*, Linda Snopes Kohl has a pre-ordered British Jaguar delivered the day after her husband Flem is killed with her assistance. To pay for it, she uses the money she will receive from Flem's insurance policy. For this former Communist Party member and worker for the goal of human equality to indulge in a luxury belying any notions of equality seems to suggest either that Faulkner was condemning his only radical character for her hypocrisy or that he was condemning the consumer society for its ability to seduce even its most serious critics. In his last book, *The Reivers*, an automobile becomes a vehicle not of destructiveness but of egalitarianism. An automobile unites a wealthy white boy, a poor black man, and a poor white man in the pleasures of a buoyant democracy that comes not only with shared experience but with escape from a rural community in which everyone knows what to expect from each other.[14] Faulkner's two portrayals of automobiles suggests that consumer goods could offer both an escape from rural poverty but also a rejection of meaningful traditions and the indulgence of the self at the expense of responsibilities for other people.

In his own life Faulkner lived out many of the primary tensions in consumer society. He was constantly in debt, partly because he insisted on keeping up a home beyond his means and partly, at least according to him, because of the spending habits of his wife Estelle. One of the many reasons for their running battles was an almost stereotypical dispute between the woman who wanted expensive clothes and the man who maintained interests in large investments but could be frugal to the point of cheapness on small expenses. When Faulkner ran a notice in Mississippi newspapers denying responsibilities for Estelle's debts, he was thinking not just about the future of their marriage but also about those debts themselves. The distinction between spending for a home and spending for clothing suggested that Faulkner thought his own purchases helped create and sustain permanence and respect in the Oxford community, whereas Estelle's purchases were selfish, flighty, and insignificant. By identifying expenses for personal pleasure as something female even as he went into debt for automobiles and an airplane, Faulkner was also sharing with much of American culture the idea that spending on personal goods was a frailty of women.[15]

The tensions between Faulkner's life in small-town Mississippi and the time he spent in Hollywood enhanced the author's concerns about the meanings of consumer goods. In Mississippi he not only tried to keep up his home, Rowan Oak, as a sign of continuity with upper-class family traditions, he also owned a farm and frequently talked as farmers did about the need to stay independent and debt-free. But to Faulkner, Hollywood always represented impermanence, economic necessity for him and greed in almost everyone else, and standards for personal and artistic life so low he hardly considered them standards. Hollywood was the place where cheap and passing pleasures were made for the rest of the country.[16]

In his work, Faulkner was able to combine his well-known respect for the past with sympathy for rebels in order to explore some of the challenges consumer society presented to both upper-class and agricultural traditions. Significantly, he presents the challenges with some fairly likable characters and scenes. Colonel Sartoris stands as a ridiculous spokesman for traditional upper-class uses of goods. Like Will Percy, Sartoris deplores the idea of a democracy of appearances. Unlike Percy, Sartoris takes steps to restore the appearances that accompany class hierarchy. First he proposes a law "that no Negro woman should appear on the streets without an apron."[17] Then, when his carriage has a confrontation with the town's first automobile, Mayor Sartoris authors a law banning automobiles from the streets.

What Faulkner called the "destiny of America" would not be denied. Manfred de Spain initiates a new generation of both political and cultural leadership simply by opposing the ban on automobiles. Faulkner turned sociologist in discussing the basis for opposition to Sartoris. First, opponents were young. The automobile ban "was the opportunity which that whole contemporary generation of young people had been waiting for, not just in Jefferson but everywhere." Second, they were part of an ambitious, nonagricultural middle class—"the clerks and bookkeepers in the stores and gins and offices." De Spain and his automobile-loving followers turn the defeat of Sartoris into a defeat of elitist traditions in the South. When they hang the automobile law in the courthouse and laugh about it along with the automobile generation from all over the country, they are celebrating the entry of Jefferson into a twentieth-century America that stresses the pursuit of pleasure, easy mobility, and wide-spread involvement in cosmopolitan culture. De Spain buys Jefferson's first automobile—a shiny red one—and then starts its first automobile dealership; from his place in the bank he gladly lends money to anyone wanting to buy a car. Thus, he not only embodies the excitement of consumer culture, he also tries to spread its availability far beyond the wealthy.[18]

Discussing the appeal of the automobile as a challenge to traditional hierarchies, Faulkner was an effective sociologist. The coming automobile age, he wrote, celebrated a particular kind of sexual pleasure. The red car was "alien and debonair, as irrevocably polygamous and bachelor as de Spain himself."[19] Part of this sexual freedom came simply with the settings cars provided for couples to escape public view. From a broader perspective, automobiles carried meanings central to consumer culture. As with Faulkner himself, whose first car was a yellow Model T Ford with a modified racer body,[20] owners took pleasure in their cars' appearance and capacity for speed. De Spain foreshadowed what Faulkner called "that new national religious cult of Cheesecake as it translated still alive the Harlows and Grables and Monroes into the hierarchy of American cherubim." The imagery that untouchable, sexually alluring women represented America's most sacred figures suggested that only constant desire could honor the country's highest ideals.[21]

That perspective posed serious threats to Faulkner's understanding of farm life and the powerful cautions it sustained. The three prevailing reasons not to make purchases of large or small items were the threat debt posed to personal independence, the commitment to self-denial demanded by evangelical religion, and an agricultural life that sought repeated renewal rather than new pleasures. All of these appear with clarity and some sympathy in Faulkner's work. But his characters often find the principles restrictive and try to over-turn them.

Two of the perspectives of traditional agricultural folk appear in *Light in August*. Faulkner portrays Lena Grove as a woman of nature for whom buying anything is a struggle. She fears that improvidence might cost her the independence that allows her to travel in her search to unite her household. At one country store, "she is waging a mild battle with that providential caution of the old earth of and with and by which she lives." Earth people, then, are born with a literally natural reluctance to become consumers. In Faulkner's perspective, a primary principle of the earth is that it needs renewal to survive. That renewal allows little room for the novelty of consumer goods. But Faulkner continues the scene. "This time she conquers. She rises and walking a little awkwardly, a little carefully, she traverses the ranked battery of maneyes and enters the store, the clerk following." The picture of a woman running a male gauntlet shows that in Yoknapatawpha County, the so-called feminization of consumer spending has not occurred, and it takes courage to go against both the conventions of the genders and the traditions of the old earth to make a purchase. " 'I'm a-going to do it,' she thinks, even while ordering the cheese and crackers; 'I'm a going to do it,' saying aloud: 'And a box of sardines.' She calls them *sourdeens*. 'A nickel box.' " By splurging on what to her is a luxury, Lena is violating one of the central characteristics that make her an earth woman.[22]

A character in the same book attempts to avoid consumer spending for religious reasons. The Presbyterian McEachern gives a heavy sigh every time he has to leave his responsibilities on the farm and face the temptations and degradations of the town. Visiting town, he cautions his stepson Joe Christmas, "is no good habit for a man who has yet to make his way." The danger lies in anything that tempts people away from their responsibilities. Specifically, McEachern sees luxury goods as signs of indulgence. When Joe sells his cow to buy a suit, his stepfather challenges him for the reason. "What else would you want with a new suit if you were not whoring." Of course it is McEachern who has given Joe the cow, with the clear goal of testing his ability to overcome temptation. Buying the suit for the reason McEachern suspected allows Joe to break free from the confining morality of his stepfather and the expectations for self-denial that accompany farm life.[23] Once again, then, Faulkner showed a degree of respect for a character who uses the ability to consume to escape the confining features of agricultural tradition.

A third scene, addressing several reasons for reluctance to spend money, occurs at the conclusion of *As I Lay Dying*. Here two of Faulkner's most exasperating characters find common and potentially sympathetic ground in the appeals of consumer pleasures. Both Anse and Cash Bundren are extremely reluctant to spend money. Anse is a poor farmer, head of a large family, and husband of a woman who believes the purpose of life is to prepare for death. As a farmer, his life centers on renewing the earth and economizing in order not to lose the farm. He lives in great fear of debt, four times stating, "we would be beholden to no man."[24] As a member of a partly religious family, he has heard about the dangers of temptation, and his home is not a setting for the pleasures of new experiences. As a rural Mississippian living in the countryside, he has little contact with the fashion and novelty of mass culture. He resents not only the power of merchants in Jefferson but also the ways they enjoy their wealth. He makes, with what is for Faulkner unusual clarity, a farmer's criticism of the locals who control the economy. "Nowhere in this sinful world can a honest, hardworking man profit. It takes them that runs the stores in the towns, doing no sweating, living off of them that sweats. It aint the hardworking man, the farmer. Sometimes I wonder why we keep at it. It's because there is a reward for us above, where they cant take their autos and such. Every man will be equal there and it will be taken from them that have and give to them that have not by the Lord." The sentiment was commonplace among rural Protestants that people who did not use their muscles made their money manipulating those who did. As usual, however, Faulkner's characters use conventions only to defy them. After spelling out the virtues of work and austerity, Anse thinks, "it's a long wait, seems like," and he repeats a desire that occurred to him when Addie died. "But now I can get them teeth. That will be a comfort."[25]

Anse's son Cash seems to be a stereotypical hard worker. He fears the temptations of consumer goods because they could interfere with his commitment to work. He wonders what a record player might cost on installment, and he imagines the pleasure recorded music might give to the evenings after days of hard work. But he decides, "I reckon it's a good thing we aint got ere a one of them. I reckon I wouldn't never get no work done a-tall for listening to it."[26]

The many objections the Bundrens raise to consumer goods indicate that they have given them considerable thought. By the end of the book, however, they finally take refuge from their troubles in the pleasures of consumer goods. First, Anse starts asking his children to lend him money for reasons he does not make clear. After all he has done for them, he says, a few dollars are not much to ask. This shows a willingness to pursue new pleasures that violate his often-stated fear. When he buys his new teeth and shows up with a new Mrs. Bundren, he is looking to a better future—not to a renewal of the work and limited expectations of his past. When the new Mrs. Bundren meets the family, she is carrying a record player, and this inspires Cash, too, to look to a future in which work will no longer dominate. "Everytime a new record would come from the mail order and us setting in the house in the winter, listening to it, I would think what a shame Darl couldn't be here to enjoy it too."[27]

To summarize, Faulkner could be sympathetic and even positive about the potential for consumer culture to offer individual liberation from traditional forms of confinement. De Spain lets loose the pleasures of the automobile age as liberation from the ideals of planter hierarchy, Lena Grove overcomes the tendency of the old earth to do nothing more than renew itself, Joe Christmas overcomes the pleasure-denying evangelicalism of his stepfather, and Cash and Anse Bundren overcome the joyless economizing that independent farm life has demanded. Finally, in *The Reivers* Boon Hogganbeck, Ned McCaslin, and Lucius Priest set off as a trio on an automobile trip that defines freedom as the experience of classlessness. In each case, the enjoyment of consumer goods undercuts traditions associated with a pantheon of white southern ideals— aristocracy, paternalism, life close to the soil, the independence of the rural household, evangelical religion, and white supremacy. One might conclude that Faulkner, so unlike Percy and Wright, could have even been a defender of consumer culture, at least in the ways it allowed people to escape the constraints into which they were born.

How did Faulkner reconcile his concern for the past as an influence worthy of attention with his apparent sympathy for characters who gain new freedoms by fulfilling consumer desires? How could he deal with a definition of freedom that sees no ultimate goals or absolute values but instead seeks constant pursuit of novelty and freedom from any goals and experiences of the past?

The group in Faulkner's work who have spending money but no ties to the past are the Snopes family.[28] The newly wealthy among the Snopeses can spend their money for pleasure without old notions of expressing leadership through display. Just as important, all of the Snopeses who make economic progress do so outside agriculture, believing as Flem Snopes says, "aint no benefit in farming."[29] Thus, they do not feel the farmer's need to deny themselves goods in order to keep the farm.

The first Yoknapatawpha Snopes, Ab, shows up in the county as a barn burner, a man for whom issues of justice outweigh concerns about economic gain. He sneers at the hierarchical pretensions of de Spain, tracks manure on the hundred-dollar rug in the front hall, and says, "If I had thought that much of a rug I don't know as I would keep it where folks coming in would have to tromp on it." Ab's two daughters, at work every time Faulkner mentions them, do not spend much, nor does anyone seem to spend money on them. One of the daughters wears a faded sunbonnet that suggests she spends considerable time in the sun and that she does not wear new clothes. The other daughter wears "a shapeless hat which at one time must have belonged to the man."[30] Wearing hand-me-downs signifies economic necessity. Wearing a man's hat shows she is outside the process that turned fashions for women into one of the most dynamic parts of the consumer economy.

Faulkner's portrait of the sharecropping Snopeses indicates neither agrarian respect for farm life nor any particular excitement over the consumer goods that threaten it. Time after time they embody the traditional approach of the agricultural poor who use goods without enjoying them. The home of Mink Snopes is a run-down two-room dogtrot with nothing to distinguish it from the homes of other poor families. It is not comfortable; the roof leaks and the roof is rotting away. It is not attractive; it has no paint or decoration. When he goes to town, he watches people going to movies, driving automobiles, and drinking soft drinks, but he does not expect to enjoy such things himself. Eventually, and most significantly, he grows accustomed to the material side of prison life, where the clothes and food are no worse than he has had outside Parchman. He has never expected economic progress, and he seems to have no problems with a lack of opportunity for novel experiences. In fact, parts of prison life offer real relief. "No more now to go to a commissary store every Saturday morning to battle with the landlord for every gram of the cheap bad meat and meal and molasses and the tumbler of snuff which was his and his wife's one spendthrift orgy."[31] Here is one more reason not to become a consumer—trying to become one put him at the mercy of a landlord. In prison he finds he can accept life without the daily conflicts that go with trying to survive.

The Snopeses who leave the farm have a changed attitude about goods. Most obvious is the extravagantly named Montgomery Ward Snopes. The not-so-simple fact of his name stands in comic contrast to that of his father, I. O. Snopes. For a Snopes to be saddled with the name I. O. suggests that his entire identity is wrapped up in the poor man's condition—I owe—and the need to economize. And for I. O. Snopes to father Montgomery Ward Snopes signals a dramatic break in that tradition. Montgomery Ward in Chicago was the nation's first mail-order catalog service, offering to rural people a variety of goods never available outside cities and exposing rural people to affordable versions of cosmopolitan styles.

In Montgomery Ward Snopes, Faulkner offers his view of consumer culture at its worst. Montgomery Ward Snopes begins his business career as a storekeeper in France in World War I. While running a canteen for soldiers, he builds a room in the back and hires a French woman to work as a prostitute. He returns to Jefferson to open Atelier Monty, an erstwhile photography studio that does at first most and eventually all of its business showing French postcards in the back room.

Faulkner had already drawn the connection between consumer goods and sexual pleasure when he described de Spain's introduction of the automobile into Jefferson as the precursor of Hollywood cheesecake and when he had Gavin Stevens call the automobile the national sex symbol. What Montgomery Ward Snopes offers is sexual excitement without responsibility or even physical contact. By portraying untouchable forms one after another on his wall, he offers the men of Jefferson pleasures without consequences. Here, as in much of consumer culture, sexuality carries few of the burdens it carried in the agricultural South—burdens of personal identity, racial identity, religious commitment, and ties to the family and household economy. The fact that the women in the pictures are French only makes them more untouchable and removed from conventional rural, agricultural, Protestant meanings of sexual experience. The pleasures are brief, they can be experienced repeatedly, and they leave the customer wanting more.

Montgomery Ward Snopes comes to represent the principle that anything is available for purchase. He ends up in the cradle of consumer pleasures, Hollywood, in what Faulkner calls a "quite lucrative adjunct or correlative to the motion-picture industry or anyway colony."[32] It seems safe to assume that Montgomery Ward Snopes has become involved in the business of pornographic films. In what was surely a slap at the crassness he endured in Hollywood, Faulkner took the commodification of immediate pleasure and turned it into one of the ugliest sides of mass culture.

Flem Snopes and Linda Snopes Kohl ultimately represent the culmination of Faulkner's thinking about the meanings of economic success. The story of Flem is a rags-to-riches tragedy, and part of its tragedy is that he never finds enjoyment in the benefits of the economic system he helps bring to Yoknapatawpha.

Flem is the leading figure in converting Yoknapatawphans into consumers. The changes he makes in marketing at Varner's store were taking place throughout the rural South in the early twentieth century as cash replaced credit as the means of payment. The Varners have traditionally offered store credit as part of the control they exercised over local farmers. The customers, mostly farmers with debts to the Varners, shopped mostly for subsistence goods. With the Varners foreclosing on one farm after another, the farmers have good reason to buy as little as they can.[33] After he takes over Varner's store, Flem moves immediately to deny store credit to customers who have learned to expect it as a right. In doing so, he also disdains the trust that has accompanied the Varners' notions of paternalism and makes clear he has no time for the male small talk that had long dominated the store. In all of those ways, Flem is trying to revolutionize the general store to make profits by selling rather than simply using the store to support the Varners' hold over the land. A key scene occurs when he brings a plug of tobacco to Will Varner and stays around until Varner pays for it in cash— a sign that Flem has successfully taken aim at the economic customs of planter domination.

What makes Flem Snopes remarkable in a discussion of the meanings of goods is that he believes in neither traditional nor modern views on what goods can do for the individual. He is more unknowable and more mysterious than depictions of materialistic Americans from George Babbitt to Thomas Sutpen because he has no goals in mind for his money. As Donald Kartiganer writes, he embodies "pure acquisitiveness but [is] indifferent to acquisitions."[34] Flem has none of the conventional reasons for wanting money. He does not adopt a traditional elite view that goods can earn the respect of the community. Nor does he adopt a modern view that consumer goods are part of a constant search for new pleasures. Flem uses extravagant forms of selling, bringing what Cleanth Brooks calls "the world of advertising and Madison Avenue, in this instance set down in a little backwater of a community,"[35] without having any interest in enjoying goods himself.

Particularly intriguing is the attention Faulkner gave to Flem's relation with the homes of Jefferson. In the original plan for the Snopes trilogy, Flem in the final volume was to bulldoze the largest homes in Jefferson and replace them with subdivisions.[36] Faulkner decided that instead of having Flem become a real estate mogul, he should instead move into a mansion but take no pleasure from it. By leaving out the overtly destructive side, Faulkner portrays Snopes as a character who cares about nothing but making money and keeping it. Were Flem to become a bulldozing realtor, he would be an active opponent of Jefferson's old upper class and its values. He would represent a wealthy and more menacing culmination of the goals of the first Snopes, who by burning barns and muddying carpets sneered at the goods that either sustained or symbolized wealth and power.

Instead of using the destruction of homes as a prominent metaphor and story line, Faulkner made the mansion itself a central feature of the book and the conclusion of the trilogy. When Flem becomes bank president, he buys and moves into de Spain's two-story mansion and adds columns to conform more clearly to an antebellum version of a classical image.[37] He makes only one addition to suit his own tastes: "a little wood ledge, not even painted, nailed to the front of that hand-carved Mount Vernon mantelpiece at the exact height for Flem to prop his feet on it."[38] The little wooden ledge distinguishes Flem from so many other materialistic characters in American fiction because it shows that he is seeking neither the novelty of consumer culture nor the symbols of upper-class respectability. Instead, the meaning of Flem's home is mercenary. As a son of the poor, he intends the mansion and its columns to earn the trust of people who have good reason not to trust him. He hopes that people with money to put in a bank will know he does not need to cheat them.

Linda Snopes Kohl rebels against countless conventions governing American and especially southern small-town life. Her identity is defined by active and often courageous forms of radical commitment. One of her many rebellions concerns her indifference to the products of American capitalism.

Until the end of the trilogy, Linda shows little interest in consumer products or shopping or expressing herself through goods. The conclusion of the trilogy, in which Flem's murder allows his wife Linda to buy one of the most extravagant consumer goods imaginable, is especially tragic, because of who she has been. The Jaguar she buys represents the end of her idealism. It is private and fast, and Linda uses it to escape the county and its people, with no intention of coming back.

The logic of consumer culture ultimately includes a powerful contradiction. One side is public, emphasizing the democracy of appearances and the irrelevance of inherited class traditions. The other side emphasizes the never-ending search for new experiences. This side is by necessity individualistic, leading eventually to self-indulgence and even self-obsession. No matter how fully a shared system of meanings links the consumer to fellow consumers, the desire for novelty ultimately drives the consumer to search for the best goods, the most exciting, the most colorful, the most powerful, the goods that offer the greatest sense of individual satisfaction. A fast car is not good enough. When Linda Snopes Kohl buys a Jaguar to get the hell out of Yoknapatawpha, she represents Faulkner's suggestion that this central contradiction of the American Dream cannot be reconciled.

Montgomery Ward Snopes, Flem Snopes, and Linda Snopes Kohl take consumer culture to three of its ugliest culminations. Montgomery Ward represents an extreme form of an empty self-indulgence that can be purchased again and again. The pornography industry becomes the culmination of the promise of the mail-order catalog. Flem embodies something close to the opposite. Uninterested in pleasures of any kind, Flem takes the desire to accumulate money to its culmination by refusing to spend it except in ways that will allow him to make more. And Linda embodies the ability of consumer culture to cut people off from shared interests with other people.

Faulkner seems torn between the personal liberation some of his characters find in becoming consumers and the ultimately destructive uses these three Snopeses make of consumer culture. To draw a conclusion about his treatment of consumer culture, we should consider the well-known importance Faulkner saw in the past. The postwar America in which Faulkner wrote *The Town* and *The Mansion* showed a remarkable respect for youth and for things that were new. This was the time when *Peter Pan* was a popular show and Walt Disney built Disneyland, when Benjamin Spock was writing about the virtues of babies exploring their universe, and when teenagers with guitars were becoming cultural heroes and spokesmen. Almost all of Faulkner's characters feel the weight of the past, for bad or good. For all his respect for the power of the past, however, he believed that any tradition could produce the need for people to free themselves from it. Had he been able to identify any tradition as the right one, he would not have experienced and fictionally embodied so many of the powerful ambivalences that drove his work. Faulkner could treat with respect characters who used goods and shopping to free themselves from the confining aspects of their own traditions. But he was hardly ready to give up on traditions. Traditions have their problems—and their tragedies—but traditions are better than nothing. In the Snopeses he created characters without traditions, and when he turned them loose to face the opportunities and contradictions of the consumer society, they ended in destructiveness and self-obsession.

Of Mississippi's four great writers in the twentieth century, Eudora Welty wrote the only tribute to shopping. Compared with Wright, Percy, and Faulkner, Welty tended to write more about the inner lives of her characters than public and political or potentially political issues. Material things do not seem to matter a great deal in themselves or as symbols of broader perspectives. Thus a childhood reminiscence that lovingly recalled her fascination with a store helps distinguish her from Mississippi's other writers.

In 1975 Welty published "The Little Store," a short essay different in tone from anything Percy, Wright, or Faulkner ever wrote. Welty grew up in a city, but she introduces the piece by placing Jackson, Mississippi, and her family in a pastoral setting. When she grew up, only "two blocks away from the Mississippi State Capitol, and on the same street with it," she begins, "it was possible to have a little pasture behind your backyard where you could keep a Jersey cow, which we did."[39] "A thrifty home maker" who milked cows and did not go to stores, her mother resembled rural farm women who did not see shopping as a significant responsibility or joy. In fact, the family lived in easy reach of rural people like the blackberry lady, the watermelon man, and "farmers driving in with their plenty."[40]

Since Welty made a point not to portray her mother as a consumer, her own fascination with the Little Store has an air of escape and intrigue. The short trip away from home allowed new freedoms and took on the air of a pilgrimage to a special site. "We children thought it was ours. The happiness of errands was in part that of running for the moment away from home, a free spirit. I believed the Little Store to be a center of the outside world, and hence of happiness."[41] Enjoying a free spirit meant a rare combination of mystery, the self-definition that came with choice, and the indulgence of the senses. Mystery began with the separation of the store from home and continued with the appearance of the place. "Running in out of the sun, you met what seemed total obscurity inside." In the darkness, powerful smells and the promise of powerful tastes held the potential for special intrigue. In this setting, surrounded by so many sensations, the child had the pleasure of choosing how to spend the extra nickel her mother always gave her. Stating almost a maxim of consumer culture, Welty wrote, "Enchantment is cast upon you by all those things you weren't supposed to have need for."[42] She felt lured by the marbles and rubber balls, bubble pipes, sparklers, and toys. Especially for a child, the counters overflowed at eye level with candy bars and Cracker Jacks; large iced barrels lured her to a choice of cold drinks.

Much of the significance of Welty's reminiscence lay in its difference from anything Faulkner, Wright, or Percy chose to write. For Wright and Percy, the American celebration of consumer goods substituted illusions of freedom for more valuable possibilities. For Faulkner, the search for novel goods ultimately worked against the importance of more valuable pasts. But Welty chose to remember her own excitement as a consumer and how trips to the store allowed her a small rebellion against the behavior of her mother. She accepted no simple agrarianism and respected shopping for the independence inherent in the ability to make choices.

Welty comes close to a critique of consumers in her treatment of two female characters who grow up poor and marry wealthy men. Twice she uses spending habits to characterize women who are uninterested in the past and interested primarily in seizing new pleasures. Fay McKelva, the lively new wife of the dying Judge McKelva in *The Optimist's Daughter*, makes clear her perspective on the past. "The past isn't a thing to me. I belong to the future."[43] Fay shows her interest in novelty and excitement by showing one of her new purchases to the Judge while he lies motionless after eye surgery. " 'Look! Look what I got to match my eardrops! How do you like 'em, hon? Don't you want to let's go dancing?' She stood on one foot and held a shoe in the air above his face. It was green, with a stilletto heel."[44] As the outsider and a new force in a small town, Fay strikes other characters as gaudy and shocking.

Welty's most extravagant spender is Bonnie Dee Peacock Ponder in *The Ponder Heart*. Another young woman from a poor background, she marries the considerably older and possibly crazy Daniel Ponder. Bonnie Dee first meets Daniel at the ten cent store, where she works the cash register. Later she turns up at a Woolworth's in Memphis. By placing her in those two stores, Welty suggests that she has left behind the norms of her big farm family to pursue the pleasures that she can afford. A fan of popular culture, she reads movie and romance magazines, and when she has access to money, she starts to order "evening dresses and street dresses and hostess dresses and brunch dresses— dresses in boxes and hanging up."[45] Then she turns to modern technology, ordering a washing machine and then a telephone. Her husband Daniel is almost a parody of Will Percy's ideal paternalist, who secures the affection of people he meets by giving his money away, but instead Bonnie Dee asserts herself by becoming a spender.

The progression of Bonnie Dee Ponder from dime store employee to maga-zine fan to wealthy consumer might be the closest Welty comes to creating her own version of a Snopes. But was she sneering at modern consumers for pursuing quick, popular pleasures at the expense of more lasting values? In marrying wealthy men and spending their money, did Bonnie Dee and Fay represent Welty's fears about cultural chaos ruled newly rich consumers?

The roles Fay and Bonnie Dee play in the two books make clear that Welty did not join Wright, Faulkner, and Percy in condemning consumers. The char-acterizations of Bonnie Dee come from Edna Earle Ponder, the small-minded narrator who is very protective of her family, especially Uncle Daniel. As a member of a wealthy family, she sees Bonnie Dee's spending habits as unsavory and threatening. Edna Earle first scoffs, "Think of something to wear. Bonnie Dee had it." Then, much as Will Percy was troubled by people who misused money and new goods, she sneers that "Bonnie Dee kept the washing machine on the front porch, just like any Peacock would be bound to do."[46] To Edna Earle, such spending was the height of ingratitude from a once poor woman who ran off her rich husband. But to Welty herself, the fascination with shop-ping carries no menacing implications, and Edna Earle's criticisms simply add to the comic quality of the book.

In *The Optimist's Daughter*, Laurel Hand, Fay's stepdaughter, has to come to terms with the issue of the desirability of change. Should she design her life to resemble her mother, who always feared change and claimed "it was unlucky to make too much of your happiness"?[47] Or should she try more to resemble her father, the optimist who was so ready to change that he married a younger woman? Her parents had differed over the meanings of material goods. Her mother saved everything and considered her most beautiful and satisfactory piece of clothing a blouse she made herself from "cloth from Mother's own spinning, and dyed a deep, rich, American Beauty color with pokeberries."[48] Her mother, very much an agrarian, valued home manufacturing and connec-tions to family tradition. In contrast, her father saved nothing and saw no problem with buying Laurel's mother an expensive New Orleans beaded crepe dress that she considered extravagant. Ultimately, Laurel's decision that she is the optimist's daughter capable of facing the future suggests that Welty uses the tensions over goods not to critique consumers but to dramatize one of issues Laurel has to confront.

The positive sides Welty sees in consumer culture show in two short stories about poor characters. "The Whistle" treats with great respect two characters who decide that comfort and pleasure are worth even enormous risks. An aging farm couple live on the margin of survival. The man and woman expect few pleasures, and above all they are cold—so cold they spread their clothes over the tomatoes that provide their only chance for economic independence. The cold tests all of the lessons they have learned about thrift, self-restraint, and sacrifice. The remarkable feature about the story is that the couple start to burn their winter's supply of firewood, first their kindling, then "the big cherry log which of course was meant to be saved for the very last of winter."[49] Then they burn their furniture. By the end of the story, they are left insecure, at the mercy of the elements and their own poverty. But they have found momentary pleasure in the experience, and Welty treats with enormous respect the decision to leave behind a past full of restraint and discomfort and seize instead pleasures—even pleasures that promise dire consequences.

That story is not about shopping and new goods, but another story about a poor character concludes with the dignity that comes with choice. In "A Worn Path," Phoenix Jackson, a very old, very poor African American woman, makes a long walk to town from her small rural home to get medicine for her grandson. Dramatizing key elements of the rural nonconsumer, she concentrates her energies on her family and makes do with what she has by wearing a "long apron of bleached sugar sacks." A white man assumes she is making the trip for her own pleasure. When he tells her, "I know you old colored people! Wouldn't miss going to town to see Santa Claus!"[50] he voices the assumption that African Americans are by nature self-indulgent spenders. Phoenix Jackson goes to town only to get medicine.

But Welty ends the story with a twist. With two nickels white people dropped or gave her, she makes new plans. "I going to the store and buy my child a little windmill they sells, made out of paper. He going to find it hard to believe there such a thing in the world."[51] The picture of a poor woman deciding to bring her sick grandchild a rare luxury again shows Welty's respect for people who made decisions to defy traditions and expectations.

For Welty, unlike Faulkner and very unlike Wright and Percy, no ultimate judgment awaits characters who buy new goods to define and enjoy themselves. Even if they offer no ultimate solutions or redemptions, goods allow significant forms of freedom. In characters like Fay McKelva and Bonnie Dee Peacock Ponder, she uses the conventional image of the free-spending social climber only to overturn it, and in Phoenix Jackson she raises the image of the poor African American as money-waster only to see dignity in the possibility of new goods. Whether Welty is unique on the issue of spending money because she once pursued a career in advertising, or because as a woman she can, like Gladys Smith Presley, see consumption as a form of rebellion, she shows a rare ability to identify with characters whose rebellions are small and quiet.

CHAPTER EIGHT

White Christmas

BOYCOTTS AND THE MEANINGS

OF SHOPPING, 1960–1990

In her 1967 book, *For Us, the Living*, Myrlie Evers described one perspective on the relationship between the civil rights movement and consumer culture. She described how her husband Medgar, like many black Mississippians, had sometimes worked in a northern city and came to imagine a more comfortable life. Unlike many Mississippi natives, Medgar Evers returned to Mississippi to work for a particular version of the American Dream. Myrlie Evers argued that "Nearly any movie, almost any page of *Life* magazine, the advertising on the billboards and in the newspapers, most of what we see each day on television—all of these constitute a kind of torture to many Negroes. For they know that this—or something like it, is what awaits the American who is willing to work for it—unless he is a Negro. American advertising is responsible for much of the Negro's current demand that he, too, be allowed to participate in the fulfillment of the American dream."[1] Advertising, so often condemned for its manipulative and politically conservative elements, served in Evers's interpretation as an unwitting inspiration for protest.

By far the most significant change in post–World War II Mississippi was the series of dramatic protests African Americans like Evers made against the lack of control over their lives. But how did those protests relate to economic and cultural changes taking place in Mississippi and the rest of the country? The rise of protest movements in the 1950s and 1960s coincided with the culmination of the decline in the number of people who made their living in agriculture, the de-

Downtown Port Gibson, Mississippi, 1940. Farming people in a wagon already seemed outsiders. By the 1960s, African Americans were spending enough money that a civil rights boycott posed a serious challenge to local power relations. (Photo by Marion Post Wolcott; courtesy Library of Congress)

cline in the demand for farm labor, and the resulting migration from rural areas. With the end of the old agricultural schedule that had for so long regulated how poor people received and spent their cash, many of the main obstacles to consumer buying deteriorated, and Mississippi, like most of the United States in the postwar period, saw a dramatic increase in the number of goods people chose to buy. Goods and forms of entertainment that had once been luxuries became more commonplace, and many new goods turned up on Mississippi shelves and in Mississippi homes. Thus, when civil rights protestors began to wonder what sort of statement they should make about goods and store life, they were confronting an economic landscape that was rapidly changing.

Workers for civil rights often recall that their first confrontations with injustice involved issues of goods and appearances. In her autobiography about becoming an activist, Anne Moody recalled the importance of goods in her childhood. After making friends with some white children, she cried for weeks when she did not receive skates like they had as a Christmas gift. Then she learned that the downstairs section of the movie theater was more comfortable than the upstairs area where African Americans had to sit. This lesson inspired a series of realizations about the differences between the possessions of blacks and whites. "Now that I was thinking about it, their schools, homes, and streets were better than mine. . . . Their homes were large and beautiful with indoor toilets and every other convenience that I knew of at the time. Every house I had ever lived in was a one- or two-room shack with an outdoor toilet. It really bothered me that they had all these nice things and we had nothing."[2] Fannie Lou Hamer said she first began to understand injustice after she started picking cotton at age six in order to buy things at a plantation store. After she realized the work was "trapping" her, she complained, "Being a very small child I thought it was because of our color that made something wrong. I remember telling my mother one day. I said, 'Mother, how come we are not white? Because white people have clothes, they can have food to eat, and we work all the time, and we don't have anything.' "[3] SNCC protestor Charles McDew, not a native southerner, began to learn about the material meanings of injustice early in his stay in Mississippi when a policeman told him, "Down here, niggas don't wear white shirts during the week unless they teachers or preachers" and threatened to put him in jail if he did not have a Bible, textbook, or a work shirt.[4]

During the 1950s and 1960s, the tensions and potential for violence that had long characterized life for African Americans who went into white-owned stores became even more pronounced. White Mississippians were on edge about any activities that hinted at demands for equality for blacks, and many African Americans were ready to overthrow the etiquette of white supremacy. It was at a small general store in Money, Mississippi, in 1955 that Emmitt Till spoke to a white woman in a jovial way that local white men found offensive. Till was a Chicago teenager who had grown up with a greater sense of freedom than young blacks in Mississippi had experienced, and he had a sense of daring his murderers found unacceptable. Eleven years later in Hattiesburg, protest leader and store owner Vernon Dahmer was killed days after he announced that people could pay their poll taxes at his store rather than at traditional sites of white supremacy.

Black Mississippians found they had a powerful way to protest in the post-agricultural era. The most forceful statements they made about their place in consumer culture came when they boycotted stores owned by whites. Beginning in the early 1960s, protestors engaged in countless consumer boycotts in Mississippi towns and cities. Boycotts could involve almost everyone in the black community and did not depend on powerful leaders, outsider protestors, student foot-soldiers, or people ready to go to prison. Almost anyone could participate in a boycott.

By staying outside the stores and using economic power for political purposes, protestors were making statements about their place in the world of goods. But what statements? Were they saying they wanted to be part of consumer culture by gaining equal access to the space and goods in the stores they were boycotting? Or by staying outside the stores, were they rejecting some the ideals of the consumer society, upholding instead notions of self-control or anti-materialism? Were they saying, with Myrlie Evers, that they wished to "participate in the fulfillment of the American dream" and were they agreeing with so many blues musicians that part of freedom meant the excitement of urban life, goods, and mobility? Or were they hoping, with Richard Wright, to redefine that dream and redirect the nature of American life away from fascination with passing pleasures available for purchase? At Christmas season during the bus boycott in Montgomery, Alabama, Martin Luther King Jr. built on the ascetic tradition of previous American boycotts by calling on protestors to refuse to shop at downtown stores and to save their Christmas-shopping money or give it to charity or the Montgomery Improvement Association.[5]

Boycotts had many goals, only a few of which concerned consumer issues. Protestors hoped to use the pressure of boycotts to force town authorities to negotiate about issues they had refused to discuss. Some boycotts immediately followed white violence on blacks, and others arose over dramatic segregation issues. One of the most aggressive efforts to inspire a major protest was the NAACP boycott of Jackson stores led by Medgar Evers. Beginning in December 1962, it included demonstrations of many kinds, most of them by native Mississippians, and it lasted for several months as part of a broad demand for desegregation of the city.[6] In 1965 the NAACP in Natchez made a list of the grievances the organization wanted to address through a long and angry boycott. Members demanded that the city's Board of Aldermen denounce the Klan and Citizens' Council and end police brutality, and they called for the hiring of blacks by the police force, immediate desegregation of schools, parks, and swimming pools, the appointment of blacks to the school board, equal police protection for African American funerals, equal city services like street cleaning and sewage, and some action toward equalizing job opportunities, housing standards, and a new code to govern relations between tenants and landlords. The NAACP urged African Americans to stay out of white-owned stores until conditions improved.[7]

Among other things, the boycotts showed that African Americans were spending enough money to use their purchasing as a weapon. It is difficult to imagine sharecroppers having much success in boycotting a plantation store, both because they lacked economic power and because their limited spending made such a strategy futile. But by the 1960s, boycotts could put considerable pressure on merchants.

Many boycotters specifically addressed what took place inside the stores. Picket signs supporting the protests confronted the issue of purchasing with slogans like "Don't Buy Segregation" and "Keep Your Money in Your Pocket."[8] A group of college students in Jackson wore T-shirts with individual letters so they could line up on a signal and spell out "DON'T SHOP ON CAPITAL STREET."[9] Two of the goals protestors pursued through the boycotts specifically addressed the experience of shopping. First, protestors demanded that African Americans be hired as store clerks. An early boycott in Clarksdale included the demand that black employees should gain promotion "above the menial level." When the Freedom Democratic Party organized a boycott in Greenwood in 1965, it demanded the right of black employees to be promoted to better jobs. In the Natchez boycott, NAACP activist Charles Evers stressed the economic component of the protest, telling participants, "Don't give your money to people who hate you. Don't shop in stores that won't hire Negroes at thirty dollars a week."[10]

Along with more employment and better wages, protesters demanded more respectful treatment for shoppers. Most of the boycotters told store employees to address African American customers as Mr., Mrs., and Miss. Myrlie Evers detailed several ways white clerks in Jackson showed disrespect to African American customers. They waited on white customers before serving black customers. They tried to sell what Evers called "cheap and flashy clothes, the kind they clearly felt was fit for Negroes." The notion that African Americans really wanted to buy outlandish things continued the old stereotype that African Americans were in their hearts the ultimate consumers who wanted to buy anything gaudy and colorful. Evers always gave her name as Mrs. Medgar Evers, but clerks insisted that she give her first name. She made a habit of leaving merchandise on the counter when a clerk asked, "Myrlie, . . . do you want to pay cash today?" Charles Evers recalled that courtesy titles might have been "the hardest demand for the bigots to swallow." Finally, Myrlie Evers recalled that clerks often refused to allow African Americans to try on clothes. She described an employee in one Capitol Street store who would not let African Americans try on hats without lining the inside with paper because, the clerk said, "you people always have such greasy hair you ruin the hats." Other merchants refused to allow blacks to try on clothing in changing rooms, as Endesha Ida Mae Holland remembered, "lest we steal them."[11]

When boycotters first made their demands, courtesy titles and the hiring of black clerks seemed minor points compared with other demands. However, as the boycotts continued and individual store owners started to feel economic pressure, some owners chose to attract African American customers by addressing those demands. Store owners could not make many of the other changes on their own even if they wanted, but boycotters had a number of individual successes on the issues of what went on inside the stores. National chain stores often made the first efforts to hire black clerks and make policies about courtesy titles. When they changed their policies, protestors shifted from general boy-cotts to what they called selective buying. Chain stores were important in part because northern civil rights protestors could boycott chains like Woolworth's and Kress to force them to change southern store practices.[12] In Natchez, for example, twenty-three stores responded to a long boycott by agreeing to hire more black employees and to have employees "treat all customers fairly cour-teously and respectfully and not to address any persons by any term which may be offensive."[13] But opponents of the boycott and its purposes hurried to claim that traditional Mississippi stores had not changed their practices. Seventeen of the twenty-three stores, according to Rowland Scott, head of a new group called the Association for the Preservation of the White Race, were chain stores "which have no local connections or affiliations."[14] The connections black Mississip-pians had started making between chain stores in Chicago and the possibility of freedom made even more sense as those stores modified their practices to accommodate the demands of protestors.

With their demands for more access to the stores, more respect inside them, and more African American employees working for them, protestors wanted full access to two central aspects of consumer culture. They saw shopping as a potentially democratic experience and hoped to find pleasure and dignity in the experience. Even if they did not emphasize the idea, they were defining the right to shop as a basic element in American freedom. Charles Evers, who said that he hated to go into stores in his youth because they were dominated by white men who wanted him to dance for their amusement, took some satisfac-tion in 1971 from the fact that he owned stores himself. "But," he wrote, "I've never made anybody dance in them."[15]

Consumer boycotts by African Americans took white merchants and town political leaders by surprise. Since emancipation, many white landlords and employers had claimed that black Mississippians spent money foolishly and recklessly. Believing African Americans to be governed mostly by their ap-petites, they were unprepared for protestors' displays of self-control.[16]

White business leaders first responded to the boycotts by blaming them on outside agitators. They usually tried to deny publicity to the protestors, believ-ing or at least hoping they would simply tire and go away. Issues of publicity had become extraordinarily important by the mid-1960s. When angry whites poured ketchup and mustard on the heads of Anne Moody and other students protesting at the Jackson Woolworth's in 1963, they were dramatizing their rejection of ideas that all people deserved dignity in stores.[17] But they also inspired considerable negative publicity of the sort that later counterprotestors hoped to avoid. Because many of the boycotts also involved picketing the stores, local politicians and newspaper editors and leaders of Citizens' Councils and

Ku Klux Klans urged whites to stay away and avoid the confrontations that might bring protestors media attention and national sympathy. On the second day of the boycott in Grenada in 1966, police urged whites to stay away from stores while protestors were picketing. Two weeks later, the mayor and aldermen proposed what they called the "starve-out strategy" to avoid giving boycotters any attention.[18]

The problem with avoiding boycotted stores became clear as the protests continued. If black potential customers were boycotting the stores and many white potential customers stayed away from areas where protestors were picketing, no one was going into the stores to buy anything. A group of merchants in Grenada ran an open newspaper letter six weeks after the boycott began. They acknowledged that most African Americans were shopping outside the town, but they worried especially "that there are far too many patriotic citizens, who ARE NOT in sympathy with this boycott, also doing their shopping outside of Grenada for one reason or another." Merchants assured potential customers that downtown was perfectly safe, they said that most protestors were "Negro children, some of whom have just shed their diapers," and they begged people to come back and shop. Those who stayed away, they argued, were "falling right into the hands of these agitators." Finally, in the tradition of American merchants, they reminded readers, "We still offer a wide selection of merchandise, courteous service, and BARGAINS for our customers."[19]

The more aggressive way to fight boycotts was to make them illegal. Merchants secured court injunctions against several boycotts by describing them as restraints on trade. As early as 1961, seven protesters in Clarksdale, including state NAACP president Aaron Henry, were arrested for "conspiring to commit acts injurious to public trade." They had organized a boycott of downtown merchants after the school board refused to allow marching bands from African American schools to appear in the Christmas parade.[20] Four years later, a chancery court judge in Natchez issued an injunction against protestors for conducting an illegal boycott and, ironically, for parading without a permit. In four days, police arrested about 500 people, sending more than 200 of them to the state prison in Parchman.[21] In the summer of 1968, a Greenwood judge issued an injunction against a long boycott, agreeing with merchants who claimed that the protestors "conspired to cause ruin 'of Greenwood businesses and others' following the assassination of the Rev. Dr. Martin Luther King in April."[22] Opponents of the boycotts repeatedly argued, in a twist on the old antipathy toward outside agitators, that boycott leaders were harassing African Americans who wanted to keep spending in white-owned stores. The solution, they argued, was to remove the boycott leaders so the blacks who wanted could come back and shop. Merchants accused protestors of intimidating potential customers and especially cited statements by Charles Evers that if protestors saw a black man buying in boycotted stores, they should "go ahead and whip him" or "break their damn necks!"[23] U.S. senator James Eastland proposed a federal law in 1966 that would make boycotting and intimidating potential shoppers federal offenses.[24] Two years later, the state legislature passed a law that prohibited two kinds of boycotts: those that tried to put pressure on public officials and those that protested grievances beyond the control of the merchants involved.[25]

The state law allowed a gigantic 1969 lawsuit against protestors who had been boycotting Port Gibson stores since 1966. Eighteen businesspeople with interests ranging from pharmacies and grocery and variety stores to laundries, auto parts stores, and auto dealers sued the NAACP, along with a group called the Mississippi Action for Progress, and 151 individuals for $3.5 million they claimed to have lost. The Mississippi Supreme Court ruled that the protestors owed $1.25 million, a decision the U.S. Supreme Court overturned in 1982. Protestors boycotting stores in Vicksburg in 1972 and Lexington in 1978 faced arrest under the same law. Finally, in 1986, the U.S. Supreme Court ruled the law unconstitutional.[26]

By putting the law on the side of the merchants, powerful white Mississippians were claiming that buying and selling were basic American rights. In condemning the methods of the boycott leaders, the editor of the *Grenada Daily Sentinel-Star* argued in 1966, "A wage earner, and he alone, has the right to say where and for what he spends his money."[27]

The idea that spending one's money was a crucial part of the definition of freedom was central to the other strategy white Mississippians used to combat the boycotts. In December 1965, more than three months after a coalition of protest groups had begun a very successful boycott in Natchez, the Citizens' Council of Louisiana came together with the local Ku Klux Klan and the Americans for the Preservation of the White Race to organize what they called Buy In Natchez Day. Soon they were referring to this method of counterprotest as a Buy-In. The Americans for the Preservation of the White Race "urged all white citizens of the surrounding area to come to Natchez on December 11 and, by their presence on the streets, sidewalks and in the stores of Natchez, give wholehearted support to concentrated efforts to restore the economy of the city to its natural balance and break the back of the boycott."[28] The group's leader, Rowland Scott, urged all whites to do their Christmas shopping on a Saturday in the city, with the goal of creating a " 'White Christmas' in Natchez."[29]

The shoppers came. They came not merely from Adams County, but they drove from as far away as New Orleans and Jackson, signed in at a cafeteria, put on name tags, and shopped all day in an atmosphere of a big party for white people. The groups organized similar buy-ins in January and February and expanded the events to include Fayette, a neighboring Mississippi town whose merchants were feeling the effects of a civil rights boycott.[30]

The events turned shopping into a weapon for white supremacy and celebrated the indulgent, carnival side of consumer culture. Rowland Scott planned the first event as "a gala, holiday occasion."[31] The large crowd and mixture of local residents and guests added to the carnival side of the events, and by February of 1966, buy-ins also included a parade of shoppers through downtown Fayette. Such events celebrated shopping and spending in an atmosphere of giddy excitement. In Fayette, robed Klansmen "posed for network cameramen as they loaded sacks of groceries into car trunks and pickup trucks." The APWR called the event Operation Locust because they said visitors descended on Fayette "like a plague of locusts to buy everything but the real estate." The strategy was long-lived. In 1978 members of the Ku Klux Klan in Tupelo responded to a boycott by African Americans protesting police brutality with a counterdemonstration to support white merchants. After protestors in 1980 boycotted a Fayette store whose owner had fired its black employees, "200 Fayette residents banded together for a group shopping trip to the store."[32]

White Mississippians had long resisted the idea that shopping and spending were significant parts of the definition of freedom. To them, freedom had meant a variety of things—freedom from government control, freedom for men to work for themselves, freedom gained by farming one's own land, freedom from racial egalitarianism. But by turning a movement for white supremacy into a celebration of shopping and by asking whites to do their duty to buy as many goods as possible, they were emphasizing the romantic side of spending as a form of excitement. Turning counterprotest into a shopping spree thus suggested that white Mississippians were coming more than ever to define shopping as part of freedom. But the other elements of consumer culture—the importance of choice, abundance, and excitement—appeared in new guises as part of the struggle for white supremacy.

In their boycotts the African American protestors were making their own statement about their place in the consumer society. Instead of emphasizing the romantic and carnival sides, their protests upheld the democratic side of consumption that stressed that all people deserve equal respect in the experience of shopping. They demanded full access to the stores and rejected notions of whites' control over the streets. As Emilye Crosby argues, the boycotts challenged both "white supremacy and the accompanying sense of entitlement and private ownership of nominally public spaces."[33] The boycotts and whites' responses to them thus represented an argument over the meanings of consumer culture.

In the 1970s and 1980s, protestors continued to use economic boycotts to address issues of local schools, police, and city hiring policies. At least fifteen times, African Americans used boycotts, partly through the actions of a new group called the United League, which emerged in 1974 during boycotts in Holly Springs and Byhalia. Those boycotts no longer addressed issues of courtesy titles and access to stores, and only a few protested the absence of black store employees. Some of those battles have been won, with the fall of legal segregation and the gradual if uneven decline of overt racism. Still, the boycotts show the power African Americans continue to have when they withhold their spending money.[34]

The boycotts were not the only approach African American protestors took toward consumer issues. Several groups tried cooperative farms that stressed the goals of shared work and shared resources rather than the private goals of enjoying goods and shopping without indignity. For example, the Freedom Farms, led by Fannie Lou Hamer, tried to help poor men and women in the Delta escape debt and set up small farms. The organization set up pig banks and seed banks to facilitate small farming according to an ideal of communal rural subsistence.[35] Some protest organizations set up cooperatives to allow African Americans to control the goods and marketing of their stores and especially to avoid the debts agricultural workers had long faced.[36]

The goals of courtesy titles and equal access to jobs seem to have had more staying power than the goals of cooperative farming and marketing. Not many African Americans today are engaged in farming, and few look to farm cooperatives as solutions to debt and dependence. The continuing use of the boycott as a method of protest shows that African Americans in Mississippi have defined the ability to spend both as part of their influence and as part of the meaning of freedom.

A "Fine New Day"?

Writers do not seem to tire of asking whether a South still exists. Perhaps the time has come that we should. The question tends to construe a few key elements in a regional past as the essence of the South and then judges whether industrialization or agricultural mechanization or the Sun Belt economy or migration or the civil rights movement or two-party politics or something else has challenged, eroded, or overcome those essential elements.[1] Consumer goods have a role in most of those discussions. Some scholars wonder if the Agrarians would have watched television, if William Faulkner would have written as he did in an air-conditioned home, if folk cultures can stand the intrusion of fast-food restaurants and shopping malls, and if commercialization may have destroyed generations of musical creativity. It is common to end a book in southern history with consumer culture helping to bring an end to something distinctive. Perhaps curiously, scholars who argue the opposite point often use consumer goods and mass entertainment to argue that southern culture has influenced national and international culture instead of succumbing to it. Kentucky Fried Chicken, Coca-Cola, and rock music show the ability of southern inventions to keep something southern alive by selling it. In either case, the question tends to be a yes or no judgment that something called southern culture is either living or dying.

This volume has tried to reach inside some aspects of southern culture and see how they worked. What meanings have goods, stores, shopping, and credit had for different Mississippians? How has shopping served as either temptation or liberation, and how has credit worked for and against different groups? How have stores changed to cater to different shoppers, and what have different people thought about them? How did the nature of shopping and goods re-affirm existing power relations, and how did they allow challenges to them? Within these questions, no single element stands out so prominently that its decline would prove that Mississippi has lost some essential characteristic that once defined the South but does no more.

In antebellum Mississippi, goods reaffirmed who had power and who did not. But with land, credit, the law, and the whip, wealthy men in Mississippi did not really need such symbolic affirmation. So along with the desire to appear well-settled and comfortable leaders of society, they also wanted connection to cosmopolitan centers unavailable to other Mississippians, and they wanted to see themselves as kindly, paternalistic figures over slaves and women. They felt the American Dream of abundance was reserved for them, and they worried little about notions of democracy that people might want to express through goods or shopping. With their urban connections, they enjoyed the excitement of shopping far more than the rest of Mississippi society, and they looked forward to new goods they or their cotton factors would buy for them. But the role of consumer did not rest easily in their minds. Within their notions of paternalism was a sense that buying things for pleasure was a sign of weak-ness, so wealthy men chose not to identify themselves as consumers but often claimed that white women and slaves were the ones who really wanted to spend money for pleasure. The slaves, seizing on their rare opportunities to spend that money in ways that broke free from the roles owners expected of them, defined themselves as something other than agricultural workers.

Men, women, and children of small farming families stood most strikingly and intentionally outside most aspects of the American dreams of a consumer culture. Both white farmers throughout the 1800s and former slaves in the postbellum period so feared debt and so valued independence that they made painful efforts to limit their purchases. The efforts of store owners to excite shoppers with new goods, to train them in the modern ways of paying cash, and to encourage more women to shop usually fell on the deaf ears of people who saw debt as a form of enslavement or reenslavement. White farming men tended to view general stores as much as sites for all-male recreation as places for buying things. Farm women rarely went into the stores and hoped instead to sew clothing without spending much money on it. In the postbellum period, black men and women had a marginal presence in such stores, making most of their purchases at plantation stores with limited inventories and powerful, mysterious account ledgers. For most small farmers, the dreams of abundance and choice posed too much of a gamble, and the dream of novelty was not a social ideal but a rare chance associated with occasional moments of plenty. Any dreams of expressing democracy through shopping for goods and owning them lay far into the future.

Economic changes in the late nineteenth and early twentieth centuries encouraged consuming habits and opportunities, but only in a halting, uneven way. White farmers who lost their land, far from leaving for factory jobs, often shifted to sharecropping, which locked them almost as fully as blacks into a cashless form of poverty they only occasionally escaped. The state's first major form of industry, logging, also placed severe limits on the ability to spend money. The passage of segregation laws, the end of a political role for blacks, and the dramatic rise in lynching around the turn of the century all made any notions of democracy of appearances impossible. In fact, appearances probably became *more* important as a way of asserting who had freedom and power and who did not.

Only in the 1920s and 1930s did consumer goods become sources of significant cultural fascination, either as threats, liberation, or problems. The increase in cash-paying jobs and the proliferation of stores—department stores, variety stores, and automobile dealerships—that dealt in either cash or installment credit gave new life to shopping in the state and brought national fashions into rural areas. Traditional rural identities—planter, farmer, would-be farmer, member of farm household—all faced serious challenges, and Mississippians of many backgrounds wondered if opportunities as consumers might offer new identities that were more meaningful and enjoyable. If people became more comfortable about their goods, more excited about shopping, and less worried about debt, many wondered if they might be giving up valuable parts of their pasts. These questions appeared in sources as diverse as the home economics reports of Dorothy Dickins, the novels of William Faulkner and Eudora Welty, the autobiographies of Richard Wright and Will Percy, and the songs of countless blues musicians.

Of those voices, it was the blues musicians who most wholeheartedly embraced the dreams associated with new goods and the pursuit of them. With the decline in agricultural jobs, the rapid decline in sharecropping, and the virtual end of the chance to own land, the traditional constraints on spending money and traditional identities rooted in rural *families* gave way to new identities of urbanizing *individuals*. Blues performers sang about the opportunities available when mobile people could visit city stores with city money and perhaps be able to impress country folk with new abilities and new goods. Far different from the traditional realities of being black in Mississippi, these opportunities promised freedom of choice, the freedom to remake themselves as nonfarming people, and the democracy of goods and shopping in chain stores outside the old agricultural power system. Abundance was still far from a reality, but the blues generation showed some hopefulness about leaving behind the look, limits, and fears of farm life.

Many of the greatest changes took place in the period after World War II. The number of farmers and agricultural laborers declined dramatically, and goods became important in new ways. Some civil rights protestors used boycotts to argue that African Americans had more important things to do than spend money at stores whose owners and employees treated them with disrespect. When many of the protestors demanded better treatment for shoppers in the stores and more and better jobs for African American employees, they were seeking inclusion in the democratic side of consumer culture. At the same time, white counterprotestors argued that boycotts were illegal if they obstructed the basic American freedom of buying and selling. Thus, both sides saw consumer spending as keys to their definitions of freedom. Through it all, the image of the black man as a self-indulgent free spender was a favorite image for white Mississippians who claimed that African Americans were immature and irresponsible.

What of contemporary Mississippi? Historians have a hard time assessing the very recent past. It has been easy for many past scholars to see the coming of consumer culture as the *end* of something important: community, ethnic identity, meaningful labor, independent farming, political commitment, radical potential, artistic creativity, and more. Consumer culture often emerges in scholarship as what we are, compared to what we used to be or what we could have been had we made other choices. Perhaps the best the historian can do is to offer a few images that show that questions about the meanings of consumer goods continue.

The shopping landscape of the state has changed dramatically. The isolated general store is something of a relic. Already by 1964, Thomas Clark, Mississippi native and leading historian of the general store, said the institutions hung on primarily as vestiges of an earlier Mississippi; most were "ancient" stores that "hold on in spite of chain-store competition."[2] By the mid-1960s, Mississippi had over 800 car dealers, over 300 women's ready-to-wear clothing stores, over 150 radio, television, and appliance stores, and over 300 variety stores.[3] In cities and many towns, shopping for new goods has moved away from town centers to large buildings on highways, usually at the edges of town. The outskirts of Jackson, Tupelo, Natchez, Meridian, and Greenville and even smaller towns like Oxford, Hattiesburg, Columbus, and West Point combine shopping centers, large chain department and specialty stores, and fast-food restaurants with automobile dealerships and large gas stations. As in most of America, people drive to shop.[4]

One of the most dramatic recent changes has been the power of Wal-Marts in Mississippi, as in much of the country, to redefine how and where people shop. By the 1990s, there were sixty of the Arkansas-based establishments in the state, including the sprawling "supercenters,"[5] and they almost always became the largest stores in their areas. Frequently locating in areas with relatively small stores as competition, Wal-Marts have gained immediate dominance with the variety and low prices of their goods. Wal-Marts are pretentious only in their lack of pretension, offering what they claim are American-made goods and displaying their goods in ways that emphasize utility and low price more than any connection to cosmopolitan culture. With wide aisles, bright white light, and lack of any obvious decoration, the huge stores emphasize the goods themselves rather than any intrigue in their display. As if to emphasize their difference from other stores, and the irrelevance of other stores, Wal-Marts are almost always located at the edges of communities, far from the town square.[6]

It is common to criticize Wal-Mart for threatening both local distinctiveness and local businesses. But for Mississippians who never felt welcome in down-town shopping districts, such stores offer considerable appeal. Recent chain stores like Wal-Mart never asked customers to go to the back door; nor have the employees who greet each customer ever used condescending terms in address-ing particular customers. Such stores, crucial in the contemporary experience of shopping, are friendly in not being unfriendly and democratic in offering everyone the same not particularly personal experience. If general stores in the nineteenth century and plantation stores well into the twentieth century rein-forced status differences simply through people's places in the process of shop-ping, stores such as Wal-Mart emphasize that all customers have the same experiences. As a young journalist observed in a study of race relations in Neshoba County in 1989, "While black or white is still an important label, everyone shops at Wal-Mart."[7]

Visible images of mass culture symbolized the changes in the Mississippi to Endesha Ida Mae Holland when she returned to the hometown she had left in sadness and anger in 1965. Far fewer African Americans worked in the fields, far more African Americans voted and held political office. And there was Wal-Mart. "Nearing Greenwood, I saw a Wal-Mart store and roadside video rentals along the highway where, a generation ago, I had turned tricks among the farmers." She concluded to a friend, "It's a fine new day."[8] Many Mississippi writers have written poignant accounts of coming home. Holland is the first to depict Wal-Mart as a sign of positive change. She does not discuss what the store represents, but it seems to offer a negation of the sides of Mississippi life she hated—violence, racism, poverty, and suspicion.

With the movement of shopping areas outside the traditional areas, the consumer boycotts that in effect desegregated downtown shopping areas proved to be only a partial victory. Many newer stores in downtown areas are small institutions that cater almost exclusively to African American consumers, some of them offering clothing with bright and proudly West African colors and stripes, others with clothes designed for young adults and teenagers who identify with basketball players and rap musicians. Here the freedom that migrant Mississippi blacks once found in urban chain stores has come to Mississippi. The names of many trumpet their ties to urban culture—New York Fashion, New York Hi-Style, Hollywood Output.[9]

The larger story, however, is that rural depopulation has decimated commercial life in the downtown areas of countless towns, as many potential shoppers have moved away and those who remain drive to larger stores like Wal-Mart or urban shopping malls. A group called the Mississippi Downtown Development Association sponsored lectures by an economist on ways small-town merchants could survive the coming of Wal-Marts,[10] but the trend is clearly toward the decline of the downtown areas of smaller towns. Many downtowns offer few stores except second-hand stores, bargain stores, perhaps a video store, and some boarded-up buildings. In the tiny Delta town of Alligator, Aaron Kline has run a general store since the 1930s, but he keeps it open out of habit rather than sales. "I don't do much business, certainly not enough to justify keeping the store open," he said in 1994. In Alligator, entire days go by without a customer.[11]

As dramatic as the changes in downtown areas, rural depopulation has brought an end to the importance of crossroads general stores and plantation stores. Many sit silent, victims of the automobiles that allow people to drive to larger stores and the agricultural changes that made plantation labor unnecessary. Some remain as gas stations that sell milk, bread, and beer, and a few retain their importance as gathering points. But even in a state that continues to have a large rural population, shopping seems to grow less rural all the time.

Among the signs of the increasing importance of consumer goods in Mississippi life are those promising that goods are available to everyone.

Installment buying has become commonplace, as store owners and creditors have finally succeeded in ridding Mississippians of their old habits of spending money according to agricultural rhythms. Already by 1959, farm-owning families—a declining breed—were buying hundreds of dollars of goods and paying on them every month. Among farm-owning families Dorothy Dickins studied that year, 63 percent of the whites and 71 percent of the blacks were buying goods on installment credit. To the question "Do you want something in the next ten years you do not have?" less than 5 percent answered no.[12]

Contemporary newspapers promise installment credit as something close to a natural right. An automobile dealership in Sardis calls itself the "Home of Second Chance Credit" and offers a plan by which first-time buyers can receive credit by showing a driver's license, pay stub, and telephone bill. Another in Neshoba County reassures potential buyers, "Credit Problems? No Problem!"[13] Stores offer furniture and televisions and video cassette recorders for a few dollars a week. One north Mississippi lending agency boasts of its 99 percent approval rate.[14] Such credit celebrates both the notion of the democracy of goods and of the joys of shopping; if everyone can have credit, everyone can shop, and everyone can enjoy the things that promise new kinds of pleasure.

Contemporary credit relations, with few exceptions, do not follow the form that tried to ensure workers for large employers. Today's poor people have unstable job prospects but plenty of chances for credit with high interest rates. They do not change residences every year or two looking for a better place to live and work as farm laborers, and agricultural rhythms do not regulate their lives any more than the old limit book and their fear of it. Nor do they have much reason to hope that if they can only limit their expenses, they might some day become landowners. Instead, poor people today receive occasional pay from low-paying jobs, or they receive small checks from government agencies.[15] While individual poor people have accomplished extraordinary things for themselves and their families by stringent thrift, it seems fair to conclude that most of the old reasons not to spend money have passed.

But for all of the ways one can see Mississippians driving to consumer institutions and shopping in chain stores, one can see numerous changes that have moved away from key elements of consumer culture. In many downtowns of depopulated areas, the stores that remain sell used goods. The rise of stores that sell antiques and secondhand goods has been a phenomenon of the twentieth century. In the 1880s the R. G. Dun Company listed no secondhand or antique stores in the state, and by 1929 Mississippi had 26, 10 of which sold old tires and car parts. The Depression enhanced the role of such stores, as their number climbed to 43 by 1933, just as many stores selling new goods went out of business.[16] But the number of secondhand and antique stores jumped from a total of 80 in 1948, to 121 in 1954, to 180 in 1967, to a startling 461 by 1977. Since then, the number of used-merchandise stores has decreased, like most kinds of stores in Mississippi, and in the 1990s, the state had well over 300 such establishments.[17]

Such stores depend on two significant developments. A growing number of cash-paying poor people want to buy goods as cheaply as possible outside the old institutions that had long confirmed their powerlessness. People who buy used goods can acquire clothing and furniture of reasonably high quality without paying high prices and without going deeper into debt. Second, the notion of Mississippi as an example of the past still alive within modern America has suited well those who want to buy and sell old things. Consumers who do not wish to tie their identities to chain stores and shopping malls find that the goods, the stores, and the process of shopping for antiques or secondhand items allows them options they find appealing.

To people drawn to the idea of Mississippi as an embodiment of the past, antique stores have become particularly attractive. As late as 1967, only about two dozen businesses in the state identified themselves as antique stores, but that number has increased dramatically.[18] By the early 1980s, both Jackson and Bay St. Louis had antique malls with over 20 stores each.[19] By the 1990s, Natchez had developed a 15-store downtown antique district, at least 11 antique stores dotted the Mississippi Delta, and one small town after another has sought to make itself a successful antique location. In 1995, 271 stores in the state sold antiques.[20]

Most interesting is the range of meanings antique sellers and buyers associate with the material past. In a three-block area in Natchez, one can shop at stores called Country Bumpkin, the Antiquarian, and Elegante.[21] That range of meanings, from friendly and rustic, to old and rare, to sophisticated, cosmopolitan, and European illustrates the visions of the past antique stores offer their customers. Some stores specialize in what they call primitive goods, catering to people troubled by the coldly standardized nature of consumer culture and attracted to the creative work of untrained rural people. Such stores offer items some call folk art—handmade, idiosyncratic things that seem to embody a past that was more creative than people today tend to be. Other stores specialize in old agricultural implements or obsolete kitchen implements that nonfarming people hang on their walls or display in their yards. A few towns seem to have no successful businesses except shops that sell the tools farm workers no longer use. Other establishments, like antique stores throughout the United States, offer goods with what they call the country look—quaint and vaguely agrarian, decorated with pastel ducks and rabbits and bonnets and magnolia blooms and cotton blossoms. Lacking associations with a specific historic period, they suggest that rural life once had a degree of comfort and security unavailable in towns and cities. Perhaps most intriguing are stores that specialize in English and French goods from the eighteenth and nineteenth centuries. The antique dealer north of Indianola who advertises "accessories personally selected in England," the dealers in Jackson who call themselves "direct importers of fine English furniture," and the Gulfport shop "specializing in choice English pieces, 1775–1825"—all promise a connection to European elite culture many buyers associate with an old upper class. The message that store owners go to England to choose the best goods themselves is one that Mississippi store owners had not conveyed to their customers since the antebellum period.[22]

Antique stores and secondhand stores appeal to customers in part because they are so different from department stores and other large institutions. Stores that sell used goods tend to be located in buildings that look, feel, and even smell different from the large institutions that sell new goods. Antique stores and secondhand stores are often in old wooden buildings lacking the powerful lights and bright colors that decorate many newer stores. If customers are unhappy with the impersonal nature of large stores, they can appreciate the small size of antique and secondhand stores. While the average department store in Mississippi employs 164 people, the average used-merchandise store has 3 employees.[23]

Unlike most antique stores, secondhand stores do not attempt to link buyers with specific pasts. They offer scattered collections of clothing, dishes, furniture, books, and household decorations. Such stores generally cater to people who cannot afford many new consumer goods. They rarely advertise in newspapers, and when they do, they promise little of the romance and excitement celebrated by most stores that sell new goods or the mystique that antique stores offer. For example, a store in the poor Delta town of Crenshaw advertised only that "We have used furniture, glassware, odds & ends, etc."[24] Such language is reminiscent of the advertisements of the nineteenth-century general stores that stated simply that they were selling inexpensive goods.

Flea markets provide the other setting for buying and selling used goods. Beginning in 1971, hundreds of people started taking their old goods to the Jackson fairgrounds for a huge flea market. The city of Vicksburg began offering space for a similar event in the mid-1970s, and by 1983, small towns like Ripley in Tippah County had begun to draw tremendous crowds to buy and sell old, generally inexpensive goods. Ripley's First Monday Flea Market was attracting 40,000 people on sunny days at its monthly events, about 10,000 more than went to the Canton Flea Market that started a few years later. By 1995, forty-six businesses in Mississippi called themselves flea markets, an increase of eleven in just six years.[25]

The attractions of flea markets combine the fascination of old goods with the good chance of finding a bargain, sometimes in a carnival atmosphere that cuts across traditional social lines. Buyers can haggle over prices and trade their goods for other people's items, and poor people's goods sometimes turn out to be worth more than they expected. The whole experience celebrates the fascinations of shopping and the potential mysteries of goods, but it does so in ways that emphasize experiences other than the goods themselves. Some flea markets, such as a large annual event in Canton, combine sales of used goods with the display and sale of handmade goods that often combine the rustic and country looks.[26]

Flea markets sometimes attract the angry attention of store owners who worry they are losing some of their business. The unofficial, untaxed nature of much of the selling has been a target for numerous opponents of such events. Almost 100 merchants in Ripley successfully petitioned the county government in 1983 to charge vendors at the First Monday Flea Market a monthly fee to make up for a loss of tax income.[27] Other store owners apparently find the aesthetics of flea markets troubling. In 1996 the chamber of commerce in Sardis called small flea markets near the railroad tracks an "eyesore" and asked the city government to regulate the times and place of such events. Representing store owners, the mayor of Sardis complained, "We must have a lot of professional spring cleaners."[28]

Unless such chambers of commerce have their way, such events will continue to offer poor people a significant form of freedom. Their decisions help set prices, they decide whether to buy used or new goods, and they determine which goods are desirable outside a national system of fashion that always tries to tell them which goods are obsolete. Along with spending money, they can also earn it. Setting up a table at a flea market or along the road to sell goods one makes or finds at home is a low-cost, low-risk way for underemployed people to make a little cash.

Finally, yard sales and garage sales offer some of the same attractions as flea markets and secondhand stores. Many shoppers head to garage sales and yard sales every weekend in hopes of finding extraordinary bargains. Few can match the prices of a Potts Camp yard sale in 1997 whose organizers promised, "Everything Free,"[29] but such events offer the certainty of inexpensive goods. People have been selling their unwanted goods for generations, but they started advertising yard and garage sales only in the 1970s. Since then, newspapers in even the smallest towns advertise several yard sales each weekend, especially in warm weather. One of the most appealing sides of yard sales is that so many of them support churches, schools, libraries, and charities, so shoppers can make purchases that ultimately support entities other than a local merchant or a large corporation.

Within the dramatic changes associated with rural depopulation, one can see Mississippians adapting rather than giving up certain themes from their pasts. In buying used goods, some continue to live on narrow economic margins, while others use material goods to evoke association with certain pasts. In shopping at large chain stores, some Mississippians are continuing the attraction earlier generations developed in northern cities for shopping in stores that refused to discriminate against anyone and offered new definitions of freedom. These are not what scholars typically see as points of continuity in southern history, but they illustrate ways recent developments in consumer culture can draw on past experiences and not simply reject all pasts.

It is equally true that the language of consumer culture can include elements of inequality. Perhaps the most significant continuity in contemporary meanings of consumer behavior lies in ideas many Mississippians express about welfare payments. Mississippi was the last state to begin its own welfare system, and even then it identified orphans, the blind, and the very old as the only worthy recipients.[30] Many planters raised their voices against New Deal welfare programs in the 1930s and continued to view welfare payments as a challenge to their labor force at least through the 1960s.[31]

A common complaint about welfare recipients is that they waste their money on luxuries and therefore take money away from those who work hard and pay taxes. Angry letters to editors frequently condemn government payments to people who seem excessively comfortable. In 1980 a self-proclaimed Concerned Citizen wrote, "Follow some of the people who buy big baskets of groceries, and pay for them with food stamps, home and you will find some of them living in $50,000 homes, driving the finest cars and dressing in the highest fashion."[32] Sometimes the criticism is simply that welfare payments encourage laziness. In 1995, for example, Republican governor Kirk Fordice said welfare reform should begin by teaching welfare recipients how to use an alarm clock.[33] But much of the criticism asserts that welfare allows people to spend money irresponsibly, whether on alcohol, drugs, or automobiles. According to a 1994 newspaper story, law enforcement officials in the state agreed that "drugs and food stamps go together like rats and cheese."[34] The most recurring image in the conservative imagination is the Welfare Cadillac. In 1980 state welfare officials placed a limit on the amount of total wealth welfare recipients could have. According to a Jackson newspaper, "a $12,000 Lincoln would eliminate anyone seeking stamps, according to welfare people. This clause was thrown into the regulations after complaints about food stamp recipients driving away with their free groceries in Cadillacs."[35]

There is no doubt that some people abuse government welfare programs, just as people abuse other government programs. But the right-wing critique suggesting that welfare recipients waste their money on luxury goods is either denying the reality of poverty or blaming poor people for their own economic problems. Those who deny it choose to believe there are few people who are actually poor. Those who blame the poor for their own poverty assume that welfare recipients tend to be self-indulgent and ultimately suffer when the government feeds their indulgence with welfare money.[36] Such claims follow in the tradition of postbellum planters who believed former slaves wasted their money as soon as they had any. In both cases, those who see the Welfare Cadillac as a significant reality minimize and oversimplify serious and complicated problems.

If the history of goods and shopping in Mississippi is the story of conversations, it should be clear that people do not always converse very clearly. One continuing story within the broad history of Mississippi consumer behavior is that different groups of white Mississippians have created images of African Americans as wasteful and indulgent consumers. Sometimes those images have been kindly and comic in a condescending way—slaves shouting "Christmas gift" or former slaves wearing formal dress in political office. More recently, the images have been more sinister, involving drugs and big cars. In most cases, the suggestion is that African Americans do not know how to spend money responsibly. And in all cases, the image-makers reveal more about themselves than about the people they are discussing.

Many of us may wish for a world in which consumer goods and those who sell them have less power in our lives. We may wish for a world where possessions mean less and human relationships, interest in work, or individual creativity mean more. But to try to understand other people's dreams rather than simply to dream our own, it is essential to see the ways goods and shopping have carried meanings some people can find subversive and liberating. African Americans in Mississippi can call on a tradition of disciplined nonspending in the postbellum struggle for land ownership and in the more recent consumer boycotts. They can also find legacies of asserting themselves through consumer spending under slavery, or in reshaping themselves as urbanizing people in the periods of migration, or in demanding dignity in consumer institutions during the civil rights movement. White Mississippians as different as Eudora Welty and Gladys Smith Presley's son have seen goods and shopping as ways people can reject the harshest sides of their past. As scholars, we can write all we want about commodity fetishism or about the hegemony of the marketplace, but until we try to understand the range of meanings goods and shopping have carried, we will continue to miss important stories in the search for American dreams.

NOTES

Abbreviations Used in the Notes

Duke   William Perkins Library, Duke University, Durham, N.C.
LSU   Special Collections, Louisiana State University Library, Baton Rouge
MDAH   Mississippi Department of Archives and History, Jackson
MHC   Oral History Collection, Mary Holmes College Library, West Point, Miss.
MStU   Mississippi State University, Starkville
SHC   Southern Historical Collection, University of North Carolina, Chapel Hill
TSLA   Tennessee State Library and Archive, Nashville
UArk   Special Collections, University of Arkansas Libraries, Fayetteville
UK   Special Collections, Mercantile Collection, University of Kentucky Library,
          Lexington
UMem   Mississippi Valley Collection, University of Memphis Libraries, Memphis, Tenn.
UMS   Special Collections, University of Mississippi Library, Oxford

Introduction

1 Potter, *People of Plenty*; Lynd and Lynd, *Middletown*; Veysey, "A Postmorten on Daniel Bell's Postindustrialism."

2 Among the works discussing a democracy of experience and ideology in consumer society are Cohen, *Making a New Deal*; McKendrick, Brewer, and Plumb, *The Birth of a Consumer Society*; Blumin, *The Emergence of the Middle Class*; Heinze, *Adapting to Abundance*; Horowitz, *The Morality of Spending*; Veblen, *The Theory of the Leisure Class*.

3 Among the works discussing the concept of the freedom of choice that different groups found in shopping are Leach, *Land of Desire*; Leach, "Transformations in a Culture of Consumption"; Barth, *City People*; Edsforth, *Class Conflict and Cultural Consensus*; Abelson, *When Ladies Go A-Thieving*; Banner, *American Beauty*; Loeb, *Consuming Angels*.

4 Among scholars addressing the issue of romantic potential in waiting for the next shopping and spending experience are Campbell, *The Romantic Ethic*; Lears, *Fables of Abundance*; Wolfenstein, "The Emergence of Fun Morality"; Schama, *The Embarrassment of Riches*. Major collections of essays that address all four of these American dreams as well as other aspects of consumer spending and goods are Fox and Lears, eds., *The Culture of Consumption*; Bronner, ed., *Consuming Visions*.

5 Among the works stressing the notion of consumer behavior as communication are Douglas and Isherwood, *The World of Goods*; McCracken, *Culture and Consumption*.

6 Jordan, *White over Black*.

Chapter One

1 *Southern Business Directory*, 140, 146–52.

2 *Southern Business Directory*, 156, 146, 141; quote from 141. On supply boats, see Owens, *Steamboats and the Cotton Economy*.

3 R. G. Dun and Company, *Mercantile Agency Reference Book*, 1883.

4 *Yazoo Democrat*, September 17, 1851, 4.

5 John Houston Bills Diary, July 2, 1851, typed vol. 2, SHC.

6 T. V. Gill to My Dear Husband (William Gill), Greensburg, La., June 21, 1877, box 1, folder 1, Gill-Price Family Papers, MDAH.

7 Annie Butler to William Paisley, Tulip, Ark., May 4, 1870, in Huckaby and Simpson, eds., *Tulip Evermore*, 179.

8 William Paisley to Emma Butler Paisley, St. Louis, Mo., September 12, 1870, in ibid., 193.

9 William Eakin Memoir, p. 24, Eakin Family Papers, TSLA.

10 *Kosciusko Chronicle*, April 12, 1851, 3.

11 *Yazoo Democrat*, July 2, 1851, 3.

12 *Greenwood Reporter*, March 18, 1845, 3.

13 *Yazoo Democrat*, July 2, 1851, 4.

14 *Hernando Press*, November 18, 1869, 3.

15 *Lexington Union*, Feb. 4, 1839, 3.

16 *Dollar Democrat* (Coffeeville), April 11, 1845, 3.

17 *Kosciusko Chronicle*, October 12, 1850, 4; April 26, 1851, 3.

18 *Dollar Democrat*, November 6, 1845, 1.

19 House, "Recollections of Coldwater," 49.

20 Clark, *Pills, Petticoats, and Plows*, 15–54.

21 All three quotes from Ownby, *Subduing Satan*, 41–42.

22 Thigpen, *Ninety and One Years*, 39.

23 Hicks, *The Song of the Delta*, 105.

24 Dickins, "Clothing and Houselinen Expenditures," 4.

25 F. B. Furr Store Ledger, 1893–94, UMS.

26 Clark, *Pills, Petticoats, and Plows*.

27 A. H. Jones Invoice Book, January 1, 1846, Duke.

28 *Holly Springs Gazette*, October 28, 1842, 3.

29 M. Jones Mercantile Store Journal, 1875, UMem.

30 Mount Prospect Trading Post Account Book, 1838, MDAH.

31 Arthur Hopkins Rice Farm Diaries, April 15, 1886, folder 287, Nannie Herndon Rice Papers, MStU.

32 Robert B. Freeman Diaries, December 30, 1876, TSLA.

33 Price, ed., "Excerpts from the Diary of Walter Alexander Overton," 192.

34 *Greenwood Reporter*, February 18, 1845, 3.

35 *Kosciusko Chronicle*, October 12, 1850, 4.

36 *Hernando Press*, December 9, 1869, 3.

37 *Holly Springs Palladium*, December 19, 1851, 3.

38 *Kosciusko Chronicle*, December 15, 1852, 2. See Atherton, *The Southern Country Store*, 69; Clark, *Pills, Petticoats, and Plows*, 98–113.

39 On responses to fears of debt, see Moore, *The Emergence of the Cotton Kingdom*, 25–27; Bond, *Political Culture in the Nineteenth-Century South*, 47–79.

40 Rhodeham Yoe Store Ledger, 1837–39, MDAH.

41 Charles Warren Lafayette Hale Account Book, 1832–33, SHC. On the problems of poor wage laborers, see Bolton, *Poor Whites of the Antebellum South*, 102.

42 Love's Station, 1901, UMem.

43 W. K. Hankinson, 1898, box 24, UK.

44 Campbell Store Ledger, 1890, Prewitt Family Collection.

45 Breen, *Tobacco Culture*. On fears of debt among antebellum Mississippians, see Bond, *Political Culture in the Nineteenth-Century South*, 47–79.

46 D. M. McKenzie to Duncan McLaurin, near Jaynesville, Miss., October 31, 1837, Duncan McLaurin Papers, Duke.

47 William Duncan to Calvin Jones, Jackson, Tenn., June 29, 1832, box 1, folder 12, Calvin Jones Papers, SHC.

48 Sim Williams to William Paisley, Tulip, Ark., February 27, 1868, in Huckaby and Simpson, eds., *Tulip Evermore*, 105. On honor, especially as it related to appearances, see Greenberg, *Honor and Slavery*; Wyatt-Brown, *Southern Honor*; Stowe, *Intimacy and Power*.

49 Bond, *Political Culture in the Nineteenth-Century South*, 6.

50 Needham Whitfield to Allen Wooten, Aberdeen, Miss., March 5, 1850, folder 2, Whitfield and Wooten Family Papers, SHC.

51 Charlie Chilton to "Aunt Dory," Clinton, Miss., February 18, 1873, folder 9, Norton, Chilton, and Dameron Family Papers, SHC.

52 Ewell Gill to William Gill, Liberty, Miss., January 16, 1892, box 1, folder 2, Gill-Price Family Papers, MDAH.

53 R. B. Mayes to O. J. E. Stuart, Yazoo City, Miss., July 4, 1867, box 1, John Bull Smith Dimitry Papers, Duke.

54 Duncan MKenzie to Charles Patterson, Covington County, Miss., April 7, 1833, box 1, folder 1, Duke. See also D. MKenzie to John McLaurin, Jaynesville, Miss., March 8, 1837, box 1, folder 2, Duncan McLaurin Papers, Duke.

55 D. McKenzie to Duncan McLaurin, near Jaynesville, Miss., June 16, 1839, box 1, folder 2, Duncan McLaurin Papers, Duke.

56 Thomas Clark to Gustavus A. Pope, Columbus, Miss., June 9, 1831, June 13, 1830, July 4, 1830, box 1, folder 1, Pope-Carter Family Papers, Duke.

57 A. J. Paxton Manuscript, n.p., MDAH.

58 Thomas Clark to Gustavus A. Pope, Columbus, Miss., November 16, 1832, box 1, folder 1, Pope-Carter Family Papers, Duke.

59 A. P. Burditt to Ellis Malone, Olive Branch, Miss., January 5, 1854, box 1, folder 4, Ellis Malone Papers, Duke.

60 Thomas B. Webber Diary, January 5, 1861, January 16, 1861, Duke.

61 Charles McClellan to Francis J. Levert, Aberdeen, Miss., May 27, 1851, box 2, folder 21, Levert Family Papers, SHC.

62 Clive Metcalfe Diary, December 7, 1889, SHC.

63 L. M. Boatner Diary, April 22, 1841, typescript, MDAH.

64 "Texas Tramp" to Clyde Bryant, San Angelo, Tex., July 22, 1885, Clyde Bryant Papers, MDAH.

65 Henry W. Ball Diary, September 5, 1890, SHC.

66 Turitz and Turitz, *Jews in Early Mississippi*, x–xiv, 11, 43.

67 Ibid., 63; *The Guard*, December 13, 1843, 2.

68 Reprint of *The Deer Creek Pilot*, Rolling Fork, Miss., September 22, 1888, 1, in Turitz and Turitz, *Jews in Early Mississippi*, 59.

69 On household as a concept, see Fox-Genovese, *Within the Plantation Household*; Bercaw, "Politics of Household." On the roles of women in preserving the independence of farm households, see McCurry, *Masters of Small Worlds*.

70 Rogers and Hearn Store Account Book, 1859–60, TSLA. Over two years 267 customers bought 72 items of men's clothing and 18 items of women's clothing that cost more than $5.00. Campbell Store Ledger, Lodi, Prewitt Family Collection.

71 Jackson, *Vinegar Pie and Chicken Bread*, 27.

72 Ibid., 35.

73 Dora Byers McFarland to Lou Hartsfield and Laura Byers, Water Valley, Miss., April 5, 1884, folder 1, Byers Family Papers, MDAH.

74 Martha Rebecca Blanton to Dr. and Mrs. George Smith, Belle Air, Washington County, Miss., January 25, 1859, Blanton-Smith Letters, UMS.

75 Octavia Otey Diary, January 24, 1871, Wyche-Otey Family Papers, SHC.

76 On sewing, see Fox-Genovese, *Within the Plantation Household*, 120–29; Morris, *Becoming Southern*, 45–47; Smith, *Mastered by the Clock*, 60.

77 Miss Hardeman's Diary, Rules for 1859, John Bull Smith Dimitry Papers, Duke.

78 William A. Gill to "My Dear Pettie," Greensburg, La., June 19, 1862, Gill-Price Family Papers, MDAH.

79 Charles B. Galloway, "The Excellent Woman," sermon, 1870s?, box 1, Charles B. Galloway Papers, MDAH.

80 Winans, *Sermons*, 291.

81 William A. Gill to "My Dear Pettie," Greensburg, La., June 21, 1862, box 1, folder 4, Gill-Price Family Papers, MDAH.

82 *The Guard*, February 7, 1844, 4.

83 John W. Brown Diary, December 21, 1853, SHC.

84 *Lexington Union*, November 24, 1838, 4.

85 Quotes about sewing as "my work" appear in the Mahala P. Roach Diary, April 9, 1868, vol. 23, box 2; March 27, 1868, vol. 23, box 2; January 23, 1853, vol. 6, box 1, Roach and Eggleston Family Papers, SHC. Other quotes appear in the Roach Diary, December 31, 1853, February 2, 1853, May 20, 1853, May 22, 1853, vol. 6, box 1.

86 Nancy R. Willard to Micajah Wilkinson, Collinsburg, La., March 30, 1876, folder 4; Nancy Willard to Micajah and Mary Wilkinson, Bossier Parish, La., November 1, 1857, folder 1, Micajah Wilkinson Papers, LSU.

87 Maria Dyer Davies Diary, December 18, 1851, September 17, 1852. Also on idleness and usefulness, August 10, 1852, Duke University Microfilm, in Stampp, ed., *Records of Antebellum Southern Plantations*.

88 Maria Dyer Davies Diary, June 3, 1852, March 25, 1852, September 22, 1852, in ibid.

89 On sermons about humility, see ibid., December 17, 1850, October 9, 1852; on extravagance and laziness, July 28, 1852; shawl quote, November 14, 1852.

90 M. Byron to Margaret Butler, Red River, La., March 21, 1864, Margaret Butler Papers, LSU; Mary Overton, in Price, ed., "Excerpts from the Diary of Walter Alexander Overton," 207; Dustin Willard and Nancy Willard to Micajah Wilkinson and Mary Wilkinson, Bossier Parish, La., January 20, 1862, folder 2, Micajah Wilkinson Papers, LSU. On sewing as a wartime sacrifice, see Faust, *Mothers of Invention*.

91 Smith-Rosenberg, *Disorderly Conduct*, 53–76.

92 Belle Strickland Diary, January 24, 1865, MDAH.

93 Jane M. Jones Diaries, April 20, 1850, TSLA.

94 Amelia T. Long to Lucy Treadwell, Lamar, Miss., October 20, 1876, box 2, Aldrich Collection, UMS.

95 Martha Rebecca Smith Blanton to Jane Smith, Greenville, Miss., November 29, 1858, typescript, Book 1; Jeanie Smith to Martha Rebecca Smith Blanton, Live Oak, Warren County, Miss., September 28, 1865, typescript, Book 1, Blanton-Smith Letters, UMS.

96 Eliza Lucy Irion Neilson Journals, Book 1, p. 4, box 12, Irion-Neilson Family Papers, MDAH.

97 Ibid., January 3, 1859, Book 3, box 12.

98 Ibid., January 23, 1861, Book 3, box 13.

99 Ibid., January 4–5, 1859, Book 3, box 12.

100 Lucy Neilson to Bess Irion, Trotwood, Miss., April 11, 1872, Book 6, p. 11, box 14, Irion-Neilson Family Papers, MDAH.

101 Neilson Diary, June 17, 1865, Book 5, pp. 16, 17, box 12, Irion-Neilson Family Papers, MDAH.

102 Lucy Neilson to Bess Irion, Sunny Slope, Miss., April 14, 1870, Book 6, p. 27, box 14, Irion-Neilson Family Papers, MDAH.

Chapter Two

1 Quoted in Genovese, *Political Economy of Slavery*, 30.

2 Robert Gordon Diaries, June 5, 1851, June 11, 1851, July 28, 1851, August 1, 1851, Robert and James Gordon Diaries, MDAH.

3 The poorest group consisted of 37 inventories of personal goods worth less than $600, the middle group, 37 inventories worth between $600 and $5,000, and the wealthy group, 38 inventories worth more than $5,000 at death. The sample includes 90 inventories from Yalobusha County, 1847–71, and 22 inventories from Lawrence County, 1828–45. Yalobusha County inventories, County Records section, MDAH; Lawrence County inventories, in *Selected Documents from 101 Chancery Court Cases, Lawrence County, Mississippi, 1815–1845*, comp. John Paul Smith (Jackson: N.d.). Probate inventories pose numerous problems as sources. Some are incomplete because family members kept some items for themselves; others are unclear because they listed items in broad categories like kitchen furniture and household furniture.

4 Among those who discuss the concept of stuffing the parlor with goods are Halttunen, "From Parlor to Living Room," and Agnew, "A House of Fiction."

5 Greene, *Pursuits of Happiness*; Isaac, *Transformation of Virginia*; Sydnor, *American Revolutionaries in the Making*; Bushman, *Refinement of America*; Bridenbaugh, *Myths and Realities*; Rozbicki, *Complete Colonial Gentleman*.

6 Genovese, *Political Economy of Slavery*, 18; Genovese, *Roll, Jordan, Roll*, 113–19.

7 James, "Ante-Bellum Natchez," 168–71. See also Jordan, *Tumult and Silence at Second Creek*, 50–52; Isaac, *Transformation of Virginia*, 18–87. Stressing the wooden construction and often impermanent nature of the housing of most antebellum Mississippians is Mactavish, "With Strangers United in Kindred Relation."

8 See Stone, *Crisis of the Aristocracy*; Isaac, *Transformation of Virginia*, 52–57; Jordan, *Tumult and Silence at Second Creek*, 10–11.

9 Martha Rebecca Smith Blanton to Dr. and Mrs. George Smith, Belle Air Plantation, Washington County, Miss., April 23, 1857, Blanton-Smith Letters, UMS.

10 Samuel Pickens to Julia Howe, Greensboro, Ala., April 25, 1855, folder 35, Chiliab Smith Howe Papers, SHC.

11 Susan Sillers Darden Diary, July 18, 1854, February 27, 1857, September 18, 1857, March 3, 1856, typescript, pp. 10, 108, 137, 61, pt. 1, Darden Family Papers, MDAH.

12 *Memphis Daily Appeal*, May 26, 1848, 1.

13 Dustin and Nancy Willard to Micajah and Mary Wilkinson, Bossier Parish, La., June 10, 1855, folder 1, Micajah Wilkinson Papers, LSU.

14 Ellen Howe to Julia Howe, Aberdeen, Mississippi, July 14, 1851, folder 30, Chiliab Smith Howe Papers, SHC.

15 Charles Whitmore to Mr. John Hooton, November 26, 1836, Charles Whitmore Book, SHC.

16 Sydnor, *American Revolutionaries in the Making*, 44.

17 Dugal McCall Plantation Journal, May 6, 1850, Dugal and Duncan McCall Papers, Duke.

18 Ibid., May 11, 1850, July 29, 1850, Duke.

19 Francis Terry Leak, June 1841, typed vol. 1, SHC.

20 Dick Hardaway Eggleston Journal, January 21, 1830, box 1, vol. 3, Roach and Eggleston Family Papers, SHC.

21 *New Orleans Price Current*, May 3, 1843.

22 Jane Randolph to Bethia Richardson, Baywood, Miss., November 3, 1839, folder 1, Caffery Family Papers, SHC.

23 Anna E. Coffee to Alexander Donelson Coffee, Florence, Ala., November 23, 1846, folder 3; January 16, 1848, folder 5, Alexander Donelson Coffee Papers, SHC.

24 Fannie Buford to My Dear Sister, Oakland, Miss., November 1865, box 1, folder 14B, Juanita Brown Collection, UMS.

25 Woodman, *King Cotton and His Retainers*, 14.

26 *New Orleans Price Current*, November 10, 1838, quoted in Woodman, *King Cotton*, 32.

27 *Memphis Daily Appeal*, advertisements, 1847–48; quote from January 25, 1848, 3. Showing that such connection to European centers were part of advertisements in early Natchez is Pennington, "Aesthetics of Everyday Life in Old Natchez," 112.

28 C. B. Champlin to Lewis Clarke, New Orleans, December 14, 1867, folder 1, Lewis Clarke Papers, Duke.

29 Copy of Charles Whitmore to Joseph Lyon, April 1839, and Charles Whitmore to Mr. John Hooton, November 26, 1836, Charles Whitmore Book, SHC.

30 See Wojak, "The Factors of Urban Development."

31 J. M. Champlin to Lewis Clarke, New Orleans, June 10, 1869, folder 1, Lewis Clarke Papers, Duke.

32 William T. Worrall to Thomas A. Watkins, New York, N.Y., February 7, 1859, in *Letters from Forest Place*, ed. Dimond and Hattaway, 137.

33 On the personal relationships between planters and factors, see Woodman, *King Cotton and His Retainers*, 30–48.

34 Kolchin, *Unfree Labor*, 59–68, 129–34.

35 Breen, *Tobacco Culture*.

36 Hundley, *Social Relations in Our Southern States*, 173–74.

37 J. Floyd King to Lin, Belize, Miss., February 19, 1866, box 18, folder 444, Thomas Butler King Papers, SHC.

38 Everard Green Baker, Diary and Plantation Notes, June 5, 1849, December 25, 1852, February 13, 1849, September 18, 1855, typed vol. 1, SHC.

39 *Lexington Union*, December 15, 1838, 1.

40 *The Coahomian*, January 26, 1866, 1.

41 Gustavus A. Henry to Marion Henry, New Orleans, March 1853; Gustavus A. Henry to Marion Henry, Vicksburg, Miss., March 15, 1853, folder 13, Gustavus A. Henry Papers, SHC.

42 Thomas A. Watkins to Letitia A. Watkins, Carrollton, Miss., March 12, 1852, p. 55; Sarah E. Watkins to Letitia A. Watkins, Carrollton, Miss., May 15, 1850, p. 36; Letita A. Watkins to Thomas A. Watkins, Holly Springs, Miss., April 11, 1852, p. 58–59, in *Letters from Forest Place*, ed. Dimond and Hattaway.

43 A. L. Pickens to Julia Howe, Greensboro, Ala., March 16, 1850, folder 29, Chiliab Howe Papers, SHC.

44 Fogel and Engerman, *Time on the Cross*; Genovese, *Roll, Jordan, Roll*, 58–63; Kolchin, *Unfree Labor*, 58–63; Fogel, *Without Consent or Contract*, 189–96.

45 Thomas P. Wyche to John Kirkland, Piney, Yazoo County, Miss., May 19, 1840, box 1, folder 3, Wyche-Otey Family Papers, SHC.

46 Gustavus A. Henry to Marion Henry, White Hall, Miss., December 12, 1849, folder 9, Gustavus A. Henry Papers, SHC. Mrs. Harris was the wife of Henry's overseer.

47 Jo. B. Somervell to Ellis Malone, Wesley, Haywood County, Tenn., November 29, 1849, box 1, folder 3, Ellis Malone Papers, Duke.

48 Joseph M. Jayne Plantation Account Books, November 1, 1855, Duke.

49 Gustavus A. Henry to Marion Henry, White Hall, Miss., December 3, 1846, November 28, 1846, folder 7, Gustavus A. Henry Papers, SHC.

50 Riley, "Diary of a Mississippi Planter," 373.

51 The inventories covered Mississippi estates from 1819 to 1882, with the great majority from 1840 to 1870. They consist of 47 from Amite County, 23 from Lawrence County, 4 from Quitman County, 6 from Sharkey County, and 100 from Yalobusha County. All are located in the County Records section, MDAH. My thanks to Bruce Mactavish for his assistance.

52 George Washington Sargent to Mr. Curry, Natchez, Miss., March 23, 1852, April 27, 1852, Letter Book, vol. 8, George Washington Sargent Papers, SHC.

53 Francis Terry Leak Diary, October 4, 1858, typed vol. 5, p. 478, SHC.

54 James H. Ruffin Plantation Record, June 1842, Ruffin, Roulhac, and Hamilton Family Papers, SHC.

55 John Houston Bills Diary, October 29, 1859, vol. 3, SHC; Y. F. Griffin to Dear Nephew, Washington County, Miss., March 20, 1853, Micajah Wilkinson Papers, LSU.

56 Killona Plantation Journals, January 1, 1837, December 31, 1838, MDAH; Charles Whitmore Book, December 1840, SHC; "Record of Clothing Given to Slaves," 1859, p. 80, Panther Burn Plantation Account Books, MDAH.

57 Bethia F. Richardson to Francis D. Richardson, Elmsley, Wilkinson County, Miss., May 29, 1843, Caffery Family Papers, SHC; William St. John Elliot to R. G. Hazard, Tilsit Plantation, near Woode, Miss., June 25, 1837, R. G. Hazard Papers, MDAH. On the concept of "negro cloth," see Owens, *This Species of Property*, 22–23; Fox-Genovese, *Within the Plantation Household*, 120–21.

58 Pernella Anderson, in Rawick, ed., *American Slave*, vol. 8 (Arkansas Series), pt. 1, 75.

59 Ike Woodward, in ibid., Supplement, ser. 1, vol. 10 (Mississippi Narratives), pt. 5, 2395.

60 On Mississippi slaves earning money, see Sydnor, *Slavery in Mississippi*. For specific examples, see Polly Turner Cancer, in Rawick, ed., *American Slave*, Supplement, ser. 1, vol. 7 (Mississippi Narratives), pt. 2, 343; Mark Oliver, in ibid., Supplement, ser. 1, vol. 9 (Mississippi Narratives), pt. 4, 1660; William Flanagan, in ibid., Supplement, ser. 1, vol. 7 (Mississippi Narratives), pt. 2, 732; Henry Gibbs, in ibid., Supplement, ser. 1, vol. 8 (Mississippi Narratives), pt. 3, 823; Callie Gray, in ibid., Supplement, ser. 1, vol. 8 (Mississippi Narratives), pt. 3, 1168; Billie Smith, in ibid., Supplement, ser. 1, vol. 10 (Mississippi Narratives), pt. 5, 1989–90; Laura Thornton, in ibid., vol. 10 (Arkansas Narratives), pt. 6, 328; "Aunt Adeline," in ibid., vol. 8 (Arkansas Narratives), pt. 1, 12; Fannie Alexander, in ibid., vol. 8 (Arkansas Narratives), pt. 1, 31. Also see Rogers and Hearn Store Account Book, TSLA; M. P. Norton to Louisa Norton, Vicksburg, Miss., December 10, 1848, Norton, Chilton, and Dameron Family Papers, SHC; William Ethelbert Ervin Journal, December 1846, p. 22, December 27, 1847, pp. 53–54, SHC; Panther Burn Plantation Account Books, 1859, p. 63, 1860–61, pp. 68–73, MDAH; Aventine Plantation Diary, 1859–60, MDAH; James Allen Plantation Book, 1860, MDAH; Killona Plantation Journals, 1836–41, MDAH; Slavery Collection, MDAH; Mont Jones Plantation Account Books, 1851–56, Calvin Jones Papers, SHC; Eliza Ann Marsh Robertson Diary, 1855, SHC; Arthur and Fannie Rice Farm Diaries, 1864–65, folders 299–300, MStU; Hermann, *Joseph E. Davis, Pioneer Patriarch*, 60–61; Smedes, *Memorials of a Southern Planter*, 54–57; Morris, *Becoming Southern*, 75.

61 Sarah Amis to Mrs. Hugh Johnston, Choctaw, Miss., December 22, 1836, Elizabeth Blanchard Papers, SHC.

62 Samuel B. Smith, "Testimony by a Former Resident of Mississippi before the American Freedmen's Inquiry Commission," November 19, 1863, in Berlin et al., eds., *Wartime Genesis of Free Labor*, ser. 1, vol. 3, 750.

63 Historians of slavery at least since U. B. Phillips have known about the ability of slaves to earn money. Many slavery scholars, building on his example, have included in their works discussions of rewards and punishments, with the ability to make small amounts of cash appearing in the sections on rewards. Among the most important scholarship on slaves who made money are the following: Phillips, *American Negro Slavery*; Stampp, *The Peculiar Institution*; Sydnor, *Slavery in Mississippi*; Fogel and Engerman, *Time on the Cross*; Fogel, *Without Consent or Contract*; Joyner, *Down by the Riverside*; Jones, *Born a Child of Freedom*. Recent scholarship treats the topic with considerable subtlety. See Wood, *Women's Work, Men's Work*; Campbell, "As 'A Kind of Freeman'?; Hudson, *To Have and to Hold*. On the coastal task system, see Morgan, "Work and Culture"; Morgan, "The Ownership of Property by Slaves"; Armstrong, "From Task Labor to Free Labor"; Joyner, *Down by the Riverside*. On urban slaves, see Johnson and Roark, eds., *No Chariot Let Down*; Wade, *Slavery in the Cities*. On large sugar plantations, see Roderick A. McDonald, *The Economy and Material Culture of Slaves*.

64 Rubin Fox, in Rawick, ed., *American Slave*, Supplement, ser. 1, vol. 7 (Mississippi Narratives), pt. 2, 771.

65 John Nevitt Journal, December 25, 1828, p. 172, SHC; John Houston Bills Diary, December 26, 1856, TSLA; Newstead Plantation Diary, December 26–27, 1858, SHC.

66 Hutchinson, *Code of Mississippi*, 1848, chap. 37, art. 2, 9–29.

67 Account Ledger, 1860, folder 62, box 6, A. H. Arrington Papers, SHC.

68 Foster Freeland to Dear Mother, Oxford, Miss., December 20, 1847, Foster and Freeman Freeland Papers, MDAH. Three other antebellum store ledgers in Mississippi revealed the presence of slaves, either as customers for themselves or as surrogates for their owners. See German and Joseph T. B. Berry Ledger, February 1831, MDAH; Mount Prospect Trading Post Account Book, 1838–58, MDAH; Alden Spooner Forbes Account Book, MDAH.

69 Rogers and Hearn Store Account Book, TSLA.

70 Newstead Plantation Diary, December 26–27, 1858, SHC; *De Bow's Review*, quoted in Kolchin, *Unfree Labor*, 86; Thigpen, *A Boy in Rural Mississippi*, 184; Rawick, ed., *American Slave*, vol. 9 (Arkansas Narratives), pt. 3, 341, 342.

71 Material from the next several paragraphs comes from the Rogers and Hearn Store Account Book, TSLA.

72 McDonald, *Economy and Material Culture of Slaves*, 69–91.

73 White and White, *Stylin'*, 24; Thompson, *Flash of the Spirit*. On cloth and African tradition, see the essays in Weiner and Schneider, eds., *Cloth and Human Experience*.

74 Fox-Genovese, *Within the Plantation Household*, 223.

75 Prince Johnson, in Rawick, ed., *American Slave*, vol. 8 (Mississippi Narratives), pt. 3, 1168; Josie Martin, in ibid., Supplement, ser. 1, vol. 10 (Mississippi Narratives), pt. 5, 1660; Pet Franks, in ibid., Supplement 1, vol. 7 (Mississippi Narratives), pt. 2, 56.

Chapter Three

1 Stone, *Studies in the American Race Problem*, 102, 105.

2 Wright, *Old South, New South*; Jaynes, *Branches without Roots*; Cohen, *At Freedom's Edge*; Ayers, *The Promise of the New South*; McKenzie, "Freedmen and the Soil in the Upper South." The dominant interpretations these works are challenging are, on the lock-in mechanism, Ransom and Sutch, *One Kind of Freedom*; on coercive debts generated by landowner-merchant collaboration, Wiener, *Social Origins of the New South*; on peonage, Daniel, *The Shadow of Slavery*; Novak, *The Wheel of Servitude*.

3 Samuel Agnew Diary, November 9, 1865, Samuel Agnew Papers, UMS; John Houston Bills Diary, October 30, 1867, p. 168; Bills Diary, December 25, 1873, p. 176, TSLA; U.S. Census Office, *Report on Cotton Production in the United States*, 154; Robert Cartmell Diary, January 14, 1880, Robert Cartmell Papers, TSLA; G. P. Collins to Anne Collins, Tunica County, Miss., December 24, 1873, Anne Cameron Collins Papers, SHC.

4 Quoted in Kirby, *Rural Worlds Lost*, 143; Dollard, *Caste and Class in a Southern Town*, 112. See also Davis, Gardner, and Gardner, *Deep South*, 388–91; Nelson, "Welfare Capitalism on a Mississippi Plantation in the Great Depression," 233.

5 H. A. Turner, "Report on the Bledsoe Plantation," LeFlore County, Miss., November 10, 1913, p. 18, in Grossman, ed., *Black Workers*; Mississippi State Board of Health, *Biennial Report*, 1927–29, 98. My thanks to Corey Lesseig for this source.

6 Cohn, *Where I Was Born and Raised*, 33–34.

7 Adelaide Lewis Stuart to Ann Hardeman, Hickory Hills, Miss., February 18, 1867, John Bull Smith Dimitry Papers, Duke.

8 *Vicksburg Times*, quoted in Glymph, "Freedpeople and Ex-Masters," 63.

9 This survey examined 2,374 contracts approved by the Freedmen's Bureau in Mississippi in 1865, 1866, and 1867 in U.S. Bureau of Refugees, Freedmen, and Abandoned Lands, *Records of the Assistant Commissioner for the State of Mississippi*, microfilm reels 46–50.

It asked whether the landowners supplied clothing to the laborers. The survey omitted contracts that were not clear. The author would like to thank graduate assistants James Baggett, Mariacristina Bortolami, Gregory Hospodor, Bruce Mactavish, and Mark Newman for their considerable work in compiling this survey.

10 Contract, Samuel L. Pinson with Dirk Henry et al., Pontotoc County, Miss., August 7, 1865, U.S. Bureau of Refugees, Freedmen, and Abandoned Lands, *Records of the Assistant Commissioner for the State of Mississippi*, reel 47; Contract, Thomas Topp with Henry et al., Pontotoc County, Miss., August 15, 1865, ibid., reel 47; Contract, J. Butcher with Freeman et al., Lauderdale County, Miss., September 28, 1865, ibid., reel 47. Hereafter cited as USBRFAL.

11 Contract, L. P. King with Gates London et al., Yazoo County, Miss., December 25, 1865, ibid., reel 49.

12 Contract, Caroline Gibson with Milia et al., Simpson County, Miss., August 1, 1865, ibid., reel 47; Contract, Mary L. King with Jacob et al., Pontotoc County, Miss., August 10, 1865, ibid., reel 47.

13 Contract, John Gregory with Mary Jane Tucker, Yazoo County, Miss., January 2, 1866, ibid., reel 49.

14 Contract, J. H. Burch and W. H. Porter with Joseph Brooks, Holmes County, Miss., January 2, 1867, ibid., reel 50. See also Contract, Todd and Banner with Nick Pearson, Warren County, Miss., 25 December 1866, reel 50; J. D. Vance and Company with Edward Epps et al., Bolivar County, Miss., November 1, 1866, reel 50.

15 Jaynes, *Branches without Roots*. On "The Long Pay," see 224–49.

16 Contract, Rebecca L. Brock with Kurt et al., Lowndes County, Miss., August 16, 1865, USBRFAL, reel 47.

17 Jaynes, *Branches without Roots*, 158–90.

18 In Rawick, ed., *American Slave*, ser. 1, vol. 10 (Mississippi Narratives), pt. 5, p. 51; Hattie Jefferson, in ibid., Supplement, ser. 1, vol. 8 (Mississippi Narratives), pt. 3, p. 1135; Lewis Jefferson, in ibid., Supplement, ser. 1, vol. 8 (Mississippi Narratives), pt. 3, p. 1144. See also Charity Jones, Supplement, ser. 1, vol. 8 (Mississippi Narratives), pt. 3, p. 1202.

19 Wayne, *The Reshaping of Plantation Society*, 31–52.

20 All accounts in John Petty Moore Plantation Book, 1903, vol. 2, box 5, Thomas Hottel Gist Plantation and Business Records, UArk.

21 Leroy Percy to J. B. Ray, Greenville, Mississippi, December 28, 1906, Percy Family Papers, ser. 1, box 1, folder 14, MDAH. I thank Wiley Prewitt for this reference.

22 C. C. Barbour, "Autobiography of C. C. Barbour, To Which Some Reminiscences Are Added" (Gulf Breeze, Fla.: Ralph E. Barbour, 1993), 49, Barbour Family Memoirs, UMS.

23 Mont Jones Plantation Account Books, 1851–66, Calvin Jones Papers, SHC. The only detailed scholarly analysis of tenant spending habits on Mississippi plantations concludes that they "were only rarely able to afford much of the store's available stock; instead they concentrated their purchases mostly on food and clothing." Adams and Smith, "Historical Perspectives on Black Tenant Farmers' Material Culture," 329–30.

24 Mont Jones Plantation Account Books, 1851–66, Calvin Jones Papers, SHC.

25 Ibid., 1865–66.

26 M. F. Lewis Plantation Book, vol. 1, Lewis Plantation Records, SHC.

27 Ivey F. Lewis Plantation Book, vol. 4, Lewis Plantation Records, SHC.

28 Mississippi Plantation Record, 1866, Mercantile Collection, box 8, UK.

29 Egg and Chicken Payments, 1864, folder 299; April 28, 1865, folder 300, Arthur and Fannie Rice Farm Diaries, Nannie Herndon Rice Papers, MStU.

30 Rice Farm Record and Account Books, 1868–69, folders 301–2, MStU.

31 *William Craig v. A. H. Pattison, Mississippi Reports*, vol. 74, 1896–97, 881; *James Alcorn v. State of Mississippi, Mississippi Reports*, vol. 71, 1893–94, 464. The court ruled against both Pattison and Alcorn.

32 Hamilton L. Parks Diaries and Ledgers, 1869–74, Rev. Hamilton L. Parks Diaries and Papers, UMem.

33 Leach, *Land of Desire*; Marchand, *Advertising the American Dream*, Barth, *City People*; Nasaw, *Children of the City*; Abelson, *When Ladies Go A-Thieving*; Benson, *Counter Cultures*.

34 H. A. Turner, "Report on the Mississippi Delta Planting Company," Bolivar County, Miss., November 14, 1913, p. 16, in Grossman, ed., *Black Workers*.

35 Mattie J. Cooks interview, May 25, 1970, Mary Holmes College interviews, vol. 4, p. 5, MHC; Josephine Beard interview, July 13, 1970, ibid., vol. 2, p. 4; Artley Blanchard interview, June 30, 1970, ibid., vol. 2, p. 14.

36 H. A. Turner, "Bledsoe Plantation," in Grossman, ed., *Black Workers*.

37 *Oxford Falcon*, December 21, 1865, 3.

38 Examples of characterizing customers as "col" appear in Collier General Store Ledger, Charlotte, Tenn., 1890–91, TSLA; Henderson's Store Records, Preston, Miss., 1902, 1904–5, 1911–13, box 29–30, UK: S. G. Burney General Store Ledger, 1869–70, MDAH; Evins Brothers Store ledger, Maury County, Tenn., 1931, box 2, Evins Brothers Store Papers, TSLA. The last ledger made the distinction between several customers labeled "col" and one labeled "Negro Teacher."

39 Hale, *Making Whiteness*, 172.

40 Cobb, in Rosengarten, *All God's Dangers*; Faulkner, *Intruder in the Dust*; Archer, *Growing Up Black in Rural Mississippi*, 39–40; Charles Evers, *Evers*, 28; Taulbert, *When We Were Colored*, 71. Among the scholars who may have overstated the freedom African Americans felt at stores in the postbellum period is Clark, *Pills, Petticoats, and Plows*.

41 Collier General Store Ledger, 1890–91, TSLA; Henderson's Store Records, 1902, UK; S. G. Burney General Store Records, 1869–70, MDAH.

42 S. G. Burney General Store Records, 1869–70, MDAH.

43 Henderson's Store Records, 1902, UK.

44 S. G. Burney General Store Records, 1869–70, MDAH; Collier General Store Ledger, 1890–91, TSLA; Henderson's Store Records, 1902, UK.

45 McMillen, *Dark Journey*, 177–94.

46 R. G. Dun and Company, *Mercantile Agency Reference Book*, 1883. My thanks to Leigh McWhite and Joe Bonica for help in compiling this data.

47 Ibid.

48 *Clarksdale, Mississippi, City Directory*. Neil McMillen details the rise of a significant group of black entrepreneurs in the early 1900s, but he does not mention store owners as a significant component of the group. McMillen, *Dark Journey*, 177–86.

49 Hale, *Making Whiteness*, 176–79.

50 Morant, *Mississippi Minister*, 20, 42.

51 Nathans, "Gotta Mind to Move, Gotta Mind to Settle Down." See also Cobb, *The Most Southern Place on Earth*, 69–124, esp. 91–92; Willis, "On the New South Frontier"; Higgs, "Accumulation of Property by Southern Blacks before World War I"; Schwen-

inger, *Black Property Owners in the South*; Daniel, *Breaking the Land*; Kirby, *Rural Worlds Lost*; Fite, *Cotton Fields No More*; McMillen, *Dark Journey*.

52 Nettie Bell interview, May 7, 1970, Mary Holmes College interviews, vol. 2, p. 15, MHC; Artley Blanchard interview, June 30, 1970, ibid., vol. 2, p. 8; William Carr interview, August 27, 1970, ibid., vol. 3, pp. 2–3; Willie Blanchard interview, August 27, 1970, ibid., vol. 2, p. 2; Amy Jane Bafford interview, August 10, 1971, ibid., vol. 1, pp. 2, 6.

53 Dickins, "A Nutrition Investigation of Negro Tenants in the Yazoo Mississippi Delta," 11; Cohn, *Where I was Born and Raised*, 122.

54 Woofter, *Land Lord and Tenant on the Cotton Plantation*, 101.

55 Clinton Anderson interview, August 24, 1971, Mary Holmes College interviews, vol. 1, p. 7, MHC; Prime Bolden interview, September 14, 1971, ibid., vol. 2, p. 4; Emily Carouthers interview, August 27, 1971, ibid., vol. 3, p. 2.

56 See Turner, *The Ritual Process*.

57 Heinze, *Adapting to Abundance*, 51–85; Cohen, "Embellishing a Life of Labor"; Lears, "Beyond Veblen"; Lears, *Fables of Abundance*.

58 For the best analyses, see Nissenbaum, *The Battle for Christmas*, 260–90; Dirks, *The Black Saturnalia*.

59 Most studies of antebellum slave life include discussions of the importance of Christmas celebrations. For examples, see Joyner, *Down by the Riverside*; Owens, *This Species of Property*; Genovese, *Roll, Jordan, Roll*; Rawick, *From Sundown to Sunup*.

Chapter Four

1 Ayers, *The Promise of the New South*, 3–33, 81–103.

2 Mississippi State Planning Commission, *Progress Report on State Planning in Mississippi*, 53–54.

3 Dickins, "Improving Levels of Living of Tenant Families," 14–15.

4 Dodd and Dodd, *Historical Statistics of the South*, 34–37.

5 On the Mississippi lumber industry, see Hickman, *Mississippi Harvest*; Crawford, "A History of the R. F. Learned Lumber Company"; Ayers, *Promise of the New South*, 123–31. On the nature of payment, see Andrew Brown and Son Ledger 134, 1871–76, and R. F. Learned Lumber Company Ledger 184, 1881, Andrew Brown and Son–R. F. Learned Lumber Company Records, UMS.

6 R. G. Dun Company, *Mercantile Agency Reference Book*, 1883 and 1905. On the rapid expansion of the timber industry in Mississippi from the 1880s through the 1910s, see Hickman, *Mississippi Harvest*, 155.

7 Hickman, *Mississippi Harvest*, 93, 252.

8 R. F. Learned Workmen's Account Books, 1929–30, vols. 347–48, Andrew Brown and Son–R. F. Learned Lumber Company Records, UMS.

9 Hamilton, *Trials of the Earth*, 37, 196. On the impermanence of lumber work, see also Beets, "Growing Up in Marion County."

10 Hamilton, *Trials of the Earth*, 84, 85.

11 Dickins, "Some Contrasts in the Levels of Living of Women Engaged in Farm, Textile Mill, and Garment Plant Work," 28.

12 Dickins, "Some Contrasts in Levels of Living in Industrial, Farm, and Part-Time Farm Families in Rural Mississippi," 251, 254.

13 Dickins, "Some Contrasts in the Levels of Living of Women Engaged in Farm, Textile Mill, and Garment Plant Work," 19.

14 *Fifteenth Census of the United States, 1930, Distribution, vol. 1, Retail Distribution,* pt. 2, p. 1379; R. G. Dun and Company, *Mercantile Agency Reference Book,* 1925.

15 On car dealers, see Lesseig, "Automobility and Social Change," 51–69.

16 *Summit Sentinel,* June 24, 1909, p. 4.

17 *Greenwood Commonwealth,* September 13, 1916, p. 4; November 15, 1916, p. 4.

18 Dickins, "Some Contrasts in the Levels of Living of Women Engaged in Farm, Textile Mill, and Garment Plant Work," 30. Dickins found that about half of the families that included textile and garment workers owned cars, while 43 percent of the farm-owning families and just 19 percent of the families who worked as farm laborers owned cars. She also noted that many of the cars owned by farm owners tended to be rather old.

19 Roberts, *Some Oaks Grow Small,* 61.

20 *Fifteenth Census, 1930, Distribution, vol. 1, Retail Distribution,* pt. 2, 1390.

21 Ibid., 1389; R. G. Dun and Company, *Mercantile Agency Reference Book,* 1925; Holman, *"Save a Nickel on a Quarter,"* 14.

22 Schlereth, "Country Stores, County Fairs, and Mail Order Catalogues," 342–49; White, "Community Portrait from Postal Records."

23 Olney, *Buy Now, Pay Later.*

24 *Fifteenth Census, 1930, Distribution, vol. 1, Retail Distribution,* pt. 2, 1389.

25 R. G. Dun and Company, *Mercantile Agency Reference Book,* 1925.

26 Leach, *Land of Desire*; Barth, *City People.*

27 *Fifteenth Census, 1930, Distribution, vol. 1, Retail Distribution,* pt. 2, 1389.

28 *Choctaw Plain Dealer,* March 9, 1906, p. 4. For the background to such practices, see Schlereth, "Country Stores, County Fairs, and Mail Order Catalogues," 350–56.

29 *Choctaw Plain Dealer,* October 19, 1906, p. 2; October 26, 1906, p. 2.

30 *Greenville Times,* June 17, 1905, p. 7.

31 Strasser, *Satisfaction Guaranteed.*

32 *Choctaw Plain Dealer,* April 13, 1906, p. 4.

33 *Columbus Commercial,* December 11, 1906, p. 5.

34 *Greenville Daily Democrat,* April 18, 1904, p. 8.

35 *Southern Advocate,* February 24, 1916, p. 1.

36 Susman, " 'Personality' and the Making of Twentieth-Century American Culture," 212–25; Lears, "From Salvation to Self-Realization."

37 Marchand, *Advertising the American Dream,* 131.

38 Ibid., 179–85.

39 *Tupelo Daily Journal,* December 12, 1936, p. 5.

40 Holman, *"Save a Nickel on a Quarter,"* 15.

41 Thigpen, *Ninety and One Years,* 28.

42 *Clarksdale Banner,* December 4, 1908, p. 1. On the rise of female store clerks, see Benson, *Counter Cultures.*

43 Howell, *Virginia's Diary,* 62.

44 *Choctaw Plain Dealer,* April 6, 1906, p. 4.

45 *Summit Sentinel,* May 13, 1909, p. 3.

46 *Laurel Chronicle,* April 22, 1910, p. 3.

47 R. G. Dun and Company, *Mercantile Agency Reference Book,* 1883; *Fifteenth Census, 1930, Distribution, vol. 1, Retail Distribution,* pt. 2, 1389; *United States Census of Business, 1948, vol. 3, Retail Trade—Area Statistics,* p. 23.02.

48 *Laurel Chronicle*, March 3, 1911, p. 4.

49 *Clarksdale Banner*, December 18, 1908, p. 1.

50 Howell, *Virginia's Diary*, 134.

51 *Hattiesburg Daily Progress*, December 18, 1903, p. 4.

52 *Tupelo Daily Journal*, November 25, 1936, p. 5.

53 *Columbus Commercial*, December 11, 1906, p. 1.

54 *Iuka Vidette*, December 18, 1919, p. 6.

55 *Tupelo Daily Journal*, December 3, 1936, 3.

56 Schmidt, *Consumer Rites*, 105–91.

57 *Yazoo City Herald*, October 13, 1936, p. 1.

58 All figures from Mississippi State Planning Commission, *Progress Report on State Planning in Mississippi*, 113–33, 158–60.

59 Dickens and Bowie, "A Guide to Planning Clothes for the Mississippi Farm Family," 16–18. On national averages, see Lebergott, *Pursuing Happiness*, 91–92.

60 Cook, *McGowah Place*, 52.

61 On separated shopping districts, see Hale, *Making Whiteness*, 184–87.

62 Cook, *McGowah Place*, 50, 85.

Chapter Five

1 Dundy, *Elvis and Gladys*, 114.

2 On southern home demonstration work, see Rieff, " 'Go Ahead and Do All You Can,' " 146–47; Keith, *Country People in the New South*, 191; Kirby, *Rural Worlds Lost*, 116; Hutchison, "Better Homes and Gullah." On such work outside the South, see Jenson, "Crossing Ethnic Barriers in the Southwest"; Babbitt, "The Productive Farm Woman and the Extension Home Economist in New York State."

3 Walker, "Home Extension Work among African American Farm Women in East Tennessee."

4 On Dickens's biography, see Stark and Kilgore, "A Tribute to Dorothy Dickins"; Jolly, "Selected Leaders in Mississippi Home Economics."

5 Dickins, "A Study of Food Habits of People in Two Contrasting Areas of Mississippi," 3.

6 Wilson, "Annual Report of Extension Work for 1927 in Agriculture and Home Economics," 72.

7 Dickins, "What the Farm Woman Can Do to Improve the Economic Status of Her Family," 6.

8 Dickins, "Improving Levels of Living of Tenant Families," 13–14.

9 Dickins, "Clothing and Houselinen Expenditures," 4, 7.

10 Midkoff, "Clothing Manual for 4-H Club Girls and Home Demonstration Women," 1.

11 The first mention of sewing machines in the reports appeared in Wilson, "Annual Report of Extension Work in Agriculture and Home Economics in Mississippi for 1919," 42.

12 Mary Cresswell, in Midkoff, "Clothing Manual for 4-H Club Girls and Home Demonstration Women," 1.

13 Jordan, "Simple Home Decoration," 8.

14 Jordan, "Clothing for First and Second Year Club Girls," 5.

15 Jordan, "Clothing for Third and Fourth Year Club Girls," 16.

16 Cresswell, in Midkoff, "Clothing Manual for 4-H Club Girls and Home Demonstration Women," 1.

17 Jordan, "Clothing for Third and Fourth Year Club Girls," 9.

18 On the goals southern extension services set for farming men, see Scott, *The Reluctant Farmer*; Kirby, *Rural Worlds Lost*, 115–54.

19 Dickins, "What the Farm Woman Can Do to Improve the Economic Status of Her Family" 4, 10.

20 See, for example, Dickins, "Some Contrasts in the Levels of Living of Women Engaged in Farm, Textile Mill, and Garment Plant Work," 50.

21 Dickins, "Improving Levels of Living of Tenant Families," 14–15, 18.

22 Dickins and Bowie, "A Guide to Planning Clothes for the Mississippi Farm Family," 5.

23 Olson, "Annual Report of Cooperative Extension Work in Agriculture and Home Economics, 1932," 42.

24 Wilson, "Annual Report of Extension Work for 1929 in Agriculture and Home Economics," 58.

25 Olson, "Annual Report, 1932," pp. 49–51.

26 Dickins, "Clothing and Houselinen Expenditures," 11; Olson, "Annual Report of Extension Work in Agriculture and Home Economics in Mississippi, 1931," 51.

27 Wilson, "Annual Report of Extension Work for 1924," 68.

28 Whisnant, *All That Is Native and Fine*.

29 Wilson, "Annual Report of Extension Work for 1925," 53.

30 Wilson, "Annual Report of Extension Work for 1928 in Agriculture and Home Economics," 90; Wilson, "Annual Report of Extension Work for 1929 in Agriculture and Home Economics," 58.

31 Dickins, "Effects of Good Household Management," 26.

32 Dickins, "Family Living on Poorer and Better Soil," 18.

33 Dickins, "A Nutrition Investigation of Negro Tenants in the Yazoo Mississippi Delta," 11, 47.

34 Dickins, "Effects of Good Household Management," 26; "A Nutrition Investigation of Negro Tenants in the Yazoo Mississippi Delta," 11.

35 See the conclusion of Jordan, *White over Black*.

36 See, for example, Heinze, *Adapting to Abundance*; Cohen, *Making a New Deal*; Ayers, *The Promise of the New South*; Peiss, *Cheap Amusements*.

37 Dickins, "Needs for Storage of Farm-Owner Families," typescript, MStU.

38 Dickins, "The Southern Family in an Era of Change," 235.

39 Dickins, "The Farm Home Improves Its Equipment," 567–70.

40 Dickins, "The Southern Family in an Era of Change," 235.

41 Dickins, "Consumption Patterns," 27.

42 Ibid., 28.

43 Dickins, "Factors Related to the Use of Credit Resources by Farm Families," 25.

Chapter Six

1 Memphis Minnie McCoy, "Me and My Chauffeur Blues," 1941, in Taft, ed., *Blues Lyric Poetry*, 201.

2 Marks, *Farewell, We're Good and Gone*; Gottlieb, *Making Their Own Way*. See also Grossman, *Land of Hope*; Jones, *Labor of Love, Labor of Sorrow*.

3 Jones, *Labor of Love, Labor of Sorrow,* 84–90; Woofter, *Land Lord and Tenant,* 164–65. See also Cohn, *Where I Was Born and Raised,* 85; Daniel, *Breaking the Land,* 158; Kirby, *Rural Worlds Lost,* 155–57; Howard A. Turner, "Runnymede Plantation Account," p. 3, in Grossman, ed., *Black Workers.*

4 Harris, *Blues Who's Who,* 409, 68; Charter, *Sweet as the Showers of Rain,* 84–85.

5 On the decline of agriculture and its effect on family life, see Douglas, *The Feminization of American Culture;* Hall et al., *Like a Family.* See also such works as Ryan, *Cradle of the Middle Class;* Zelizer, *Pricing the Priceless Child;* Zaretsky, *Capitalism, the Family, and Personal Life.*

6 Tanner Thomas, in Rawick, ed., *American Slave,* ser. 2, vol. 10 (Arkansas Narratives), pt. 6, 305; Alice Johnson, in ibid., ser. 2, vol. 9, (Arkansas Narratives), pt. 4, 62.

7 Kirby, *Rural Worlds Lost,* 115; Lillie Williams, in Rawick, ed., *American Slave,* ser. 2, vol. 11 (Arkansas Narratives), pt. 7, 178.

8 Isaac Stier, in ibid., Supplement, ser. 1, vol. 10 (Mississippi Narratives), pt. 5, 2059.

9 Josephine Ann Barnett, in ibid., ser. 2, vol. 8 (Arkansas Narratives), pt. 1, 111; William Henry Rooks, in ibid., ser. 2, vol. 10 (Arkansas Narratives), pt. 6, 79; Absalom Jenkins, in ibid., ser. 2, vol. 9 (Arkansas Narratives), pt. 4, 49.

10 Jeff Davis, in ibid., ser. 2, vol. 8 (Arkansas Narratives), pt. 2, 120; Lillie Williams, in ibid., ser. 2, vol. 11, (Arkansas Narratives), pt. 7, 178.

11 See Levine, *Black Culture and Black Consciousness.*

12 Among the blues musicians who worked on farms are Will Batts, Eddie Boyd, Big Bill Broonzy, Willie Brown, Charlie Burse, Gus Cannon, Armenter Chatmon, Arthur "Big Boy" Crudup, Walter Davis, Honeyboy Edwards, Sleepy John Estes, Bill Gillum, Son House, Mississippi John Hurt, Robert Johnson, Tommy Johnson, Floyd Jones, Noah Lewis, Robert Jr. Lockwood, Albert Luandrew (Sunnyland Slim), Robert Lee McCoy, Tommy McClennan, Sonny Boy Nelson, Hammie Nixon, Charley Patton, Yank Rachell, J. D. Short, Houston Stackhouse, Frank Stokes, Roosevelt Sykes, Muddy Waters, Booker White. The best single biographical source for Mississippi blues musicians is Harris, *Blues Who's Who.* Information on musicians' backgrounds is from Charters, *The Country Blues;* Neff and Connor, *Blues;* Shaw, *Honkers and Shouters;* Pearson, *"Sounds So Good to Me";* Charters, *The Legacy of the Blues;* Barlow, *"Looking Up at Down";* Palmer, *Deep Blues;* Charters, *Sweet as the Showers of Rain;* Olsson, *Memphis Blues and Jug Bands;* and numerous interviews in *Living Blues.* My thanks to David Nelson for his help in compiling material for this list.

13 Charters, *The Country Blues,* 130.

14 Lockwood, "Living Blues Interview," 18; Robert Johnson, "Rambling on My Mind," 1936, in Taft, ed., *Blues Lyric Poetry,* 146.

15 Hammie Nixon, in Nixon and Estes, "Living Blues Interview," 17; Neff and Connor, *Blues,* 26, 120. See also Lockwood, "Living Blues Interview," 18; House, "Living Blues Interview," 17; Boyd, "Living Blues Interview," pt. 3, p. 8; Pearson, *Sounds So Good to Me,* 21. See also Garon and Garon, *Woman with Guitar,* 242–43.

16 James "Son Ford" Thomas, quoted in Ferris, *Local Color,* 136.

17 Among the Mississippi and Memphis blues performers who played in medicine shows were Ishman Bracey, Gus Cannon, Sleepy John Estes, Jim Jackson, Furry Lewis, Robert Nighthawk, Hammie Nixon, Charley Patton, Frank Stokes, and Will Shade. See Harris, *Blues Who's Who;* Olson, *Memphis Blues and Jug Bands;* Charters, *Country Blues;* Charters, *Sweet as the Showers of Rain;* Palmer, *Deep Blues;* Nixon and Estes, "Living Blues Interview," 17.

18 See Boyd, "Living Blues Interview," pt. 1, pp. 12–13; Palmer, *Deep Blues*, 120.

19 Furry Lewis, "I Will Turn Your Money Green," 1928, in Taft, ed., *Blues Lyric Poetry*, 169; Pearson, *Sounds So Good to Me*, 9–10; Joe McCoy, "That Will Be Alright," 1929, in Taft, ed., *Blues Lyric Poetry*, 179.

20 Memphis Minnie McCoy, "It's Hard to Please My Man," 1940, in Taft, ed., *Blues Lyric Poetry*, 201.

21 Peter Chatman (Memphis Slim), "Grinder Man Blues," 1940, in Taft, ed., *Blues Lyric Poetry*, 59.

22 Marchand, *Advertising the American Dream*, 208–16. See also Lears, "From Salvation to Self-Realization"; Susman, " 'Personality' and the Making of Twentieth-Century Culture."

23 Big Bill Broonzy, "C and A Blues," 1935, in Taft, ed., *Blues Lyric Poetry*, 22; Tommie Bradley, "Please Don't Act That Way," 1931, in ibid., 40. William Barlow describes Charley Patton as "a flashy dresser who always wore expensive suits, ties, and shoes and a Stetson hat." Barlow, *"Looking Up at Down,"* 35.

24 Broonzy, *Big Bill Blues*, 48; Garon and Garon, *Woman with Guitar*, 63. On bluesmen's desire for stylish clothing, also see Boyd, "Living Blues Interview," pt. 1, p. 15; Palmer, *Deep Blues*, 78; Charters, *Sweet as the Showers of Rain*, 32; Shaw, *Honkers and Shouters*, 18, 30.

25 Joe McCoy, "Evil Devil Woman Blues," 1934, in Taft, ed., *Blues Lyric Poetry*, 181; Robert Brown (Washboard Sam), "Sophisticated Mama," 1938, in ibid., 23; Bo Chatman, "Bo Carter Special," 1934, in ibid., 54; Sonny Boy Williamson, "T.B. Blues," 1939, in ibid., 316; Williamson, "Christmas Morning Blues," 1938, in ibid.

26 Eurreal "Little Brother" Montgomery, "The Woman I Love Blues," 1935, in ibid., 202; Mississippi John Hurt, "Got the Blues Can't Be Satisfied," 1928, in ibid., 116; Sonny Boy Williamson, "Low Down Ways," 1938, in ibid., 315.

27 Oliver, *Screening the Blues*, 213–16. On blues songs, sexuality, and automobiles, see also Ewen, *Captains of Consciousness*. On the automobile as the ultimate item, see Edsforth, *Class Conflict and Cultural Consensus*; Flink, *The Car Culture*. On automobiles and their roles in Mississippi, see Lesseig, "Automobility and Social Change."

28 Walter Roland, "T Model Blues," 1933, in Taft, ed., *Blues Lyric Poetry*, 226.

29 Robert Johnson, "Terraplane Blues," 1936, in ibid., 147.

30 Robert Johnson, "Terraplane Blues," 1936, in ibid., 147; Sonny Boy Williamson, "You Give an Account," 1938, in ibid., 313. See also Rachell, "Living Blues Interview," 15. An exception to this concentration on speed can be found in Sleepy John Estes, "Poor Man's Friend," 1935, in Taft, ed., *Blues Lyric Poetry*, 84.

31 McMillen, *Dark Journey*. On the desires of black Southerners for automobiles and the privacy and freedom they offered, see Brownell, "A Symbol of Modernity"; Lesseig, "Automobility and Social Change."

32 Palmer, *Deep Blues*, 187.

33 Neff and Connor, *Blues*, 52; Memphis Minnie McCoy, "Garage Fire Blues," 1930, in Taft, ed., *Blues Lyric Poetry*, 197; Sonny Boy Williamson, "Project Highway," 1937, in ibid., 312.

34 Robert Johnson, "Phonograph Blues," 1936, in Taft, ed., *Blues Lyric Poetry*, 147; Sonny Boy Williamson, "Christmas Morning Blues," 1938, in ibid., 314; Bill Jazz Gillum, "I'm Gonna Leave You on the Outskirts of Town," 1942, in ibid., 97; Hattie Hart, "I Let My Daddy Do That," 1934, in ibid., 103.

35 Sleepy John Estes, "Need More Blues," 1935, in ibid., 84.

36 As William Barlow writes in his study of early blues musicians, "By choosing a life of travel and recreation rather than unrelenting labor and unrewarded abstinence, they signaled their alienation from the established cultural norms in their communities." Barlow, *"Looking Up at Down,"* 5.

37 McMillen, *Dark Journey*, 267.

38 Waters, "Living Blues Interview," 16; Nelson, "Living Blues Interview," 14. B. B. King ordered his first book of guitar instruction from the Sears Roebuck catalogue. King, *Blues All Around Me*, 42.

39 *Chicago Defender*, July 23, 1938, 13; July 16, 1938, 2. On the central role the *Defender* played in black Mississippians' views of the city and their decision to migrate, see Grossman, *Land of Hope*.

40 Associated Negro Press Clipping, February 9, 1963, folder 4, box 262, Claude A. Barnett Papers, CHS.

41 Cohen, *Making a New Deal*, 149; letters in Claude A. Barnett Papers, box 261, folders 6–7, box 262, folders 1–5, CHS.

42 Cohen, *Making a New Deal*, 159.

43 Grossman, *Land of Hope*, 150–51. The Chicago Urban League flyer was in a Library of Congress photograph in the exhibition "The Great Migration, 1915–1940," Smith Robertson Museum and Cultural Center, Jackson, Miss.

44 Evans, "Claude A. Barnett and the Associated Negro Press," 44–56.

45 Nile Queen Products advertising pamphlet, p. 1, Claude A. Barnett Papers, box 262, folder 2, CHS.

46 Kashmir Chemical Company advertisement, 1919, Claude A. Barnett Papers, box 262, folder 2, CHS.

47 Claude A. Barnett to Dr. Robert Moton, Chicago, September 22, 1930, Claude A. Barnett Papers, box 131, folder 6, CHS.

48 Edwards, *The Southern Urban Negro as a Consumer*, 47.

49 Ibid., 48, 96–97, 79. On African Americans' opposition to racist advertising, see Hale, *Making Whiteness*, 181–97.

50 "The Black Market," *All American News*, 1949, Claude A. Barnett Papers, box 131, folder 2, CHS.

51 "Nation within a Nation," *Premium Practice*, May 1957, Claude A. Barnett Papers, box 131, folder 2, CHS.

52 D. Parke Gibson Associates, "The Gibson Report on the Negro Market," vol. 4, no. 13 (June 1964), box 131, folder 2, Claude A. Barnett Papers, CHS. See also Gibson, *The $30 Billion Negro*. The image of the free-spending African American also stimulated a series of scholarly articles in the 1950s and early 1960s. See, for example, Klein and Mooney, "Negro-White Savings Differentials and the Consumption Function Problem"; Yoshima, "The Stereotype of the Negro and His High-Priced Car"; Alexis, "Some Negro-White Differences in Consumption."

53 Taylor, *"The Friendship" and "The Gold Cadillac,"* 8, 19, 20.

54 Ibid., 56.

55 Ibid., 68, 70.

56 Ibid., 85.

Chapter Seven

1 Young, *The Pavilion*, 66–67.

2 Percy, *Lanterns on the Levee*, 7, 41, 61, 62.

3 Ibid., 143, 13, 62.

4 Ibid., 380.

5 Wright, *Black Boy*, 166, 251.

6 Wright, *American Hunger*, 12–13, 14.

7 Ibid., 13, 21, 45.

8 Wright, "Long Black Song," *Uncle Tom's Children*, 124.

9 Ibid., 109.

10 Ibid., 108–9.

11 Ibid., 110.

12 Ibid., 108.

13 Faulkner, *Intruder in the Dust*, 238–39.

14 Faulkner, *The Mansion*; Faulkner, *The Reivers*.

15 On the Faulkner family conflicts, see Minter, *William Faulkner*, 113–64. On the feminization of consumer spending, see Marchand, *Advertising the American Dream*; Bowlby, *Just Looking*; Abelson, *When Ladies Go A-Thieving*; Loeb, *Consuming Angels*.

16 See Minter, *William Faulkner*, 137–64.

17 Faulkner, "A Rose for Emily," *Collected Stories of William Faulkner*, 119–20.

18 Faulkner, *The Town*, 11, 13.

19 Ibid., 14.

20 Faulkner, *My Brother Bill*, 119–20.

21 Faulkner, *The Town*, 14.

22 Faulkner, *Light in August*, 23–24.

23 Ibid., 171, 154.

24 Faulkner, *As I Lay Dying*, 19, 110, 111, 218.

25 Ibid., 104–5.

26 Ibid., 247–48.

27 Ibid., 249–50.

28 As David Minter has argued, the Snopeses are unique among Faulkner characters in that no ghosts of past generations haunt them, either with the ideals of the ages or the sins of the fathers. Minter, *William Faulkner*, 83. See also Dunn, "The Illusion of Freedom in *The Hamlet* and *Go Down, Moses*."

29 Faulkner, *The Hamlet*, 23.

30 Ibid., 15, 20.

31 Faulkner, *The Mansion*, 92. On the distance between Mink and cosmopolitan culture, see Millgate, *The Achievement of William Faulkner*, 295; Beck, *Man in Motion*, 175.

32 Faulkner, *The Mansion*, 368.

33 See Moreland, *Faulkner and Modernism*, 137.

34 Kartiganer, *Fragile Thread*, 119.

35 Brooks, *William Faulkner*, 185–86. See also Matthews, "Shortened Stories," 18; Kartiganer, *Fragile Thread*, 115; Watson, *The Snopes Dilemma*, 60–65.

36 Minter, *William Faulkner*, 177.

37 My understanding of the significance of housing in the Snopes trilogy draws on Ruzicka, *Faulkner's Fictive Architecture*, 69–82; Hines, *William Faulkner and the Tangible Past*.

38 Faulkner, *The Mansion*, 155, 156.

39 Welty, "The Little Store," 639.

40 Ibid.

41 Ibid., 644.

42 Ibid., 642.

43 Welty, *The Optimist's Daughter*, 179.

44 Ibid., 28.

45 Welty, *The Ponder Heart*, 67.

46 Ibid., 67, 68.

47 Welty, *The Optimist's Daughter*, 124.

48 Ibid., 136.

49 Welty, "The Whistle," *Collected Stories*, 60.

50 Welty, "The Worn Path," *Collected Stories*, 142, 145.

51 Ibid., 149.

Chapter Eight

1 Evers, *For Us, the Living*, 32, 30–31.

2 Moody, *Coming of Age in Mississippi*, 38–39.

3 Mills, *This Little Light of Mine*, 10–11.

4 Charles McDew, quoted in National Civil Rights Museum, "Honoring the Struggle of a Generation," 5–11.

5 Branch, *Parting the Waters*, 149.

6 Payne, *I've Got the Light of Freedom*, 284–87.

7 *Natchez Democrat*, August 29, 1965, 1–2.

8 *Grenada Daily Sentinel-Star*, July 20, 1966, 1; *Greenwood Commonwealth*, August 10, 1968, 1.

9 Evers, *For Us, the Living*, 280–81.

10 Payne, *I've Got the Light of Freedom*, 323–25; Evers and Szanton, *Have No Fear*, 185–86.

11 Evers, *For Us, the Living*, 194, 195; Evers and Szanton, *Have No Fear*, 156; Holland, *From the Mississippi Delta*, 160–61.

12 Payne, *I've Got the Light of Freedom*, 78.

13 *Natchez Democrat*, December 4, 1965, 1.

14 Ibid., December 5, 1965, 3.

15 Evers, "From *Evers*," 200.

16 Charles Payne shows that black Mississippians had occasionally boycotted white-owned stores to protest violence from the 1930s through the 1950s. Payne, *I've Got the Light of Freedom*, 38.

17 On the growing importance of national publicity in the civil rights movement, see Goldfield, *Black, White, and Southern*. On the Woolworth's sit-in, see Payne, *I've Got the Light of Freedom*, 285; Moody, *Coming of Age in Mississippi*, 263–68.

18 *Grenada Daily Sentinel-Star*, July 13, 1966, 1.

19 Ibid., August 25, 1966, 5.

20 *Clarksdale Press Register*, December 7, 1961, 1.

21 *Natchez Democrat*, October 1, 1965, 1, 6; October 2, 1965, 1; October 3, 1965, 1; October 4, 1965, 1; October 5, 1965, 1.

22 *Greenwood Commonwealth*, June 11, 1968, 1; July 5, 1968, 1.

23 *Grenada Daily Sentinel-Star*, July 26, 1966, 1; *Jackson Clarion-Ledger*, April 27, 1969, 15. Evers largely confirmed those reports in his autobiography, *Have No Fear*, 187.

24 *Grenada Daily Sentinel-Star*, August 17, 1966, 1.

25 State of Mississippi, *Laws, 1968*, chap. 244, 476–78.

26 *Port Gibson Reveille*, November 6, 1969, 1; *Jackson Clarion-Ledger*, June 7, 1986, B1; *Jackson Daily News*, March 16, 1974, 1; *Memphis Commercial Appeal*, December 22, 1978, 22; *Jackson Clarion-Ledger*, June 7, 1986, B1.

27 *Grenada Daily Sentinel-Star*, August 23, 1966, 1.

28 *Natchez Democrat*, December 2, 1965, 1–2.

29 Ibid., December 5, 1965, 3.

30 Ibid., December 20, 1965, 1; January 13, 1966, 1; February 27, 1966, 1, 3.

31 Ibid., December 5, 1965, 3.

32 Ibid., February 27, 1966, 3; *Jackson Daily News*, October 5, 1978, C1; *Jackson Clarion-Ledger*, January 18, 1980, 1.

33 Crosby, "White Only on Main Street," 37–41.

34 An incomplete list of the locations of boycotts in the 1970s and 1980s would include the following: Byhalia, Brookhaven, Coffeeville, Coldwater, Fayette, Holly Springs, Indianola, Lexington, Marks, McComb, Natchez, Oxford, Raymond, Senatobia, Tupelo, Vicksburg, and Weir.

35 Mills, *This Little Light of Mine*, 255–61.

36 See Payne, *I've Got the Light of Freedom*; Dittmer, *Local People*, 365–68.

Epilogue

1 Ownby, " 'Does the South Still Exist?' "

2 Clark, *Pills, Petticoats, and Plows*, vii.

3 *1967 Census of Business*, vol. 2, *Retail Trade—Area Statistics*, pt. 2, 26-4, 26-5.

4 Cohen discusses the same phenomenon in urban life in "From Town Center to Shopping Center."

5 Wal-Mart, *Annual Report*, 1993, 5; Wal-Mart, *Annual Report*, 1997, 19.

6 Vance and Scott, *Wal-Mart*, 136–55.

7 Pepper Smith, in *The Daily Mississippian* (Oxford), February 3, 1989, 5. My thanks to Sarah Torian for this reference.

8 Holland, *From the Mississippi Delta*, 312.

9 *Mississippi Business Directory, 1994–1995*, 537–38.

10 Vance and Smith, *Wal-Mart*, 139–40.

11 *Memphis Commercial Appeal*, January 24, 1994, A1. My thanks to Corey Lesseig for this reference.

12 Dickins, "Levels of Living of Young White Farm-Operator Families in Mississippi," 10–11; Dickins, "Levels of Living of Young Negro Farm-Operator Families in Mississippi," 10–11.

13 *Southern Reporter*, February 13, 1997, 7A; *Neshoba Democrat*, November 13, 1996, 11B.

14 *Pigeon Roost News*, April 9, 1997, 4.

15 Especially effective on the nature of recent jobs as low-paying and transient is Cobb, *The Selling of the South*.

16 R. G. Dun and Company, *Mercantile Agency Reference Book*, 1883; *Fifteenth Census of the United States, 1930, vol. 1, Retail Distribution*, pt. 2, 1380; *Census of American Business: 1933, Retail Distribution, vol. 1, United States Summary: 1933 and Comparisons with 1929*, A-57.

17 *United States Census of Business, 1948, vol. 3, Retail Trade—Area Statistics*, 23.02; U.S. Bureau of the Census, *1958 Census of Business, vol. 2, Retail Trade—Area Statistics*, pt. 1, 24-7; *1967 Census of Business, vol. 2, Retail Trade—Area Statistics*, pt. 2, 26-7; *1977 Census of Retail Trade, vol. 2, Geographic Area Statistics*, pt. 2, 25-9 to 25-10; *1987 Census of Retail Trade, Geographic Area Series, Mississippi*, MS-11 to MS-12; *1992 Census of Retail Trade, Geographic Area Series, Mississippi*, MS-13; *Mississippi Business Directory, 1994–1995*.

18 *1967 Census of Business, vol. 2, Retail Trade—Area Statistics*, pt. 2, 26-7.

19 *Jackson Clarion-Ledger*, November 16, 1981, 1C; Antiques file folder, MDAH.

20 Antiques Shopping Guide, Natchez, Miss., 1992–93; "Discover Delta Antiques," brochure, June 1987, Antiques file folder, MDAH; *Mississippi Business Directory, 1994–1995*, 282–83.

21 Antiques Shopping Guide, Natchez, Miss., 1992–93, Antiques file folder, MDAH.

22 "Discover Delta Antiques," brochure, June 1987; Antique Guide and Points of Interest, Jackson, Miss., n.d.; "Antique Dealers on the Mississippi Gulf Coast," brochure, n.d., Antiques file folder, MDAH.

23 *1992 Census of Retail Trade, Geographic Area Series, Mississippi*, MS-10 to MS-11.

24 *Southern Reporter*, September 26, 1996, 3B.

25 On the Jackson flea market, see *Jackson Clarion-Ledger*, November 9, 1979, 1C; on Vicksburg, "Flea Market Day in Vicksburg, Mississippi," brochure, April 27, 1974; on Ripley, *Jackson Daily News*, July 3, 1986, C2; on Canton, *Jackson Clarion-Ledger*, December 18, 1988, 16, Flea Markets file folder, MDAH; *Mississippi Business Directory, 1994–1995*, 440; *Mississippi Business Directory, 1988–1989*, 172.

26 "But Where Are the Fleas?" *Mainstream Mississippi*, Fall 1981, 23–25.

27 *Jackson Clarion-Ledger*, June 19, 1986, B1; *Jackson Daily News*, July 3, 1986, CS.

28 *Southern Reporter*, May 16, 1996, 1–2.

29 *Pigeon Roost News*, April 16, 1997, 14.

30 On the late origins of the Mississippi Department of Public Welfare, see Mississippi Department of Public Welfare, *Fifth Biennial Report*, 1943–45, p. 9. In the early 1940s, Mississippi spent less per person than any other state, spending about 40 percent of the national average. See Mississippi Department of Public Welfare, *Public Welfare in Mississippi*, vol. 2, no. 3 (January–March 1941): 19.

31 James C. Cobb quotes the criticism of food stamps by Mississippi congressman Jamie Whitten, "When you start giving people something for nothing . . . I wonder if you don't destroy character more than you might improve nutrition." Cobb, *Most Southern Place on Earth*, 261. On planters and welfare, see Kirby, *Rural Worlds Lost*, 58–59, 158; Whayne, *A New Plantation South*.

32 *Jackson Daily News*, January 22, 1980, 3A, Food Stamp Program file folder, MDAH.

33 *Tupelo Daily Journal*, May 9, 1995, 16A. See also *New York Times*, October 23, 1995, A1, A13.

34 *Jackson Clarion-Ledger*, March 4, 1994, A1, Food Stamp Program file folder, MDAH.

35 *Jackson Daily News*, January 22, 1980, 3A, Food Stamp Program file folder, MDAH.

36 On elements of permissiveness and self-indulgence in ideas about contemporary poverty, see Katz, *The Undeserving Poor*, 156–65.

BIBLIOGRAPHY

Manuscript Collections

Baton Rouge, Louisiana
Louisiana State University Library, Special Collections
    Harrod C. Anderson Papers
    Bennett Family Papers
    Margaret Butler Correspondence
    E. John and Thomas C. W. Ellis Family Papers
    C. L. Lauve Account Book
    Mrs. M. F. Surghnor Diary
    Micajah Wilkinson Papers

Chapel Hill, North Carolina
University of North Carolina, Southern Historical Collection
    Samuel A. Agnew Diary
    James Trooper Armstrong Papers
    Archibald Hunter Arrington Papers
    Everard Green Baker Diary and Plantation Notes
    Henry W. Ball Diary
    Daniel Moreau Barringer Papers
    Mary Bateman Diary
    H. L. Bedford Account Book
    John Houston Bills Diary
    Elizabeth Amis Cameron Blanchard Papers
    Breckinridge Family Reminiscences
    John W. Brown Diary
    Buchanon-McClellan Family Papers
    Caffery Family Papers
    Kate Carney Diary
    Alexander Donelson Coffee Papers
    Anne Cameron Collins Papers
    John Fletcher Comer Farm Journal
    William Cooper Diary
    Burwell J. Corban Papers
    Craft-Fort Papers
    William Ethelbert Ervin Journal
    Andrew Flinn Plantation Book
    James F. Gwinner Diary
    Elizabeth Seawell Hairston Papers
    Hairston and Wilson Family Papers

Charles Warren Lafayette Hale Account Book
William S. Hamilton Papers
Pinckney Cotesworth Harrington Papers
John Gideon Harris Diary
James Thomas Harrington Papers
Gustavus A. Henry Papers
Chiliab Smith Howe Papers
Calvin Jones Papers
Thomas Butler King Papers
Francis Terry Leak Diary
Levert Family Papers
George W. Lewis Papers
Lewis Plantation Records
William S. Lovell Plantation Diary
William McCorkle Papers
James Mallory Papers
Clive Metcalfe Diary
John Nevitt Journal
Newstead Plantation Diary
Norton, Chilton, and Dameron Papers
Jehu A. Orr Papers
Philip Rainey Papers
Randolph and Yates Family Papers
Roach and Eggleston Family Papers
Ruffin, Roulhac, and Hamilton Family Papers
George Washington Sargent Papers
Mary Stubblefield Letter
Walton Family Papers
Whitfield and Wooten Family Papers
Charles Whitmore Book
Wyche-Otey Family Papers

Chicago, Illinois
Chicago Historical Society
    Claude A. Barnett Papers

Durham, North Carolina
Duke University, William P. Perkins Library, Manuscript Department
    Elizabeth J. (Holmes) Blanks Papers
    Eliza F. Caldwell Papers
    Lewis Clarke Papers
    John Bull Smith Dimitry Papers
    James K. English Account Book
    Placebo Houston Papers
    Joseph M. Jayne Plantation Account Book
    A. H. Jones Invoice Book
    Dugal and Duncan McCall Papers
    Duncan McLaurin Papers

Ellis Malone Papers
Allen Moragne Papers
Pope-Carter Family Papers
Prices Current Bulletins
James Sheppard Papers
Benjamin H. Vester Papers
Thomas B. Webber Diary

Fayetteville, Arkansas
University of Arkansas University Libraries, Special Collections Division
Elms Planting Company Record Books
Thomas Hottel Gist Plantation and Business Records
W. W. West Company Records

Jackson, Mississippi
Mississippi Department of Archives and History
Francis Marion Aldridge Papers
James Allen Plantation Book
Antiques File Folder
Aventine Plantation Diary
German and Joseph T. B. Berry Ledgers
Jefferson J. Birdsong Plantation Journal
Narcisa L. Black Diaries
L. M. Boatner Diary
Edwin C. Bolton Papers
Boycotts File Folder
Clyde Bryant Papers
S. G. Burney Ledger
Byers Family Papers
Chain Store File Folder
County Records
    Amite County Inventories
    Lawrence County Inventories
    Quitman County Inventories
    Sharkey County Inventories
    Yalobusha County Inventories
Darden Family Papers
E. Dickinson Daybook
Drake-Satterfield Papers
William Dubard and Company Records
William R. Ellen Plantation Records
Flea Markets File Folder
Food Stamp Program File Folder
Helen E. Foote Diaries
Alden Spooner Forbes Account Book
Nathan Jackson Fox Papers
Tryphena Holder Fox Collection
Foster and Freeman Freeland Papers

Charles B. Galloway Papers
Gill-Price Family Papers
F. Goodman Dry Goods Company Papers
Robert and James Gordon Diaries
John Gideon Harris Diary
R. G. Hazard Papers
Irion-Neilson Family Papers
Jones-Smith Plantation Records
Killona Plantation Journals
John Albert King and Sons Store Records
Joseph Benjamin Lightsey Diary
McCool Family Papers
Samuel M. Meek and Family Papers
Mount Prospect Trading Post Account Book
Flavellus G. Nicholson Diary
Panther Burn Plantation Account Book
A. J. Paxton Manuscript
Percy Family Papers
Slavery Collection
Belle Strickland Diary
Taylor-Ballentine Family Papers
Jacob P. Welch Autobiography
Rhodeham Yoe Store Records

Lexington, Kentucky
University of Kentucky Library, Special Collections, Mercantile Collection
Bennett Brothers and McMillin General Store Account Book
W. S. Hankinson Daybooks and Ledgers
Henderson's Store Records
Ike Jones Store Records
Mississippi Plantation Record
Vaiden General Store Ledger

Memphis, Tennessee
University of Memphis Libraries, Mississippi Valley Collection
M. Jones Mercantile Store Journal
Love's Station, Mississippi, Ledger Book
Margarette J. Lucy Diary
Northwest Tennessee General Store Account Book
Rev. Hamilton L. Parks Diaries and Papers
Persis Garland Smith Diary

Nashville, Tennessee
Tennessee State Library and Archive
Bills, Polk, and Wood Letters and Diaries
Carson General Store Account Book
Robert H. Cartmell Papers
Clay and Sinclair's General Store Account Book
Collier Family Account Books and Papers

Eakin Family Papers
Evins Brothers Store Papers
Robert B. Freeman Papers
Herndon Haraldson Diary
Jane M. Jones Diaries
Plautus Iberus Lipsey, "Memories of His Early Life"
Mrs. Frank Robbins Diary
Rogers and Hearn Store Account Book

Oxford, Mississippi
University of Mississippi Library, Special Collections
Samuel A. Agnew Diary
Aldrich Collection
Barbour Family Memoirs
Blanton-Smith Letters
Andrew Brown and Son–R. F. Learned Lumber Company Records
Juanita Brown Collection
Goodloe Warren Buford Diary
Craft-Fort Papers
F. B. Furr Store Ledger
William Decatur Howell Collection
Duncan McCollum Diary
Harriet S. Pegues Diary
Ann Rayburn Collection

Starkville, Mississippi
Mississippi State University Library, Special Collections
Dorothy Dickins, "Needs for Storage of Farm-Owner Families," 1948, unpublished
  typescript
Nannie Herndon Rice Papers

West Point, Mississippi
Mary Holmes College Library
Oral History Collection

Private Manuscripts

F. H. Campbell Store Ledger, Prewitt Family Collection, Winona, Mississippi

Newspapers

Aberdeen Tri-Weekly Examiner
Baptist Record, The (Jackson)
Brookhaven Ledger
Carthaginian, The (Carthage)
Chicago Defender
Choctaw Plain Dealer (Ackerman)
Clarksdale Banner

Clarksdale Press Register
Coahomian, The (Friar's Point)
Columbus Commercial
Columbus Democratic Whig
Copiah County News
Crystal Springs Monitor
Delta Democrat (Tunica)
Dollar Democrat (Coffeeville)
Dollar Democrat (Oxford)
Fayette Chronicle
Fayette Watch Tower
Greenville Daily Democrat
Greenville Daily Democrat-Times
Greenville Times
Greenwood Commonwealth
Greenwood Reporter
Greenwood Times
Grenada Daily Sentinel-Star
Grenada Herald
Grenada Morning Herald
Grenadian, The (Grenada)
Guard, The (Holly Springs)
Hattiesburg Daily Progress
Hattiesburg News
Hernando Free Press and States Rights Democrat
Hernando Phoenix
Hernando Press
Holly Springs Free Trade Advocate
Holly Springs Gazette
Holly Springs Marshall County Republican
Holly Springs Palladium
Holly Springs Reporter
Holly Springs Southern Banner
Iuka Vidette
Jackson Advocate
Jackson Clarion
Jackson Clarion Ledger
Kosciusko Chronicle
Laurel Chronicle
Lexington Advertiser
Lexington Union
Mainstream Mississippi (Jackson)
Memphis Commercial Appeal
Memphis Daily Appeal
Mississippi Leader (Brookhaven)
Monroe Democrat (Aberdeen)
Natchez Democrat

Neshoba Democrat
New Orleans Price Current
North Mississippi Herald (Water Valley)
Oxford Falcon
Pigeon Roost News (Holly Springs)
Port Gibson Reveille
Southern Advocate (Ashland)
Southern Reporter (Sardis)
Sunflower Tocsin (Indianola)
Tallahatchie Herald
Tupelo Daily Journal
Yazoo Banner (Benton)
Yazoo City Herald
Yazoo Democrat

County, State, and Federal Government Documents

Ayres, W. E. "Vegetables and Truck for Home Use." *Mississippi Agricultural Experiment Station Bulletin*, no. 210, March 1922.

Census of American Business: 1933, Retail Distribution. Vol. 1, United States Summary: 1933 and Comparisons with 1929. Washington, D.C.: U.S. Department of Commerce, Bureau of the Census, 1933.

Dickins, Dorothy. "Agricultural High School Dormitories of Mississippi." *Mississippi Agricultural Experiment Station Bulletin*, no. 293, August 1931.

———. "Changing Pattern of Food Preparation of Small Town Families in Mississippi." *Mississippi Agricultural Experiment Station Bulletin*, no. 415, May 1945.

———. "Clothing and Houselinen Expenditures of 99 Rural Families of Mississippi during 1928–1929." *Mississippi Agricultural Experiment Station Bulletin*, no. 294, September 1931.

———. "Effects of Good Household Management on Family Living." *Mississippi Agricultural Experiment Station Bulletin*, no. 380, May 1943.

———. "Factors Related to the Use of Credit Resources by Farm Families." *Mississippi Agricultural Experiment Station Bulletin*, no. 658, March 1963.

———. "Family Living on Poorer and Better Soil." *Mississippi Agricultural Experiment Station Bulletin*, no. 320, September 1937.

———. "Food and Health." *Mississippi Agricultural Experiment Station Bulletin*, no. 255, July 1928.

———. "Food Consumption of Boys and Girls in Six Typical Agricultural High Schools of Mississippi." *Mississippi Agricultural Experiment Station Bulletin*, no. 292, June 1931.

———. "Improving Levels of Living of Tenant Families." *Mississippi Agricultural Experiment Station Bulletin*, no. 365, January 1942.

———. "Levels of Living of Young Negro Farm-Operator Families in Mississippi." *Mississippi Agricultural Experiment Station Bulletin*, no. 580, July 1959.

———. "Levels of Living of Young White Farm-Operator Families in Mississippi." *Mississippi Agricultural Experiment Station Bulletin*, no. 579, June 1959.

———. "Market Basket Wisdom." *Mississippi Agricultural Experiment Station Bulletin*, no. 263, January 1929.

———. "A Nutrition Investigation of Negro Tenants in the Yazoo Mississippi Delta." *Mississippi Agricultural Experiment Station Bulletin*, no. 254, August 1928.

———. "Occupations of Sons and Daughters of Mississippi Cotton Farmers." *Mississippi Agricultural Experiment Station Bulletin*, no. 318, May 1937.

———. "Owner Farm Families in Poor Agricultural Areas and Cropper Farm Families in Rich Agricultural Areas." *Mississippi Agricultural Experiment Station Bulletin*, no. 359, June 1941.

———. "Some Contrasts in the Levels of Living of Women Engaged in Farm, Textile Mill, and Garment Plant Work." *Mississippi Agricultural Experiment Station Bulletin*, no. 364, November 1941.

———. "A Study of Food Habits of People in Two Contrasting Areas of Mississippi." *Mississippi Agricultural Experiment Station Bulletin*, no. 245, November 1927.

———. "Time Expenditures in Homemaking Activities by White and Negro Town Families." *Mississippi Agricultural Experiment Station Bulletin*, no. 424, October 1945.

———. "Traditional Food Preparation Rules." *Mississippi Agricultural Experiment Station Bulletin*, no. 418, June 1945.

———. "What the Farm Woman Can Do to Improve the Economic Status of Her Family." *Mississippi Agricultural Experiment Station Bulletin*, no. 346, July 1940.

Dickins, Dorothy, and Alice Bowie. "A Guide to Planning Clothes for the Mississippi Farm Family." *Mississippi Agricultural Experiment Station Bulletin*, no. 372, December 1942.

Dickins, Dorothy, and Virginia Ferguson. "Practices and Preferences of Teen-Age Girls in the Selection of Blouses, Skirts, Dresses, and Sweaters." *Mississippi Agricultural Experiment Station Bulletin*, no. 636, February 1962.

Dickins, Dorothy, Olive Sheets, and Ernestine Frazier. "Conservation of Iron in Vegetables by Methods of Preparation and Cooking." *Mississippi Agricultural Experiment Station Bulletin*, no. 291, May 1931.

Fifteenth Census of the United States, 1930, Distribution. Vol. 1, Retail Distribution, Part 2. Washington, D.C.: U.S. Department of Commerce, Bureau of the Census, 1931.

Hutchinson, A., comp. *Code of Mississippi, Analytical Compilation, 1798 to 1848.* Jackson: State of Mississippi, 1848.

"Instructions for Negro 4-H Club Girls and Negro Home Demonstration Women." *Mississippi State College Extension Bulletin*, no. 74, October 1935.

Jordan, Anne O. "Clothing for First and Second Year Club Girls." *Mississippi Agricultural and Mechanical College Extension Department Bulletin*, no. 42, December 1927.

———. "Clothing for Third and Fourth Year Club Girls." *Mississippi Agricultural and Mechanical College Extension Department Bulletin*, no. 45, December 1927.

———. "Furnishing the Farm Home: 4-H Club Girl's Bedroom." *Mississippi Agricultural and Mechanical College Extension Department Bulletin*, no. 60, January 1932.

———. "Simple Home Decoration." *Mississippi Agricultural and Mechanical College Extension Bulletin*, no. 40, November 1926.

Laws of the State of Mississippi, 1968. Jackson: State of Mississippi, 1968.

Midkoff, Ouida. "Clothing Manual for 4-H Club Girls and Home Demonstration Women." *Mississippi Agricultural and Mechanical College Extension Bulletin*, no. 61, March 1937.

Mississippi Department of Public Welfare. *Biennial Report.* Jackson, 1935–51.

———. *Public Welfare in Mississippi.* Vols. 1–2. Jackson, 1939–41.

Mississippi Reports. Vols. 71 (1893–94) and 74 (1896–97).

Mississippi State Board of Health. *Biennial Report*. Jackson, 1927–29.

Mississippi State Planning Commission. *Progress Report on State Planning in Mississippi*. Jackson, 1938.

1958 Census of Business. Vol. 2, Retail Trade—Area Statistics, Part 1, U.S. Summary and Alabama–Mississippi. Washington, D.C.: U.S. Department of Commerce, Bureau of the Census, 1958.

1967 Census of Business. Vol. 2, Retail Trade—Area Statistics, Part 2, Iowa–North Carolina. Washington, D.C.: U.S. Department of Commerce, Bureau of the Census, 1967.

1977 Census of Retail Trade. Vol. 2, Geographic Area Statistics. Part 2, Iowa–North Carolina. Washington, D.C.: U.S. Department of Commerce, Bureau of the Census, 1977.

1987 Census of Retail Trade, Geographic Area Series, Mississippi. Washington, D.C.: U.S. Department of Commerce, Bureau of the Census, 1987.

1992 Census of Retail Trade, Geographic Area Series, Mississippi. Washington, D.C.: U.S. Department of Commerce, Bureau of the Census, 1992.

Olson, L. A. "Annual Report of Cooperative Extension Work in Agriculture and Home Economics for 1931." *Mississippi State College Extension Department Bulletin*, no. 62, December 1931.

——. "Annual Report of Cooperative Extension Work in Agriculture and Home Economics, Mississippi, 1932." *Mississippi State College Extension Department Bulletin*, no. 66, August 1932.

——. "Annual Report of Cooperative Extension Work in Agriculture and Home Economics for 1935." *Mississippi State College Extension Department Bulletin*, no. 72, June 1935.

Report on Cotton Production in the United States. Vol. 5. Ed. Eugene W. Hilgard. Washington, D.C.: U.S. Census Office, 1884.

Stark, Betsy, and Lois Kilgore. "A Tribute to Dorothy Dickins." Starkville: Mississippi Agriculture and Forestry Experiment Station, October 1974.

United States Census of Business, 1948. Vol. 3, Retail Trade—Area Statistics. Washington, D.C.: U.S. Department of Commerce, Bureau of the Census, 1948.

Wilson, R. S. "Annual Report of Extension Work in Agriculture and Home Economics in Mississippi for 1919." *Mississippi Agricultural and Mechanical College Extension Bulletin*, no. 16, July 1920.

——. "Annual Report of Extension Work in Agriculture and Home Economics in Mississippi for 1923." *Mississippi Agricultural and Mechanical College Extension Bulletin*, no. 27, July 1924.

——. "Annual Report of Extension Work in Agriculture and Home Economics in Mississippi for 1924." *Mississippi Agricultural and Mechanical College Extension Bulletin*, no. 31, January 1925.

——. "Annual Report of Extension Work for 1925." *Mississippi Agricultural and Mechanical College Extension Bulletin*, no. 35, January 1926.

——. "Annual Report of Extension Work for 1926 in Agriculture and Home Economics in Mississippi." *Mississippi Agricultural and Mechanical Extension Bulletin*, no. 41, July 1927.

——. "Annual Report of Extension Work for 1927 in Agriculture and Home Economics." *Mississippi Agricultural and Mechanical College Extension Bulletin*, no. 49, July 1928.

——. "Annual Report of Extension Work for 1928 in Agriculture and Home Economics." *Mississippi Agricultural and Mechanical College Extension Bulletin*, no. 50, July 1929.

———. "Annual Report of Extension Work for 1929 in Agriculture and Home Economics." *Mississippi Agricultural and Mechanical College Extension Bulletin*, no. 54, July 1930.

Woofter, Thomas Jackson. *Land Lord and Tenant on the Cotton Plantation*. Works Progress Administration Research Monograph, no. 5. Washington, D.C.: WPA, 1936.

Published Material

Abelson, Elaine S. *When Ladies Go A-Thieving: Middle-Class Shoplifters in the Victorian Department Store*. New York: Oxford University Press, 1989.

Adams, William Hampton, and Steven D. Smith. "Historical Perspectives on Black Tenant Farmers' Material Culture: The Henry C. Long General Ledger at Waverly Plantation, Mississippi." In *The Archeology of Slaves and Plantation Life*, ed. Theresa Singleton, 309–34. New York: Academic Press, 1985.

Agnew, Jean-Christophe. "A House of Fiction: Domestic Interiors and the Commodity Aesthetic." In *Consuming Visions*, ed. Bronner, 133–56.

Alexis, Marcus. "Some Negro-White Differences in Consumption." *American Journal of Economics and Sociology* 21 (January 1962): 11–28.

Archer, Chalmers, Jr. *Growing Up Black in Rural Mississippi: Memories of a Family, Heritage of a Place*. New York: Walker and Company, 1992.

Armstrong, Thomas F. "From Task Labor to Free Labor: The Transition along Georgia's Rice Coast, 1820–1880." *Georgia Historical Quarterly* 44 (Winter 1980): 432–47.

Atherton, Lewis Eldon. *The Southern Country Store, 1800–1860*. Baton Rouge: Louisiana State University Press, 1949.

Ayers, Edward L. *The Promise of the New South: Life after Reconstruction*. New York: Oxford University Press, 1992.

Babbitt, Kathleen R. "The Productive Farm Woman and the Extension Home Economist in New York State, 1910–1940." *Agricultural History* 67 (Spring 1993): 83–101.

Banner, Lois W. *American Beauty*. Chicago: University of Chicago Press, 1983.

Barlow, William. *"Looking Up at Down": The Emergence of Blues Culture*. Philadelphia: Temple University Press, 1989.

Barth, Gunther Paul. *City People: The Rise of Modern City Culture in Nineteenth-Century America*. New York: Oxford University Press, 1980.

Beck, Warren. *Man in Motion: Faulkner's Trilogy*. Madison: University of Wisconsin Press, 1963.

Beets, Eva Davis. "Growing Up in Marion County: A Memoir by Eva Davis Beets." Ed. Christine Wilson. *Journal of Mississippi History* 47 (August 1986): 199–214.

Benson, Susan Porter. *Counter Cultures: Saleswomen, Managers, and Customers in American Department Stores*. Urbana: University of Illinois Press, 1986.

Berlin, Ira, ed. *The Wartime Genesis of Free Labor: The Lower South*. Ser. 1, vol. 3. Cambridge: Cambridge University Press, 1990.

Berlin, Ira, and Philip D. Morgan, eds. *Culture and Cultivation: Labor and the Shaping of Slave Life in the Americas*. Charlottesville: University Press of Virginia, 1993.

Blotner, Joseph. *Faulkner: A Biography*. New York: Random House, 1984.

Blumin, Stuart M. *The Emergence of the Middle Class: Social Experience in the American City, 1760–1900*. Cambridge: Cambridge University Press, 1989.

Bolton, Charles C. *Poor Whites of the Antebellum South: Tenants and Laborers in Central North Carolina and Northeast Mississippi*. Durham: Duke University Press, 1994.

Bond, Bradley G. *Political Culture in the Nineteenth-Century South*. Baton Rouge: Louisiana State University Press, 1995.

Bowlby, Rachel. *Just Looking: Consumer Culture in Dreiser, Gissing, and Zola*. New York: Methuen, 1985.

Boyd, Eddie. "Living Blues Interview." 3 pts. *Living Blues*, no. 35 (November/December 1977): 11–15; no. 36 (January/February 1978): 14–23; no. 37 (March/April 1978): 6–15.

Branch, Taylor. *Parting the Waters: America in the King Years, 1954–1963*. New York: Simon and Schuster, 1988.

Breen, T. H. *Tobacco Culture: The Mentality of the Planters on the Eve of Revolution*. Princeton: Princeton University Press, 1985.

Bridenbaugh, Carl. *Myths and Realities: Societies of the Colonial South*. New York: Atheneum, 1980.

Bronner, Simon, ed. *Consuming Visions: Accumulation and Display of Goods in America, 1880–1920*. New York: Norton, 1989.

Brooks, Cleanth. *William Faulkner: The Yoknapatawpha Country*. New Haven: Yale University Press, 1963.

Broonzy, William, as told to Yannick Bruynoghe. *Big Bill Blues: William Broonzy's Story*. 1955. Reprint. New York: Da Capo Press, 1992.

Brownell, Blaine. "A Symbol of Modernity: Attitudes toward the Automobile in Southern Cities in the 1920s." *American Quarterly* 24 (March 1972): 20–44.

Burke, Timothy. *Lifebuoy Men, Lux Women: Commodification, Consumption, and Cleanliness in Modern Zimbabwe*. Durham: Duke University Press, 1996.

Bushman, Richard L. *The Refinement of America: Persons, Homes, Cities*. New York: Knopf, 1992.

Campbell, Colin. *The Romantic Ethic and the Spirit of Modern Consumerism*. Oxford: Basil Blackwell, 1987.

Campbell, John. "As 'A Kind of Freeman'?: Slaves' Market-Related Activities in the South Carolina Up Country, 1800–1860." In *Culture and Cultivation*, ed. Berlin and Morgan, 243–74.

Campbell, Will D. *Brother to a Dragonfly*. New York: Continuum, 1977.

Cashin, Joan E. *A Family Venture: Men and Women on the Southern Frontier*. New York: Oxford University Press, 1991.

Charters, Samuel. *The Country Blues*. New York: Da Capo Press, 1975.

——. *The Legacy of the Blues: A Glimpse into the Art and the Lives of Twelve Great Bluesmen. An Informal Study*. London: Calder and Boyars, 1975.

——. *Sweet as the Showers of Rain: The Bluesmen*. Vol. 2. New York: Oak Publications, 1977.

Clark, Thomas D. *Pills, Petticoats, and Plows: The Southern Country Store*. 1944. Reprint. Norman: University of Oklahoma Press, 1963.

Clarksdale, Mississippi, City Directory. Asheville, N.C.: Piedmont Directory Company, 1916–17.

Cobb, James C. *The Most Southern Place on Earth: The Mississippi Delta and the Roots of Regional Identity*. New York: Oxford University Press, 1992.

——. *The Selling of the South: The Southern Crusade for Industrial Development, 1936–1990*. 2d ed. Urbana: University of Illinois Press, 1993.

Cohen, Lizabeth A. "Embellishing a Life of Labor: An Interpretation of the Material Culture of American Working-Class Homes, 1885–1915." *Journal of American Culture* 3 (Winter 1980): 752–75.

———. "From Town Center to Shopping Center: The Reconfiguration of Community Marketplaces in Postwar America." *American Historical Review* 101 (October 1996): 1050–81.

———. *Making a New Deal: Industrial Workers in Chicago, 1919–1939*. Cambridge: Cambridge University Press, 1990.

Cohen, William. *At Freedom's Edge: Black Mobility and the Southern White Quest for Racial Control, 1861–1915*. Baton Rouge: Louisiana State University Press, 1991.

Cohn, David. *Where I Was Born and Raised*. Boston: Houghton Mifflin, 1948.

Cook, Robert Cecil. *McGowah Place and Other Memoirs*. Hattiesburg, Miss.: Educators' Biographical Press, 1973.

Crosby, Emilye. "White Only on Main Street: A Community Showed Its True Character When Exuberant Artists Didn't Paint within the Lines." *Southern Exposure* 24 (Winter 1996): 37–41.

Daniel, Pete. *Breaking the Land: Transformation of Cotton, Tobacco, and Rice Cultures since 1880*. Urbana: University of Illinois Press, 1985.

———. *The Shadow of Slavery: Peonage in the South, 1901–1969*. Urbana: University of Illinois Press, 1972.

Davis, Allison, Burleigh B. Gardner, and Mary R. Gardner. *Deep South: A Social Anthropological Study of Caste and Class*. Chicago: University of Chicago Press, 1941.

DeGrazia, Victoria, with Ellen Furlough, eds. *The Sex of Things: Gender and Consumption in Historical Perspective*. Berkeley: University of California Press, 1996.

Des Champs, Margaret Burr, ed. "Some Mississippi Letters to Robert Fraser, 1841–1844." *Journal of Mississippi History* 15 (July 1953): 181–89.

Dickins, Dorothy. "Consumption Patterns of Cotton-Farm Families and an Agricultural Program for the South." *Rural Sociology* 13 (March 1948): 22–31.

———. "The Farm Home Improves Its Equipment." *Journal of Home Economics* 40 (December 1948): 567–70.

———. "Some Contrasts in Levels of Living in Industrial, Farm, and Part-Time Farm Families in Rural Mississippi." *Social Forces* 18 (December 1939): 247–55.

———. "The Southern Family in an Era of Change." *Rural Sociology* 15 (September 1950): 232–41.

Dimond, E. Gray, and Herman Hattaway, eds. *Letters from Forest Place: A Plantation Family's Correspondence, 1846–1881*. Jackson: University Press of Mississippi, 1993.

Dirks, Robert. *The Black Saturnalia: Conflict and Its Ritual Expression on British West Indian Slave Plantations*. Gainesville: University Press of Florida, 1987.

Dittmer, John. *Local People: The Struggle for Civil Rights in Mississippi*. Urbana: University of Illinois Press, 1994.

Dodd, Donald B., and Wynelle S. Dodd. *Historical Statistics of the South, 1790–1970*. University: University of Alabama Press, 1973.

Dollard, John. *Caste and Class in a Southern Town*. New York: Doubleday, 1957.

Douglas, Ann. *The Feminization of American Culture*. New York: Avon Books, 1977.

Douglas, Mary, and Baron Isherwood. *The World of Goods: Towards an Anthropology of Consumption.* New York: W. W. Norton and Co., 1982.

Dundy, Elaine. *Elvis and Gladys*. New York: Macmillan, 1984.

Dunn, Margaret M. "The Illusion of Freedom in *The Hamlet* and *Go Down, Moses*." In *On Faulkner: The Best from American Literature*, ed. Louis J. Budd and Edwin H. Cody, 235–51. Durham: Duke University Press, 1989.

Eaton, Clement. *The Growth of Southern Civilization, 1790–1860*. New York: Harper and Row, 1961.

Edsforth, Ronald W. *Class Conflict and Cultural Consensus: The Making of a Mass Consumer Society in Flint, Michigan*. New Brunswick, N.J.: Rutgers University Press, 1987.

Edwards, Paul K. *The Southern Urban Negro as a Consumer*. New York: Prentice-Hall, 1932.

Evans, Linda J. "Claude A. Barnett and the Associated Negro Press." *Chicago History* 12 (Spring 1983): 44–56.

Evers, Charles. *Evers*. Ed. Grace Halsell. New York: World Publishing Company, 1971.

——. "From *Evers*." In *Mississippi Writers: Reflections of Childhood and Youth. Vol. 2: Nonfiction*, ed. Dorothy Abbott, 196–208. Center for the Study of Southern Culture Series. Jackson: University Press of Mississippi, 1986.

Evers, Charles, and Andrew Szanton. *Have No Fear: The Charles Evers Story*. New York: John Wiley and Sons, 1997.

Evers, Mrs. Medgar, with William Peters. *For Us, the Living*. Garden City, N.J.: Doubleday and Co., 1967.

Ewen, Stuart. *Captains of Consciousness: Advertising and the Social Roots of the Consumer Culture*. New York: McGraw-Hill, 1976.

Ewen, Stuart, and Elizabeth Ewen. *Channels of Desire: Mass Images and the Shaping of American Consciousness*. New York: McGraw-Hill, 1982.

Faulkner, John. *My Brother Bill: An Affectionate Reminiscence*. New York: Trident Press, 1963.

Faulkner, William. *As I Lay Dying*. 1930. Reprint. New York: Vintage Books, 1964.

——. *Collected Stories of William Faulkner*. New York: Random House, 1950.

——. *Intruder in the Dust*. New York: Random House, 1948.

——. *Light in August*. 1932. Reprint. New York: Vintage Books, 1964.

——. *The Hamlet*. 1940. Reprint. New York: Random House, 1964.

——. *The Mansion*. 1955. Reprint. New York: Vintage Books, 1965.

——. *The Reivers: A Reminiscence*. New York: Vintage Books, 1962.

——. *The Town*. New York: Vintage Books, 1957.

Faust, Drew Gilpin. *Mothers of Invention: Women of the Slaveholding South in the American Civil War*. Chapel Hill: University of North Carolina Press, 1996.

Ferris, William. *Local Color: A Sense of Place in Folk Art*. Ed. Brenda McCallum. New York: Doubleday, Anchor Books, 1982.

Fite, Gilbert. *Cotton Fields No More: Southern Agriculture, 1865–1980*. Lexington: University Press of Kentucky, 1980.

Flink, James. *The Car Culture*. Cambridge, Mass.: MIT Press, 1975.

Fogel, Robert William. *Without Consent or Contract: The Rise and Fall of American Slavery*. New York: W. W. Norton, 1989.

Fogel, Robert William, and Stanley Engerman. *Time on the Cross: The Economics of American Negro Slavery*. Boston: Little, Brown, 1974.

Fox, Richard Wightman, and T. J. Jackson Lears, eds. *The Culture of Consumption: Critical Essays in American History, 1880–1980*. New York: Norton, 1989.

——, eds. *The Power of Culture: Critical Essays in American History*. Chicago: University of Chicago Press, 1993.

Fox-Genovese, Elizabeth. *Within the Plantation Household: Black and White Women of the Old South*. Chapel Hill: University of North Carolina Press, 1988.

Garon, Paul, and Beth Garon. *Woman with Guitar: Memphis Minnie's Blues*. New York: Da Capo Press, 1992.

Genovese, Eugene D. *The Political Economy of Slavery: Studies in the Economy and Society of the Slave South*. New York: Vintage Books, 1965.

———. *Roll, Jordan, Roll: The World the Slaves Made*. New York: Vintage Books, 1974.

Gibson, D. Parke. *The $30 Billion Negro*. London: Macmillan, 1969.

Glymph, Thavolia. "Freedpeople and Ex-Masters: Shaping a New Order in the Postbellum South." In *Essays on the Postbellum Southern Economy*, ed. Thavolia Glymph and John J. Kushma, 48–72. College Station: Texas A&M University Press/University of Texas at Arlington, 1985.

Goings, Kenneth W. *Mammy and Uncle Mose: Black Collectibles and American Stereotyping*. Bloomington: Indiana University Press, 1994.

Goldfield, David. *Black, White, and Southern: Race Relations and Southern Culture, 1940 to the Present*. Baton Rouge: Louisiana State University Press, 1990.

Gottlieb, Peter. *Making Their Own Way: Southern Blacks' Migration to Pittsburgh, 1916–1930*. Urbana: University of Illinois Press, 1987.

Greenberg, Kenneth S. *Honor and Slavery: Lies, Duels, Noses, Masks, Dressing as a Woman, Gifts, Strangers, Humanitarianism, Death, Slave Rebellions, the Proslavery Argument, Baseball, Hunting, and Gambling in the Old South*. Princeton: Princeton University Press, 1996.

———. *Masters and Statesmen: The Political Culture of American Slavery*. Baltimore: Johns Hopkins University Press, 1985.

Greene, Jack. *Pursuits of Happiness: The Social Development of Early Modern British Colonies and the Formation of American Culture*. Chapel Hill: University of North Carolina Press, 1988.

Grossman, James R. *Land of Hope: Chicago, Black Southerners, and the Great Migration*. Chicago: University of Chicago Press, 1989.

Hale, Grace Elizabeth. *Making Whiteness: The Culture of Segregation in the South, 1890–1940*. New York: Pantheon Books, 1998.

Hall, Jacquelyn Dowd, James Leloudis, Robert Korstad, Mary Murphy, Lu Ann Jones, and Christopher B. Daly. *Like a Family: The Making of a Southern Cotton Mill World*. Chapel Hill: University of North Carolina Press, 1987.

Halttunen, Karen. "From Parlor to Living Room: Domestic Space, Interior Decoration, and the Culture of Personality." In *Consuming Visions*, ed. Bronner, 157–90.

Hamilton, Mary. *Trials of the Earth: The Autobiography of Mary Hamilton*. Ed. Helen Dick Davis. Jackson: University Press of Mississippi, 1992.

Harmon, J. W. *Select Sermons on a Variety of Subjects*. Paulding, Miss: Privately printed, 1894.

Harris, Sheldon. *Blues Who's Who: A Biographical Dictionary of Blues Singers*. New York: Da Capo Press, 1979.

Heinze, Andrew. *Adapting to Abundance: Jewish Immigrants, Mass Consumption, and the Search for American Identity*. New York: Columbia University Press, 1990.

Hermann, Janet Sharp. *Joseph E. Davis, Pioneer Patriarch*. Jackson: University Press of Mississippi, 1990.

Hickman, Nollie. *Mississippi Harvest: Lumbering in the Longleaf Pine Belt, 1840–1915*. University: University of Mississippi, 1962.

Hicks, Ruby Sheppeard. *The Song of the Delta*. Jackson: Howick House, 1976.

Higgs, Robert J. "Accumulation of Property by Southern Blacks before World War I." *American Economic Review* 72 (September 1982): 725–37.

Hines, Thomas S. *William Faulkner and the Tangible Past: The Architecture of Yoknapatawpha.* Berkeley: University of California Press, 1996.

Holland, Endesha Ida Mae. *From the Mississippi Delta: A Memoir.* New York: Simon and Schuster, 1997.

Holman, William Henry, Jr. *"Save a Nickel on a Quarter": The Story of Jitney Jungle Stores of America.* Address to the Newcomen Society in North America. Jackson, Miss.: N.p., 1973.

Horowitz, Daniel. *The Morality of Spending: Attitudes toward the Consumer Society in America, 1875–1940.* Baltimore: Johns Hopkins University Press, 1985.

House, Boyce. "Recollections of Coldwater, A Vanished Town." *Journal of Mississippi History* 21 (January 1959): 40–55.

House, Son. "Living Blues Interview." *Living Blues,* no. 31 (March/April 1977): 14–22.

Howell, Virginia M. *Virginia's Diary.* Ed. David B. Howell. N.p.: David B. Howell, 1991.

Huckaby, Elizabeth Paisley, and Ethel Simpson, eds. *Tulip Evermore: Emma Butler and William Paisley, Their Lives in Letters, 1857–1887.* Fayetteville: University of Arkansas Press, 1985.

Hudson, Larry E. *To Have and To Hold: Slave Work and Family Life in Antebellum South Carolina.* Athens: University of Georgia Press, 1997.

Hundley, Daniel R. *Social Relations in Our Southern States.* Ed. William J. Cooper. Baton Rouge: Louisiana State University Press, 1979.

Hunt, Patricia K. "Clothing as an Expression of History: The Dress of African-American Women in Georgia, 1880–1915." *Georgia Historical Quarterly* 76 (Summer 1992): 459–71.

Hutchison, Janet. "Better Homes and Gullah." *Agricultural History* 67 (Spring 1993): 102–18.

Isaac, Rhys. *The Transformation of Virginia, 1740–1790.* Chapel Hill: University of North Carolina, 1982.

Jackson, Nannie Stillwell. *Vinegar Pie and Chicken Bread: A Woman's Diary of Life in the Rural South, 1890–1891.* Ed. Margaret Jones Bolsterli. Fayetteville: University of Arkansas Press, 1982.

James, Dorris Clayton. *Ante-Bellum Natchez.* Baton Rouge: Louisiana State University Press, 1968.

Jaynes, Gerald David. *Branches without Roots: Genesis of the Black Working Class in the American South.* New York: Oxford University Press, 1986.

Jenson, Joan M. "Crossing Ethnic Barriers in the Southwest: Women's Agricultural Extension Education, 1914–1940." *Agricultural History* 60 (Spring 1986): 169–81.

Johnson, John L. *Occasional Sermons.* New York: Burr Printing House, 1889.

Johnson, Michael, and James Larry Roark, eds. *No Chariot Let Down: Charleston's Free People of Color on the Eve of the Civil War.* Chapel Hill: University of North Carolina Press, 1984.

Jones, Jacqueline. *Labor of Love, Labor of Sorrow: Black Women, Work, and the Family from Slavery to the Present.* New York: Basic Books, 1985.

Jones, Norrece T., Jr. *Born a Child of Freedom, Yet a Slave: Mechanisms of Control and Strategies of Resistance in Antebellum South Carolina.* Hanover, Conn.: Wesleyan University Press, 1990.

Jordan, Winthrop D. *Tumult and Silence at Second Creek: An Inquiry into a Civil War Slave Conspiracy*. Baton Rouge: Louisiana State University, 1993.

——. *White over Black: American Attitudes toward the Negro, 1550–1812*. New York: Norton, 1977.

Joyner, Charles. *Down by the Riverside: A South Carolina Slave Community*. Urbana: University of Illinois Press, 1984.

Kartiganer, Donald M. *The Fragile Thread: The Meaning of Form in Faulkner's Novels*. Amherst: University of Massachusetts Press, 1979.

Katz, Michael B. *The Undeserving Poor: From the War on Poverty to the War on Welfare*. New York: Pantheon Books, 1989.

Keith, Jeanette. *Country People in the New South: Tennessee's Upper Cumberland*. Chapel Hill: University of North Carolina, 1995.

Kern-Foxworth, Marilyn. *Aunt Jemima, Uncle Ben, and Rastus: Blacks in Advertising, Yesterday, Today, and Tomorrow*. Westport, Conn.: Greenwood Press, 1994.

King, B. B., with David Ritz. *Blues All Around Me: The Autobiography of B. B. King*. New York: Avon Books, 1992.

Kirby, Jack Temple. *Rural Worlds Lost: The American South, 1920–1960*. Baton Rouge: Louisiana State University Press, 1987.

Klein, L. R., and W. H. Mooney. "Negro-White Savings Differentials and the Consumption Function Problem." *Econometrica* 21 (July 1953): 435–56.

Kolchin, Peter. *Unfree Labor: American Slavery and Russian Serfdom*. Cambridge: Harvard University Press, 1987.

Leach, William R. *Land of Desire: Merchants, Power, and the Rise of a New American Culture*. New York: Vintage Books, 1993.

——. "Transformations in a Culture of Consumption: Women and Department Stores, 1890–1925." *Journal of American History* 71–72 (September 1984): 319–42.

Lears, Jackson. "Beyond Veblen: Rethinking Consumer Culture in America." In *Consuming Visions*, ed. Bronner, 73–98.

——. *Fables of Abundance: A Cultural History of Advertising in America*. New York: Basic Books, 1994.

——. "From Salvation to Self-Realization: Advertising and the Therapeutic Roots of the Consumer Culture, 1880–1930." In *The Culture of Consumption*, ed. Fox and Lears, 3–38.

Lebergott, Stanley. *Pursuing Happiness: American Consumers in the Twentieth Century*. Princeton: Princeton University Press, 1993.

Lee, Peter. "Robert Jr. Lockwood: Unlocking Some Secrets." *Living Blues* 90 (March/April 1990): 32–35.

Lesseig, Corey T. " 'Out of the Mud': The Good Roads Crusade and Social Change in Twentieth-Century Mississippi." *Journal of Mississippi History* 60 (Spring 1998): 51–72.

Levine, Lawrence W. *Black Culture and Black Consciousness: Afro-American Folk Thought from Slavery to Freedom*. New York: Oxford University Press, 1977.

Lockwood, Robert Jr. "Living Blues Interview." *Living Blues*, no. 12 (Spring 1973): 15–39.

Loeb, Lori Anne. *Consuming Angels: Advertising and Victorian Women*. New York: Oxford University Press, 1994.

Lynd, Robert S., and Helen Merrill Lynd. *Middletown: A Study of Modern American Culture*. New York: Harcourt Brace Jovanovich, 1956.

McCracken, Grant. *Culture and Consumption: New Approaches to the Symbolic Character of Consumer Goods and Activities*. Bloomington: Indiana University Press, 1990.

McCurry, Stephanie. *Masters of Small Worlds: Yeoman Households, Gender Relations, and the Political Culture of the Antebellum South Carolina Low Country*. New York: Oxford University Press, 1995.

McDonald, Roderick A. *The Economy and Material Culture of Slaves: Goods and Chattels on the Sugar Plantations of Jamaica and Louisiana*. Baton Rouge: Louisiana State University Press, 1993.

McKendrick, Neil, John Brewer, and J. H. Plumb. *The Birth of a Consumer Society: The Commercialization of Eighteenth-Century England*. Bloomington: Indiana University Press, 1982.

McKenzie, Robert Tracy. "Freedmen and the Soil in the Upper South: The Reorganization of Tennessee Agriculture, 1865–1880." *Journal of Southern History* 59 (February 1993): 63–84.

McMillen, Neil R. *Dark Journey: Black Mississippians in the Age of Jim Crow*. Urbana: University of Illinois Press, 1989.

Manring, M. M. *Slave in a Box: The Strange Career of Aunt Jemima*. Charlottesville: University Press of Virginia, 1998.

Marchand, Roland. *Advertising the American Dream: Making Way for Modernity, 1920–1940*. Berkeley: University of California Press, 1985.

Marks, Carole. *Farewell, We're Good and Gone: The Great Black Migration*. Bloomington: Indiana University Press, 1989.

Matthews, John. "Shortened Stories: Faulkner and the Market." In *Faulkner and the Short Story, Faulkner and Yoknapatawpha, 1990*, ed. Evans Harrington and Ann J. Abadie, 3–37. Jackson: University Press of Mississippi, 1992.

Miller, Michael B. *The Bon Marche: Bourgeois Culture and the Department Store*. Princeton: Princeton University Press, 1981.

Millgate, Michael. *The Achievement of William Faulkner*. New York: Random House, 1966.

Mills, Kay. *This Little Light of Mine: The Life of Fannie Lou Hamer*. New York: Plume, 1994.

Mississippi Business Directory, 1988–1989. Omaha: American Directory Publishing, 1989.

Mississippi Business Directory, 1994–1995. Omaha: American Directory Publishing, 1995.

Mississippi County Basic Data. Philadelphia: Farm Journal, Inc., Market Research Department, 1944.

Minter, David. *William Faulkner, His Life and Work*. Baltimore: Johns Hopkins University Press, 1980.

Moody, Anne. *Coming of Age in Mississippi*. New York: Laurel, 1968.

Moore, John Hebron. *The Emergence of the Cotton Kingdom in the Old Southwest: Mississippi, 1770–1860*. Baton Rouge: Louisiana State University Press, 1988.

Morant, Jonathan J. *Mississippi Minister*. New York: Vantage Press, 1958.

Moreland, Richard C. *Faulkner and Modernism: Rereading and Rewriting*. Madison: University of Wisconsin Press, 1990.

Morgan, Philip D. "The Ownership of Property by Slaves in the Mid-Nineteenth-Century Low Country." *Journal of Southern History* 49 (August 1983): 399–420.

———. "Work and Culture: The Task System and the World of Lowcountry Blacks, 1770 to 1880." *William and Mary Quarterly*, 3d ser., 39 (July 1982): 563–99.

Morris, Christopher. *Becoming Southern: The Evolution of a Way of Life, Warren County and Vicksburg, Mississippi, 1770–1860*. New York: Oxford University Press, 1995.

Nasaw, David. *Children of the City: At Work and at Play*. New York: Oxford University Press, 1986.

Nathans, Sydney. "Gotta Mind to Move, Gotta Mind to Settle Down: Afro-Americans and the Plantation Frontier." In *A Master's Due: Essays in Honor of David Herbert Donald*, ed. William J. Cooper et al., 204–22. Baton Rouge: Louisiana State University Press, 1985.

National Civil Rights Museum. "Honoring the Struggle of a Generation: The National Civil Rights Museum." *History News* 51 (Autumn 1996): 5–11.

Neff, Robert, and Anthony Connor. *Blues*. Boston: David R. Godine, 1975.

Nelson, Lawrence J. "Welfare Capitalism on a Mississippi Plantation in the Great Depression." *Journal of Southern History* 50 (May 1984): 225–50.

Nissenbaum, Stephen. *The Battle for Christmas: A Cultural History of America's Most Cherished Holiday*. New York: Vintage Books, 1996.

Nixon, Hammie, and Sleepy John Estes. "Living Blues Interview." *Living Blues*, no. 19 (January/February 1975): 13–19.

Novak, Daniel. *The Wheel of Servitude: Black Forced Labor after Slavery*. Lexington: University Press of Kentucky, 1978.

Obrecht, Jas. "Johnny Shines: Whupped Around and Screwed Around but Still Hanging On." *Living Blues* 90 (March/April 1990): 24–31.

Oliver, Paul. *Screening the Blues; Aspects of the Blues Tradition*. New York: Da Capo Press, 1968.

Olney, Martha L. *Buy Now, Pay Later: Advertising, Credit, and Consumer Durables in the 1920s*. Chapel Hill: University of North Carolina Press, 1991.

Olsson, Bengt. *Memphis Blues and Jug Bands*. London: Studio Vista, 1970.

Osterud, Nancy Grey. "Gender and the Transition to Capitalism in Rural America." *Agricultural History* 67 (Spring 1993): 14–29.

Otken, Charles H. *The Ills of the South, or Related Causes Hostile to the General Prosperity of the Southern People*. New York: G. P. Putnam's Sons, 1894.

Owens, George W. *"I Was There . . .": An Autobiographical Sketch of Education, Legislative, and Rehabilitation Experiences during the Changing Systems of Government in Mississippi*. Pontotoc, Miss.: Itawamba County Times, 1973.

Owens, Harry P. *Steamboats and the Cotton Economy: River Trade in the Yazoo-Mississippi Delta*. Jackson: University Press of Mississippi, 1990.

Owens, Leslie Howard. *This Species of Property: Slave Life and Culture in the Old South*. New York: Oxford University Press, 1976.

Ownby, Ted. " 'Does the South Still Exist?': A Historian's Critique of the Question." *Crossroads: A Journal of Southern Culture* 5 (Spring 1998): 3–12.

———. "The Snopes Trilogy and the Emergence of Consumer Culture." In *Faulkner and Ideology, Faulkner and Yoknapatawpha*, ed. Donald M. Kartiganer and Ann J. Abadie, 95–128. Jackson: University Press of Mississippi, 1995.

———. *Subduing Satan: Recreation, Religion, and Manhood in the Rural South, 1865–1920*. Chapel Hill: University of North Carolina Press, 1990.

Palmer, Robert. *Deep Blues*. New York: Penguin Books, 1981.

Payne, Charles M. *I've Got the Light of Freedom: The Organizing Tradition and the Mississippi Freedom Struggle*. Berkeley: University of California Press, 1995.

Pearson, Barry Lee. *"Sounds So Good to Me": The Bluesman's Story*. Philadelphia: University of Pennsylvania Press, 1984.

Peiss, Kathy. *Cheap Amusements: Working Women and Leisure in Turn-of-the-Century New York*. Philadelphia: Temple University Press, 1986.

Pennington, Estill Curtis. "Aesthetics of Everyday Life in Old Natchez." In *Natchez before 1830*, ed. Noel Polk, 109–23. Jackson: University Press of Mississippi, 1989.

Percy, William Alexander. *Lanterns on the Levee: Recollections of a Planter's Son*. 1941. Reprint. Baton Rouge: Louisiana State University Press, 1973.

Phillips, U. B. *American Negro Slavery*. 1916. Reprint. Baton Rouge: Louisiana State University Press, 1966.

Pope, Daniel. *The Making of Modern Advertising*. New York: Basic Books, 1983.

Potter, David B. *People of Plenty: Economic Abundance and the American Character*. Chicago: University of Chicago Press, 1954.

Price, Beulah M. D'Olive, ed. "Excerpts from the Diary of Walter Alexander Overton." *Journal of Mississippi History* 17 (July 1955): 191–211.

Rachell, James "Yank." "Living Blues Interview." *Living Blues*, no. 97 (March/April 1988): 12–21.

R. G. Dun and Company. *The Mercantile Agency Reference Book (and Key) Containing Ratings of the Merchants, Manufacturers, and Traders Generally, Throughout the United States and Canada*. New York: R. G. Dun and Company, 1883, 1905, and 1925.

Ransom, Roger L., and Richard Sutch. *One Kind of Freedom: The Economic Consequences of Emancipation*. Cambridge: Cambridge University Press, 1977.

Rawick, George, ed. *The American Slave: A Composite Autobiography*. Westport, Conn.: Greenwood, 1972.

——. *From Sundown to Sunup: The Making of the Black Community*. Westport, Conn.: Greenwood, 1972.

Rieff, Lynne A. " 'Go Ahead and Do All You Can': Southern Progressives and Alabama Home Demonstration Clubs, 1914–1940." In *Hidden Histories of Women in the New South*, ed. Virginia Bernhard, Betty Brandon, Elizabeth Fox-Genovese, Theda Perdue, and Elizabeth Hayes Turner, 134–49. Columbia: University of Missouri Press, 1994.

Riley, Franklin L., ed. "Diary of a Mississippi Planter, January 1, 1840, to April 1863." *Publications of the Mississippi Historical Society* 10 (1909): 305–482.

Roberts, Cyrus Tapscott. *Some Oaks Grow Small*. Fulton, Miss.: Itawamba County Times, 1961.

Roche, Daniel. *The People of Paris: An Essay in Popular Culture in the 18th Century*. Trans. Marie Evans with Gwynne Lewis. Berkeley: University of California Press, 1987.

Rosengarten, Theodore. *All God's Dangers: The Life of Nate Shaw*. 1974. Reprint. New York: Vintage, 1989.

Rothstein, Morton. " 'The Remotest Corner': Natchez on the American Frontier." in *Natchez before 1830*, ed. Noel Polk, 92–108. Jackson: University Press of Mississippi, 1989.

Rozbicki, Michal J. *The Complete Colonial Gentleman: Cultural Legitimacy in Plantation America*. Charlottesville: University Press of Virginia, 1998.

Ruzicka, William T. *Faulkner's Fictive Architecture: The Meaning of Place in the Yoknapatawpha Novels*. Ann Arbor: UMI Research Press, 1987.

Ryan, Mary P. *Cradle of the Middle Class: The Family in Oneida County, New York, 1790–1865*. Cambridge: Cambridge University Press, 1981.

Schama, Simon. *The Embarrassment of Riches: An Interpretation of Dutch Culture in the Golden Age*. Berkeley: University of California Press, 1988.

Schlereth, Thomas J. "Country Stores, County Fairs, and Mail-Order Catalogues: Consumption in Rural America." In *Consuming Visions*, ed. Bronner, 339–76.

Schmidt, Leigh Eric. *Consumer Rites: The Buying and Selling of American Holidays*. Princeton: Princeton University Press, 1995.

Schudson, Michael. *Advertising, the Uneasy Persuasion: Its Dubious Impact on American Society*. New York: Basic Books, 1984.

Schweninger, Loren. *Black Property Owners in the South, 1790–1915*. Urbana: University of Illinois Press, 1990.

Scott, Roy V. *The Reluctant Farmer: The Rise of Agricultural Extension to 1914*. Urbana: University of Illinois Press, 1970.

Seidl, Joan M. "Consumers' Choices: A Study of Household Furnishing, 1880–1920." *Minnesota History* 48 (Spring 1982): 182–97.

Shaw, Arnold. *Honkers and Shouters: The Golden Years of Rhythm and Blues*. New York: Collier Books, 1978.

Smedes, Susan Dabney. *Memorials of a Southern Planter*. Ed. Fletcher M. Green. 1888. Reprint. Jackson: University Press of Mississippi, 1981.

Smith, Mark M. *Mastered by the Clock: Time, Slavery, and Freedom in the American South*. Chapel Hill: University of North Carolina Press, 1997.

Smith-Rosenberg, Carroll. *Disorderly Conduct: Visions of Gender in Victorian America*. New York: Oxford University Press, 1985.

Southern Business Directory and General Commercial Advertiser. Vol. 1. Charleston: Walker and James, 1854.

Stampp, Kenneth. *The Peculiar Institution: Slavery in the Antebellum South*. New York: Alfred A. Knopf, 1956.

Stone, Alfred Holt. *Studies in the American Race Problem*. New York: Doubleday, Page and Company, 1908.

Stone, Lawrence. *The Crisis of the Aristocracy, 1558–1641*. 1965. Reprint. Oxford: Clarendon Press, 1979.

Stowe, Steven M. *Intimacy and Power in the Old South: Intimacy in the Lives of the Planters*. Baltimore: Johns Hopkins University Press, 1987.

Strasser, Susan. *Satisfaction Guaranteed: The Making of the American Mass Market*. New York: Pantheon Books, 1989.

Susman, Warren. " 'Personality' and the Making of Twentieth-Century American Culture." In *New Directions in American Intellectual History*, ed. John Higham and Paul K. Conkin, 212–26. Baltimore: Johns Hopkins University Press, 1979.

Sydnor, Charles S. *American Revolutionaries in the Making: Political Practices in Washington's Virginia*. 1952. Reprint. New York: Free Press, 1965.

———. *Slavery in Mississippi*. 1933. Reprint. Gloucester, Mass.: Peter Smith, 1965.

Taft, Michael, ed. *Blues Lyric Poetry: An Anthology*. New York: Garland Publishing, 1983.

Taulbert, Clifton L. *When We Were Colored*. New York: Penguin Books, 1989.

Taylor, Mildred D. *"The Friendship" and "The Gold Cadillac."* New York: Bantam Skylark, 1989.

Thigpen, Julia Arledge, *Ninety and One Years*. Kingsport, Tenn.: Kingsport Press, 1965.

Thigpen, S. G. *A Boy in Rural Mississippi and Other Stories*. Picayune, Miss.: N.p., 1966.

———. *Next Door to Heaven*. Kingsport, Tenn.: Kingsport Press, 1965.

Thompson, Robert Farris. *Flash of the Spirit: African Art and Afro-American Art and Philosophy*. New York: Random House, 1983.

Turitz, Leo E., and Evelyn Turitz. *Jews in Early Mississippi*. Jackson: University Press of Mississippi, 1983.

Turner, Victor. *The Ritual Process: Structure and Anti-Structure*. Chicago: Aldine, 1969.

Vance, Sandra S., and Roy V. Scott, *Wal-Mart: A History of Sam Walton's Retail Phenomenon*. New York; Twayne Publishers, 1994.

Veblen, Thorstein. *The Theory of the Leisure Class: An Economic Study of Institutions*. New York: New American Library, 1953.

Veysey, Lawrence. "A Postmorten on Daniel Bell's Postindustrialism." *American Quarterly* 34, no. 1 (Spring 1982): 49–69.

Wade, Richard. *Slavery in the Cities: The South, 1820–1860*. New York: Oxford University Press, 1967.

Walker, Melissa. "Home Extension Work among African American Farm Women in East Tennessee, 1920–1939." *Agricultural History* 70 (Summer 1996): 487–502.

Wal-Mart. *Annual Report*. Bentonville, Ark., 1993, 1997.

Waters, Muddy. "Living Blues Interview." *Living Blues*, no. 64 (March/April 1985): 15–39.

Watson, James Gray. *The Snopes Dilemma: Faulkner's Trilogy*. Coral Gables, Fla.: University of Miami Press, 1968.

Wayne, Michael. *The Reshaping of Plantation Society: The Natchez District, 1860–1880*. Baton Rouge: Louisiana State University Press, 1983.

Weiner, Annette B., and Jane Schneider, eds. *Cloth and Human Experience*. Washington, D.C.: Smithsonian Institution Press, 1989.

Welty, Eudora. *The Collected Stories of Eudora Welty*. New York: Harcourt Brace Jovanovich, 1980.

——. *Delta Wedding*. 1946. Reprint. New York: Harcourt Brace and Co., 1973.

——. *One Writer's Beginnings*. 1984. Reprint. New York: Warner Books, 1991.

——. *The Optimist's Daughter*. 1972. Reprint. New York: Vintage Books, 1990.

——. "The Little Store." In *Mississippi Writers: Reflections of Childhood and Youth. Vol. 2: Nonfiction*. Ed. Dorothy Abbott, 639–46. Center for the Study of Southern Culture Series. Jackson: University Press of Mississippi, 1986.

——. *The Ponder Heart*. 1954. Reprint. New York: Harcourt Brace and Co., 1982.

Whayne, Jeannie M. *A New Plantation South: Land, Labor, and Federal Favor in Twentieth-Century Arkansas*. Charlottesville: University Press of Virginia, 1996.

Whisnant, David E. *All That Is Native and Fine: The Politics of Culture in an American Region*. Chapel Hill: University of North Carolina Press, 1983.

Whiteis, David. "A Tender Heart and a Hustler's Soul: Sunnyland Slim's Long Life in the Blues." *Living Blues* 90 (March/April 1990): 14–23.

Wiener, Jonathan M. *Social Origins of the New South: Alabama, 1860–1885*. Baton Rouge: Louisiana State University Press, 1978.

White, Shane, and Graham White. *Stylin': African American Expressive Culture from Its Beginnings to the Zoot Suit*. Ithaca: Cornell University Press, 1998.

White, William W. "A Community Portrait from Postal Records: Bywy, Mississippi, 1881–1900." *Journal of Mississippi History* 25 (1963): 33–37.

Williams, Rosalind H. *Dream Worlds: Mass Consumption in Late Nineteenth-Century France*. Berkeley: University of California Press, 1982.

Williams, Tennessee. *Cat on a Hot Tin Roof*. 1955. Reprint. New York: Signet, 1985.

Winans, William. *The Citizen of Zion: Substance of a Sermon on Psalm XV*. Natchez: Daily Courier, 1857.

——. *Sermons: or, A Series of Discourses on Fundamental Religious Subjects; Including a Preliminary Discourse on the Divine Revelation of the Holy Scriptures*. Ed. W. P. Harrison. Nashville: Publishing House of the Methodist Episcopal Church, South, 1891.

Wolfenstein, Martha. "The Emergence of Fun Morality." *Journal of Social Issues* 7 (1951): 15–25.

Wood, Betty. *Women's Work, Men's Work: The Informal Slave Economies of Lowcountry Georgia*. Athens: University of Georgia Press, 1995.

Woodman, Harold D. *King Cotton and His Retainers: Financing and Marketing the Cotton Crop of the South, 1800–1925*. 1968. Reprint. Columbia: University of South Carolina Press, 1990.

Wright, Gavin. *Old South, New South: Revolutions in the Southern Economy Since the Civil War*. New York: Basic Books, 1986.

Wright, Richard. *American Hunger*. New York: Harper and Row, 1944.

——. *Black Boy: A Record of Childhood and Youth*. 1945. Reprint. New York: Harper and Row, 1966.

——. *Uncle Tom's Children*. 1940. Reprint. New York: Harper and Row, 1965.

Wyatt-Brown, Bertram. *Southern Honor: Ethics and Behavior in the Old South*. New York: Oxford University Press, 1985.

Yoshima, J. Roger. "The Stereotype of the Negro and His High-Priced Car." *Sociology and Social Research* 44 (November–December 1959): 112–18.

Young, Stark. *The Pavilion: Of People and Times Remembered, Of Stories and Places*. New York: Charles Scribner's Sons, 1951.

Zaretsky, Eli. *Capitalism, the Family, and Personal Life*. Rev. ed. New York: Harper and Row, 1986.

Zelizer, Viviana. *Pricing the Priceless Child: The Changing Social Value of Children*. New York: Basic Books, 1985.

Unpublished Works

Bercaw, Nancy Dunlap. "Politics of Household during the Transition from Slavery to Freedom in the Yazoo-Mississippi Delta, 1861–1876." Ph.D. diss., University of Pennsylvania, 1996.

Crawford, Charles Wann. "A History of the R. F. Learned Lumber Company, 1865–1900." Ph.D. diss., University of Mississippi, 1968.

Jolly, Helen Sue. "Selected Leaders in Mississippi Home Economics: An Historical Inquiry." Ph.D. diss., Mississippi State University, 1995.

Lesseig, Corey T. "Automobility and Social Change: Mississippi, 1909–1939." Ph.D. diss., University of Mississippi, 1997.

Mactavish, Bruce Duncan. "With Strangers United in Kindred Relation: Education, Religion, and Community in Northern Mississippi, 1836–1880." Ph.D. diss., University of Mississippi, 1993.

Willis, John Charles. "On the New South Frontier: Life in the Yazoo-Mississippi Delta, 1865–1920." Ph.D. diss., University of Virginia, 1991.

Wojak, Joe. "The Factors of Urban Development: Cotton Brokers and Merchants in Antebellum Memphis, 1850–1860." M.A. thesis, University of Mississippi, 1996.

Microfilm Collections

Grossman, James R., ed. *Black Workers in the Era of the Great Migration, 1916–1925.* Frederick, Md.: University Publications of America, 1985.

Fannie Lou Hamer Papers. New Orleans: Amistad Research Center, 1985.

Stampp, Kenneth M., ed. *Records of Antebellum Southern Plantations from the Revolution through the Civil War.* Frederick, Md.: University Publications of America, 1985.

U.S. Bureau of Refugees, Freedmen, and Abandoned Lands. *Records of the Assistant Commissioner for the State of Mississippi*, reels 47–50.

INDEX

Birmingham, Ala., 97

Black Boy (Wright), 132

Blacksmiths, 75

Blanchard, Artley, 78

Blanton, Martha, 26, 30, 37

Blues, 4, 29, 31, 110–22, 127–29, 151, 161–62, 186 (nn. 12, 17), 188 (n. 36)

Blum, C. H., 23

Blum, Isaac, 23

Boatner, L. M., 22

Bolivar, Tenn., 31, 68

Bolivar County, Miss., 8, 71

Bond, Bradley G., 21

Bonnets, 9, 14–15, 17, 30, 33, 39–40

Books, 14–15, 74

Bossier Parish, La., 37

Boston, Mass., 33, 39, 52

Boxes, 34

Boycotts, 4, 150–58, 162, 164, 170, 190 (n. 16), 191 (n. 34); responses of whites to, 154–57

Bradley, Tommie, 117

Brand-name goods, 6, 90–92, 94, 124, 126, 133

Breen, T. H., 20, 42

Brooks, Cleanth, 143

Brooks, Joseph, 66

Broonzy, Big Bill, 111, 117–18

Buckets, 14, 69

Bucksnort, Tenn., 12

Buggies, 34, 40–41

Bundren, Addie, 139

Bundren, Anse, 138–40

Bundren, Cash, 138–40

Bundren, Darl, 139

Burney, S. G., General Store, 73–74

Bustles, 45

Butcher, J. (landowner), 66

"Buy-ins," 156–57

Byhalia, Miss., 22, 158

Cadillac, 119, 121, 127–29

Calico, 9, 21, 30, 55

Campbell, Colin, 2

Campbell, F. H., Store, 15, 19

Candles, 14, 54

Candy, 8, 14, 19, 54, 72, 79, 84, 93, 128, 146

Canton, Miss., 167–68

Carby, Thomas, 35, 38

Carouthers, Emily, 79

Carpeting and rugs, 14, 34–35, 37–38, 40, 42, 102, 128, 140, 143

Carr, William, 78

Carriages, 8, 33–38, 42, 136

Carrollton, Miss., 45

Cartmell, Robert, 63

Cash payments, 9–11, 19–20, 25, 32, 52–54, 63–71, 74, 82–88, 95, 103, 106, 112, 142, 161, 165

Cash stores, 3, 86, 88, 94

Catalogs, 2, 75–79, 87, 91, 100, 115, 122, 141, 144

Cattle, 8, 100, 138, 145

Cely (slave), 47

Chain stores, 86–87, 124, 132–33, 153–54, 162–66, 168

Chairs, 14, 34–35, 37–38, 79

Chambers of commerce, 131, 168

Champion, J. W., 46

Charles (freedman), 69

Charles (slave), 47

Charlotte, Tenn., 73

Cheese and crackers, 96–97, 138

Chevrolet, 91, 119–20

Chicago, Ill., 1, 75, 87, 111, 122–27, 132–33, 141, 151, 154

Chicago Defender, 122–24, 127

Chickens, 50, 70, 79

Children and childhood, 19–21, 27–28, 30–31, 36, 43, 70, 72, 75, 89–90, 93–94, 102, 104, 111–12, 127–29, 131–35, 145–46, 155

Christmas, Joe, 138, 140

Christmas, 18–19, 23, 43, 51, 53–54, 57–58, 63, 72, 79–81, 84, 92–95, 118, 150, 152, 155–56, 170, 182 (n. 59)

Churches, 86, 168

Circus, 64, 90

Citizens' Councils, 152, 154, 156

Civil rights movement, 4, 149–59, 162, 170

Civil War, 26, 30–31, 39, 66, 131

Clark, Thomas (historian), 11, 13, 162

Clark, Thomas (store employee), 21–22
Clarke, Lewis, 40–41
Clarksdale, Miss., 11–12, 75, 92, 94, 153, 155
Clarksdale Banner, 92
Clocks, 35, 40, 134, 169
Cloth, 9, 14–19, 25–27, 36, 39, 49, 55–57,
　66–67, 69–70, 74, 88–89, 101–2
Clothing, 8–9, 13, 15, 20, 25–33, 36, 39,
　44–95 passim, 100–104, 109, 112, 116–18,
　121, 123, 126–27, 132, 136, 140–41, 147,
　153, 160, 166–67, 170, 174 (n. 70), 180
　(nn. 9, 23)
Coahoma County, Miss., 63
Coats, 14, 17, 39–40, 49, 55, 66, 91, 95, 118
Cobb, Ned, 72
Coffee, Anna, 39
Coffee, 14, 63, 73, 84
Coffeeville, Miss., 10
Coffin tacks, 74
Cohen, Lizabeth, 123–24
Cohn, David, 63–64, 79
Coldwater, Miss., 11
Collier General Store, 73–74
Collins, G. P., 63
Columbus, Miss., 8, 32, 90, 94, 96–97, 162
Conally, Robert, 53
Confectioners, 8, 72
Consumer culture: definitions of, 1–2, 5–6;
　and idea of progress, 2–3
—and American Dreams: of abundance,
　1, 38–40, 58, 89–90, 94, 103, 112, 116–22,
　127–30, 145–46, 157, 160–61; of democ-
　racy of goods, 1–2, 5–6, 18, 51, 55, 58, 61,
　64, 71–73, 75, 91, 93, 96–99, 104, 112, 115,
　121, 123, 126–32, 137, 144, 146, 148–49,
　152–54, 157, 161–65; of freedom of choice,
　2, 5–6, 16, 29, 38–39, 55, 59, 67–68, 70–71,
　87–95, 98–99, 122, 130, 135–36, 145–47,
　154–57, 161, 165, 169; of novelty, 2–3, 16,
　25, 29–32, 38–45, 59, 77, 85–88, 91, 93,
　98–99, 117–23, 127, 130–48 passim, 157,
　167
—critiques of: ascetic, 5–6, 99–108, 111–13,
　135, 162, 170; radical, 5–6, 130, 132–35,
　162, 170; regionalist, 6; conservative, 6,
　61–65, 81, 99–108, 130–32, 162, 169–70

Contracts, labor, 65–70
Cook, Cecil, 96–97
Cooks, Mattie J., 71
Cooperative farming, 158
Corinth, Miss., 31
Corona College, 31
Corn, 19, 35, 46, 69, 71
Corsets, 28, 45, 89
Cosmetics and cosmetics companies,
　123–26
Cotton, 19, 46, 50, 61, 65–67, 69–71, 106,
　127; factors, 33–34, 40–42, 160; gins, 71
Country look, 166, 168
Country music, 122
Courtesy titles, 128, 153, 157–58, 162
Crawford, Miss., 8
Credit, 9–11, 19–26, 42, 61–79 passim,
　85–87, 112, 137, 139, 142, 159–60, 164–65
Credit cards, 6, 72
Crenshaw, Miss., 167
Cresswell, Mary, 101–2
Crosby, Emilye, 157
Curtains, 35, 104, 131

Dahmer, Vernon, 151
Daleville, Miss., 8
Dancing, 29, 36–37
Daniel, Wilober, 74
Darden, Susan Sillers, 37
Davis, Walter, 120
Debt, 3, 6–7, 19–26, 36, 42–46, 52–53,
　58–62, 67–72, 74–79, 85–87, 98, 102–4,
　109, 112, 116–17, 122–23, 136–42, 158,
　160–61, 164–66
Delta and Pine Land Company, 63
Demopolis, Ala., 69
Department stores, 3, 71, 87–93, 96, 161, 163,
　167
DeSoto County, Miss., 19
De Spain, Manfred, 136–37, 139–40, 143
Diamonds, 118–19
Dickins, Dorothy, 4, 79, 83, 85, 95, 99–109,
　161, 164–65
Dime stores. *See* Five and dime stores
Dining table, 35, 38
Dinnerware and dishes, 14–16, 35, 55, 167

Goods: differences between classes in ownership of, 30–39, 47–48, 183 (n. 13)
Gordon, Caroline, 66
Gordon, Mary, 33–34
Gordon, Robert, 33–34, 38–39
Grable, Betty, 137
Greaves, E. M., 18
Greene County, Ala., 69
Greene County, Miss., 8, 83–84
Greenville, Miss., 22, 52, 90, 162
Greenwood, Miss., 10, 18, 86, 151, 155, 163
Greenwood Commonwealth, 86
Gregory, John, 66
Grenada, Miss., 155–56
Grenada Sentinel Star, 156
Groceries, 8, 14, 18, 72, 74, 86, 92, 96, 156–57
Grossman, James, 124
Grove, Lena, 137–38, 140
Guitars, 115, 122, 144
Gulfport, Miss., 166
Guns, 8, 14, 110, 119

Hair straighteners, 123
Hall, G. D., 94
Hamer, Fannie Lou, 151, 158
Hamilton, Mary, 84
Hancock, Miss., 8
Hand, Laurel, 147
Handkerchiefs, 14, 40, 49, 55, 74, 89
Hankinson, W. S., Store, 12
Hardeman, Miss., 27
Hardware stores, 8, 96
Harlow, Jean, 137
Hart, Hattie, 121
Hats and caps, 8–10, 14, 31, 39–40, 45, 49, 56–57, 64–66, 69, 89–90, 93, 100, 118, 124, 126, 140, 153
Hattiesburg, Miss., 75, 94, 151, 162
Head rags, 124
Helena, Ark., 67
Help Yourself Store, 87
Henderson's Store, 12, 73–74
Henry, Aaron, 155
Henry, Gustavus, 44–47
Henry, Marion, 44–45

Henry, Sue, 44
Hernando, Miss., 10, 18
Hicks Mercantile Store, 93
Hierarchy, 1, 35–43, 58–60, 130–32, 136–37, 140
Hinds County, Miss., 47
Hogganbeck, Boon, 140
Holcombe, William Henry, 33, 42, 45
Holidays, 18–19, 23, 43, 51, 53–54, 57–58, 63, 72, 79–81, 84, 92–95, 118, 150, 152, 155–56, 170, 182 (n. 59)
Holland, Endesha Ida Mae, 153, 163
Holly Springs, Miss., 14, 19, 23, 27, 52, 158
Hollywood, Calif., 92, 136, 141–42
Holmes County, Miss., 49, 72
Home demonstration agents, 98–109
Homemade goods, 25–31, 46–50, 66, 95, 100–109, 131, 147, 168
Honor, 20–21, 41
Hoop skirts, 29, 55, 65, 131
Horse racing, 36, 38
Horses, 11, 37, 49
Hosiery. *See* Socks and stockings
Hospitality, 35–38, 41–43, 131, 143, 146
House, Boyce, 11
Housing, 9, 36, 59, 62, 67, 81, 83, 123, 136, 141, 143–44, 150–51
Howell, Virginia, 93–94
Hundley, Daniel R., 42–43

Independence: rural whites' ideas about, 3–5, 7, 9–10, 15–16, 18–31 passim, 56, 83–84, 98, 100, 103, 109, 135–40, 146–47; planters' ideas about, 42–47; rural African Americans's ideas about, 61, 67, 75, 112–13, 116–17, 133–34, 158, 160
Indianola, Miss., 166
Indulgence: rural whites' ideas about, 19–21, 25–31; planters' ideas about, 43–46, 59–65; rural African Americans' ideas about, 76–81, 112–13; town shoppers' ideas about, 84–90, 96–97; home demonstration workers' ideas about, 98–109; blues performers' ideas about, 110–22; urban African Americans' ideas about, 122–29, 149, 152; Faulkner's ideas

Rodney, Miss., 39

Rogers and Hearn General Store, 50–59

Roggenburger Brothers (store owners), 10

Roland, Walter, 119

Rolling Fork, Miss., 123

Rooks, William Henry, 112

Roosevelt, Franklin D., 1

Rose-Meta Cosmetics, 123

Ross, Nat, 70

Rounsaville, Miss., 83–84

Rowan Oak (Faulkner's home), 136

Ruffin, James, 49

Sacks (feed, sugar, flour, fertilizer): as clothing, 50, 104–6, 148

Saddles, 8, 17, 40

Saint Louis, Mo., 8–9, 93, 123

Salem, Miss., 8

Sales: as events, 89–90

Saloons, 8, 74

Sam (slave), 57

Santa Claus, 94, 118, 121, 148

Sarah (fictional character), 133–34

Sardis, Miss., 165

Sargent, George Washington, 47

Sartoris, Colonel (fictional character), 136–37

Schmidt, Leigh Eric, 94

Schools, 152, 155, 158, 168

Scott, Evelyn, 11

Scott, Rowland, 154, 156–57

Scott County, Miss., 73

Sears, Richard W., 124

Sears and Roebuck, 75, 115, 122, 124

Second-hand stores, 76, 164–68

Seeds, 51, 69, 158

Self-control, 4–5, 21, 26–31, 43–45, 59–60, 76–80, 102–4, 112–15, 137–38, 148, 152

Self-service shopping, 86–88

Seward and Company, 90, 93

Sewing, 6, 15, 19, 25–31, 41, 45–47, 50, 66, 88, 95, 99–103; by slaves, 46–47, 50, 54–56; supplies and equipment for, 14–16, 47, 50, 66; machines, 41, 100–101

Sharecropping, 62–72, 77, 79, 81, 83–84, 95,
98–99, 103, 106, 110–11, 116, 118, 123, 132, 140, 152, 161, 180 (n. 23)

Shawls, 40, 74

Shines, Johnny, 115

Shirts, 19, 45, 49, 66, 74, 104, 151

Shoemakers, 50

Shoes and boots, 8, 10, 14–19, 39–40, 45, 47, 49–51, 53–54, 57, 62, 64–66, 68–71, 74–75, 79–81, 84–85, 90–91, 97, 109, 118, 124, 187 (n. 23); blue suede, 109

Shoe shops, 75

Shopping: by wealthy individuals, 3, 33–35, 37–45, 130–31; in cities, 4, 7, 33–34, 36–45, 108–9, 122–29, 133, 162–64, 168; for supplies, 13–19, 25–26, 38, 53–55, 69–74, 101–2, 160; for pleasure, 19, 29, 31–39, 41–46, 71, 85–99, 101–2, 108, 123–25, 160; through cotton factors, 40–42; by slaves, 50–60; goal of efficient, 99–109. *See also* African Americans: as shoppers; Men: as shoppers; Self-service shopping; Women: as shoppers

Shopping malls and centers, 86, 159, 163–64, 166

Shotgun shells, 64

Shubuta, Miss., 8

Silas (fictional character), 133–34

Silk, 21, 31, 55, 58, 94, 113

Skin bleaching, 123

Skirts, 45, 89, 93

Slavery, 2–3, 5, 7, 20–21, 25, 35, 36, 41, 43, 65–70, 94, 111–12, 160, 170; goods owned by slaves, 31, 46–60, 81; arguments supporting, 46, 59–60; money earned by slaves, 50–51, 57, 59, 68, 81, 178 (n. 63)

Smith, Bob, 98

Smith, Clettes, 98

Smith, Doll, 98

Smith, Gladys. *See* Presley, Gladys Smith

Smith, Jane, 30

Smith-Rosenberg, Caroll, 30

Smokehouses, 70–71

Snopes, Ab, 140

Snopes, Flem, 135, 140–44

Snopes, I. O., 140

Snopes, Mink, 140